D1629877
To
Derek
From
Bob,
on reaching
½ ton!

history of the
GERMAN
AIR FORCE

history of the
GERMAN AIR FORCE

BRYAN PHILPOTT

GALLERY BOOKS
An imprint of W.H. Smith Publishers Inc.
112 Madison Avenue
New York, New York 10016
A Bison Book

Published by Gallery Books
A Division of W H Smith Publishers Inc.
112 Madison Avenue
New York, New York 10016

Produced by
Bison Books Corp.
17 Sherwood Place
Greenwich, CT 06830

ISBN 0–8317–4208–9

Printed in Hong Kong

1 2 3 4 5 6 7 8 9 10

Page 1: An interesting photograph of the interior of a World War I Zeppelin under construction.
Pages 2-3: Symbol of the Blitzkrieg, a formation of Ju 87 Stuka bombers.
This page: A Transall cargo aircraft of the present-day West German Luftwaffe.

CONTENTS

INTRODUCTION

Since the beginning of time the ability to fly like a bird has been a challenge to man; in many ways it is a challenge that has still to be met, for although air travel and the use of the aircraft as a weapon are commonplace, man is merely the inventor, user and passenger of a mechanical device that only resembles a bird in that it operates in the same environment.

The closest man gets to flying just like a bird, is perhaps the hang-glider, and in the context of this book there would appear to be no military application for it: but then the Wright brothers thought the same about their *Flyer*.

On 17 December 1903 the Wright brothers finally achieved a sustained flight by a man-carrying heavier-than-air, powered aircraft, and a whole new era was ready to break upon an unsuspecting world. Who at that time, would have dared to predict that sixty years later man would not only be travelling at speeds far in excess of any dreamed of by the early pioneers, but also have journeyed to and landed on the moon? There has been nothing, apart from the micro-chip, that has revolutionized the world in which we live in such a short space of time, like the aircraft. Despite the thoughts of the Wrights (and others) that the aircraft would either be of no use as a weapon, or would be so terrible that all war would be rendered obsolete by it, events proved otherwise. In two major World Wars plus countless other minor conflicts throughout the world, the aircraft has gone from strength to strength, and although today's modern technology has turned it into a highly sophisticated weapon, there is one element that has been constant; that is the man who flies or crews it.

It is the comradeship and fascination of the air that is common to all such men irrespective of their race, colour, creed or even political leanings. So any account of any nation's air forces must lean strongly on the contributions by such men as well as the machines in which they either achieved glory or met their end.

It is often said that war is started by politicians and waged by young men; this is of course very true, and although no doubt many of the German aviators did have some political views one way or the other, the majority, like those they fought against, were defending their homeland in an environment they had chosen because of their closeness to flying. At the end of any war it is the vanquished that come in for the closest scrutiny and analysis, therefore over the years much has been written about the aircraft, men, tactics and strategy of the German air forces.

Any account such as this, by virtue of the limited space, can only present a general overall framework to which the reader must add his own covering within the area he is particularly interested in. Some of the most profitable lines of further investigation have been listed elsewhere, and they will enlarge on the exploits of men and machines I have only been able to mention *en passant*. Although this is primarily a story of a nation's air forces, as such it must be the story of a nation's young men who lived in a world that is known only to those who fly.

Right: Adolf Galland, fighter general and ace pilot.
Far right: Hitler and Goering pictured in 1934 before the official establishment of Goering's Luftwaffe.
Below right: An F-104G Starfighter of the new Luftwaffe takes off.
Below: A 30 horsepower Grade monoplane takes off in 1910.

BIRTH OF AN AIR FORCE

The Franco-Prussian War of 1870 was probably the first occasion that a German army commander encountered the value and indeed frustration of the use of the air as an element in warfare. At the outbreak of this war an Englishman, Henry Coxwell, went to Köln and convinced the German authorities that the man-carrying balloon he was selling was a far better product than an American design they were then in the process of evaluating. Such was the persuasive power of Coxwell's tongue that he sold two complete units comprising balloons and all their associated equipment to the military authorities. The equipment was used to equip two balloon sections which officially came into being on 31 August 1870, but such was the administrative problem created that these were soon merged into one. The planned debut of the equipment was at the siege of Strasbourg, but problems in inflating the envelopes and prevailing high winds, saw only a few non-productive ascents before the city capitulated. The unit moved on to Paris and after many trials and tribulations with transport, arrived outside the French capital only to find that there was no gas available. This is somewhat ironic because by 18 September the Germans had completely isolated the French city, and were calling on the garrison to surrender.

On 23 September the besiegers were amazed to see a balloon ascend from the city and float over their heads; this was the first of 65 to leave Paris carrying mail and passengers, one of whom was the French Premier, Gambetta. This evacuation, although not having any marked influence on the final outcome, incensed Count von Bismarck to such a degree that he advised the French that any balloonists captured would be treated as spies. It also led to a contract being placed with Alfred Krupp for the very first anti-aircraft weapons, the initial order being for twenty of which only a few reached service before the end of the war. So although the French balloons had been used entirely as a means of transportation with no regard to military application, in fact the military use in the American Civil War and the earlier Battle of Fleurus, had been discarded as unsuccessful, the die had been cast in associating the use of the air as a means of obtaining military advantage and ideas for a counter measure already put into production, thus to a certain extent coloring thoughts which might in more peaceful surroundings never have occurred.

But the Germans persisted with their own experiments only until 10 October when Coxwell's two balloons were returned to Germany and the associated unit disbanded.

The army authorities had little faith in the balloon and although some experiments were carried out in 1872 by a detachment of engineers, lack of finance doomed these from the start and they soon came to an end.

But ballooning was such a popular sport in Germany that in 1881 the German Balloon Society was established and one of its declared aims was to 'forward aeronautics on a patriotic basis.' The society attracted many influential people so when it began to agitate for a renewed interest by the military authorities, the government of the time was put under pressure from within. Several high ranking army officers were members and their presence added weight to the society's suggestion that a balloon unit should again be established within the German army. Eventually the Minister of War detailed an officer to

Previous page: A Parseval drachen or 'sausage' steerable balloon which started to replace the more conventional round type in 1896.
Above right: The rear gondola and crew of LZ 13 adequately illustrates the exposed situation in these early airships.
Below: The maiden flight on 2 July 1900 of the Zeppelin LZ 1. Scale is added by the lighter and people on its deck.

Limitations with the spherical balloon's performance caused some concern, for unless weather conditions were near perfect it was very unstable and gave the observer who was housed in a basket beneath it, a very rough ride. This not only led to physical discomfort but also difficulty in observing, which after all was the prime function of the equipment. Major August von Parseval and Hauptmann Hans Bartsch Sigsfeld, came up with the answer in the form of a kite balloon which could be rigged to use the wind to help stability.

Its shape led to it being given the appellation 'sausage' and from 1896 it gradually replaced the unreliable spherical type, despite a strong lobby supporting the latter because of its ability to ascend to greater heights. But the fact that the sausage or drachen balloon (to give it its other name) could be used at a 30 percent higher rate, finally won the day.

The many problems both real, and manufactured by those within the army who still regarded the balloon as unnecessary,

Above: Count Ferdinand von Zeppelin, the father of the airship.
Right: Zeppelin LZ 3 in December 1909, note the three bladed propellers in the forward positions.

become a member, and in November 1883 following an appraisal of activities in France and England – although the latter was not considered to be a potential military rival – Hauptmann Buchholtz was ordered to set up a balloon section. The following June this was established with a strength of four officers (all members of the society), four non-commissioned officers, and twenty-nine men. The four officers had no worthwhile practical experience of ballooning so a civilian, Richard Opitz, was employed to carry out instruction.

Opitz was a skilled and talented aeronaut who made his living by constructing balloons, and using them to entertain the public at country shows, in very much the same way as barnstorming was to sweep America after WWI. His contribution to military aviation in Germany continued for many years and was in fact quite considerable, but because he was an entertainer he was looked down on by the army high command and the ground work he did in Germany has never been fully acknowledged.

By 1887 the small Luftschiffer Detachement which had been initially attached to a railway troop, was separated into a self-contained Luftschiffer Abteilung and by the turn of the century had grown into two companies using both free and tethered balloons. In the early days these had been constructed within the units but later this was put out to tender and the balloons were subsequently made by private industry under contract to the war office.

make for fascinating study and include such problems as their recovery by horse and later steam driven winches, the difficulty in communicating via a telephone link, the length of the barrels of rifles used by those in attendance, the problems created by officers having to wear spurs (as laid down in military regulations) and spiked helmets tearing the envelopes. All added to the question of survival for the small Luftschiffer Bataillon; but survive it did.

The wind of change was however beginning to blow, and in 1906 the War Ministry decided that the airship, whose performance up to this time had looked to have greater potential than the airplane, should be the vehicle adopted and developed for German military aviation.

Graf von Zeppelin had been experimenting with large rigid airships for a number of years, his first, LZ 1, having made its maiden flight over Lake Constance on 2 July 1900. His concept of using a rigid structure with a number of gas bags carried inside it was thought to be the wrong one, since the military authorities' thinking was still colored by their experience with balloons and they saw the powered airship as an extension of this. They therefore opted for a semi-rigid type which they believed could be transported in much the same way as the balloon, erected near the field of action and then used operationally. A von Parseval semi-rigid design was chosen after much influence had been exerted at the War Office by Major Gross the commander of the Luftschiffer Bataillon, a known supporter of the semi-rigid type. This craft was constructed by the Bataillon as was the second machine which was ordered in May 1907.

The following month the craft now known as Militärluftschiff 1 (M1) made its debut, and although in August a non-rigid ship designed by Parseval (P1) was also commissioned, a new dimension was entering in the background. The authorities felt they could not ignore the gradual advent of the heavier-

than-air type machine, and so appointed Hauptmann de le Roi to be aviation adviser to the airship battalion with a special brief to evaluate the many types of aircraft which were then becoming available.

In the meantime Graf Zeppelin had continued with his designs which were capturing the imagination of the German public. The LZ 1 had been scrapped because of a financial crisis in 1901, and the LZ 2 was destroyed soon after its second flight in 1906, but LZ 3 and 4 gradually began to justify the faith of those who supported the rigid type construction. LZ 4 set out to prove once and for all that this type of airship was capable of prolonged operation under varying conditions by undertaking a 24 hour endurance flight. On 4 August 1908 LZ 4 set off across Lake Constance from Friedrichshafen and followed the Rhine toward Mainz which it reached about midnight. On the return the engines which had given problems on the outbound flight, once again played up and the airship was forced to land at Echterdingen having spent over 20 hours in the air. During the enforced stay a sudden squall lifted the ship from its mooring and equally as quickly dropped it, whereupon it burst into flames and was destroyed. Graf von Zeppelin was devastated and saw in that moment his life's work crumble. He was practically penniless and his dreams for a rigid type airship looked to have come to nothing. But his machines had captured the imagination of the German public to a greater degree than even he realized, and within a short space of time over 6 million Marks had been collected in a national fund which was to establish the Zeppelin Airship Construction Company GmbH to build airships that were to become symbols of German pride and nationalism.

In October 1908 the War Ministry General Staff formed a Technical Section to look after developments in wireless communication, motor transport and aeronautics, this separate section long being advocated by Hauptmann Thomsen and Oberstleutnant Ludendorff who had long been a supporter of military aeronautics and in the airship saw a valuable weapon that should be developed into at least a fifteen strength unit by 1910. The General Staff, obviously much under the influence of Ludendorff, set these plans into motion and in March 1909 helped von Zeppelin to realize his ambition when they took on charge his LZ 3 and commissioned it into the army as Zeppelin Luftschiff 1 (Z.1).

Left: The crews of a balloon unit pose with the basket of their spherical observation craft. The ballast and different uniforms are of interest.
Below: The LZ 5 photographed in 1909 just prior to its maiden flight.

Another important step taken by the General Staff was a decision taken in October 1908 that the airplane must also qualify as part of future military aviation equipment, and consequently the War Office was persuaded to put forward funds for the building of 'a plane with a capacity for two people, a speed of at least 60 km per hour, and the possibility of landing without danger to the occupants' (sic).

Grants were made to several potential aircraft manufacturers but as was to be expected under the conditions prevailing at the time, several expensive mistakes were made including the official financing and building by the Luftschiffer Bataillon of an aircraft designed by Hoffman, that proved totally incapable of flight.

Among the more successful constructors to whom awards were made were Hermann Dorner and Hans Grade. Dorner was the only German competitor at the first German flying meeting held in the late summer of 1909 at the newly completed airfield at Johannisthal near Berlin, and Grade scooped the 40,000 Mark prize put up by the industrialist Karl Lanz for the first flight by a German aircraft powered by a German aero-engine; this event also taking place at Johannisthal but in October 1909. So, although at this time the airship seemed to be well established as the main military weapon, the progress of the airplane was such that it was becoming increasingly obvious to the more astute observers, that it had a big future in the development of military flying.

It was clear that as progress in this direction was made there would be a need for trained pilots, so in 1910 a Flying School was founded at Döberitz with the initial brief to train officer volunteers to fly. The first aircraft was a privately owned Farman put at the disposal of the school by Dr Walther Huth whose chauffeur had taught him to fly. With the aircraft also went the intrepid driver, Simon Brunnhaber, who soon had ten students under his wing. There was still a marked reluctance on the part of some of the General Staff to accept the airplane, consequently the school struggled for a long time and much of the equipment was loaned by patriotic benefactors.

Among the first ten pilots to complete their training at

Döberitz was Hauptmann de le Roi who did a great deal to swing the views of those who wavered, toward the advantages of Germany possessing an efficient air force. It was de le Roi who helped overcome many of the problems encountered in setting up an air arm ranging from the reluctance of units to release men, to the need of a proper training syllabus. He also made the first cross-country flight in Germany in September 1910, this taking place during a military investigation into the suitability of available designs for military service. On this occasion his mount was a Farman which covered the 12 miles between Döberitz and Bornstedt in 20 minutes, later at the same event he took Oberstleutnant Ludendorff on a local flight thus perhaps adding the final ingredient to his known enthusiasm. These trials resulted in the allocation of 150,000 Marks for the purchase of nine airplanes, these being: one Etrich Taube, two licence built Farmans, one each from Aviatik and Albatros, two Frey biplanes, the original Farman demonstrated by de le Roi, and a Sommer biplane which was also built by Albatros.

During 1910 there was no increase in the size of the airship fleet but an interesting move did take place when many of the existing craft used by commercial companies were subsidized by the military on the understanding that in the event of war, they would be impressed; this provided a nucleus of trained crews under a civil guise; shades of the future after Versailles?

The army suffered its first fatal accident at Döberitz on 6 February 1911 when Leutnant Stein fell from his Farman biplane which was numbered B3; oddly enough every aircraft at the school subsequently carrying this code seemed fated to misadventure, so even in the very early days of military aviation superstitions pertaining to certain numbers or aircraft, can be found.

Before looking at the administration and strengths of the German air force on the eve of the Great War, it is necessary to take a brief look at an alternative airship that is often overshadowed by the Zeppelin, and how aviation had its tentative beginnings in the German navy.

The use of the word Zeppelin has become synonymous with all airships and this of course means that other designs are passed over and notable among these was the series of Schütte-Lanz airships which first appeared in 1911. Dr Schütte was a teacher of ship construction at Danzig and had been attracted to the airship as a result of the disaster to the Zeppelin at Echterdingen.

Like Zeppelin he favored the rigid type and his ideas gained the support of the industrialist Karl Lanz whose name was added to the title. August Röchling, who made generous donations to the Zeppelin fund, also supported the new design which made its maiden flight on 17 October 1911.

In an attempt to increase the flexibility of the framework, Schütte used laminated wooden girders instead of aluminum, which he believed was too rigid. The prototype had a lattice structure not unlike the geodetic structure later produced by the British designer Dr Barnes Wallis, but on later models Schütte reverted to the circular formers and longitudinal stringers of the more conventional airships. The prototype was a beautifully streamlined craft and was purchased by the army in December 1912; it was known as the SL 1 and was unfortunately destroyed at Schneidemühl on 17 July 1913 after a forced landing. By this time tests, many of which had been carried out under the control of Korvettenkapitän von Jena, had so impressed the authorities that they had ordered a second craft which was designated SL 2 and made its maiden flight on 28 February 1914. The design of the SL 2 incorporated many

Above: The ill-fated LZ 2 which was destroyed soon after its second flight in 1906.
Below: An early Taube two-seat trainer at Döberitz with trainee pilots being shown the method of rigging.

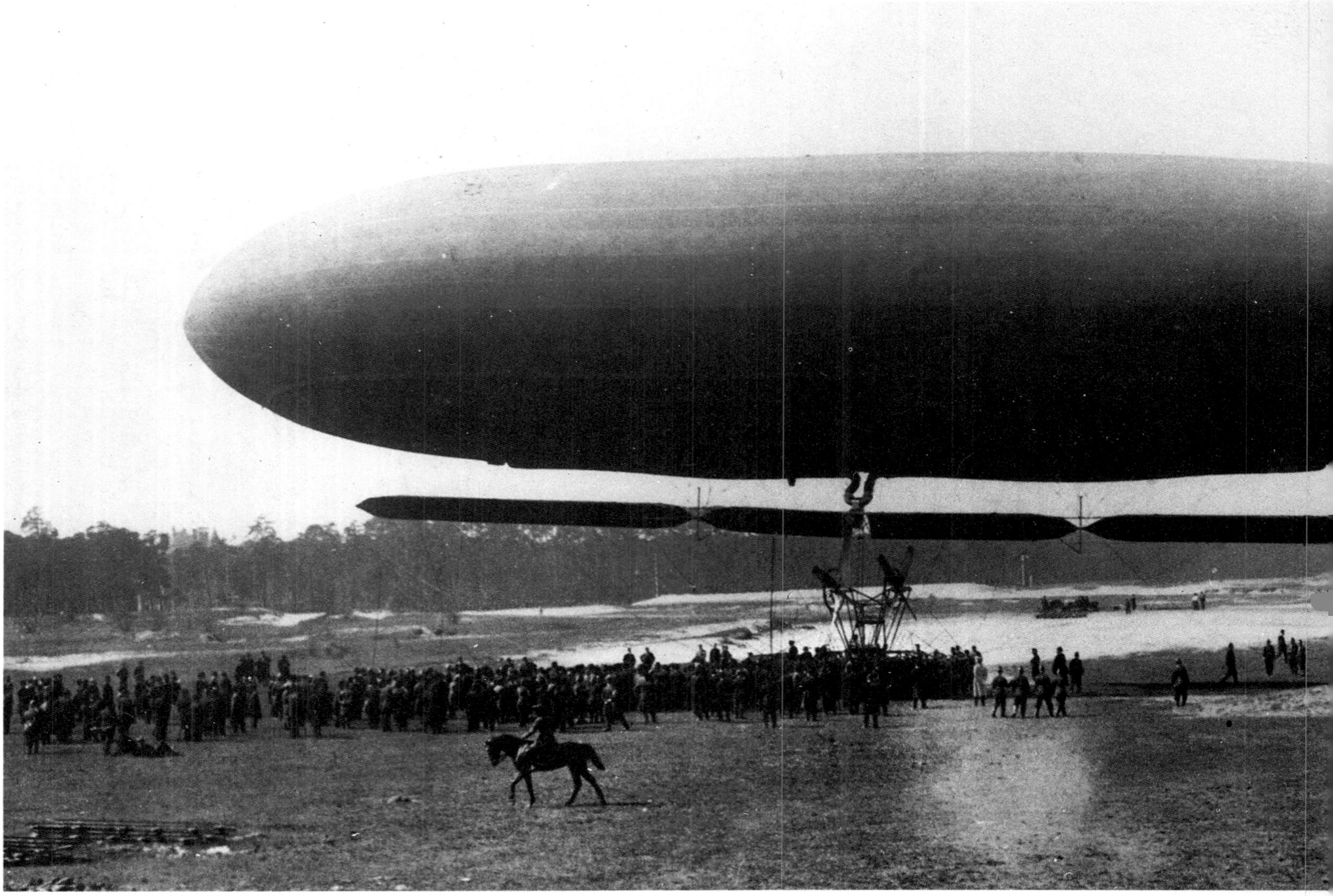

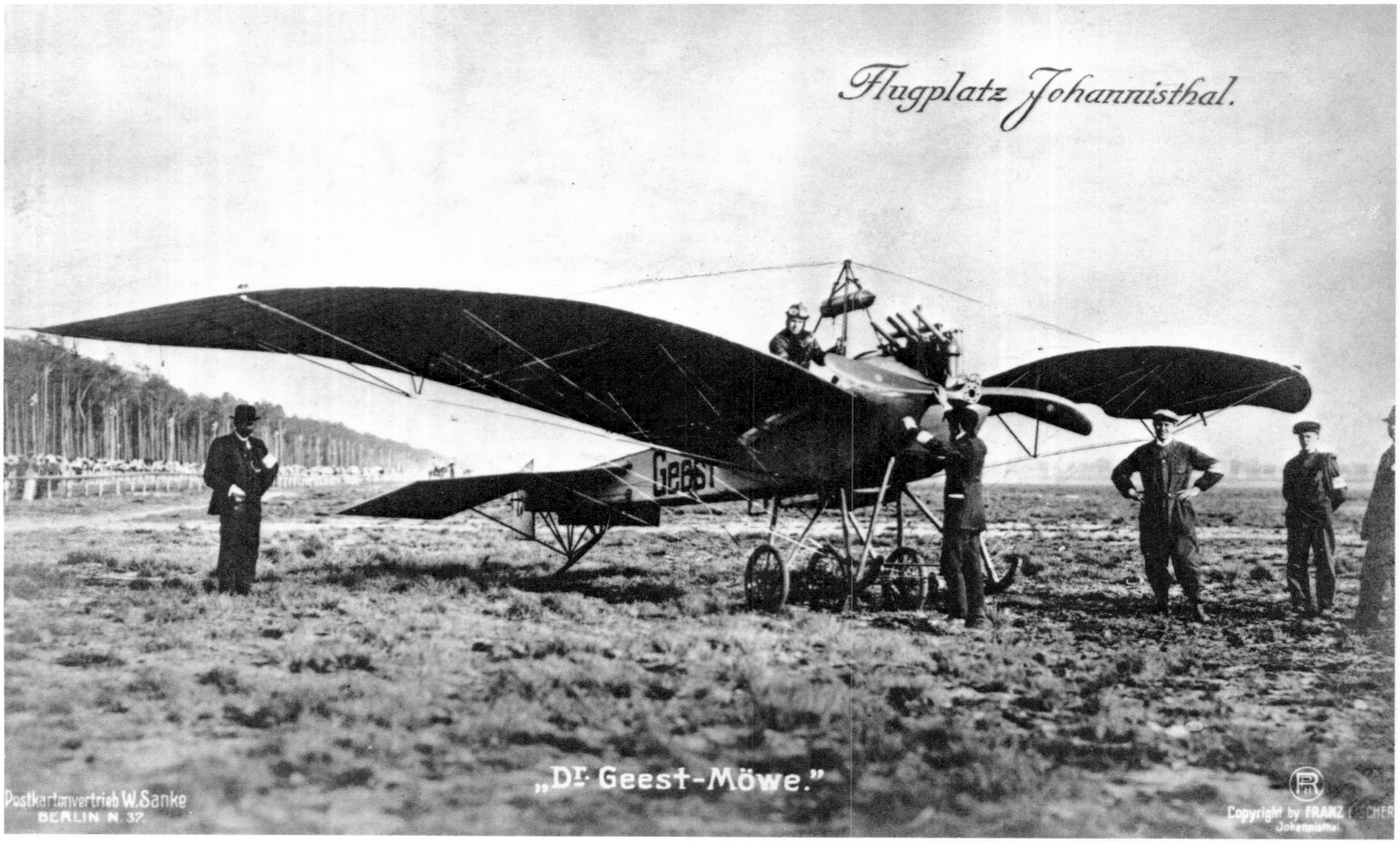

Flugplatz Johannisthal.

„Dr. Geest-Möwe."

Postkartenvertrieb W. Sanke
BERLIN N. 37.

Above: The Militärluftschiff 3 (M 3) at Döberitz in 1910. First flight was on 31 December 1909. Power came from four 75hp Körting Motors that gave a top speed of 60kmph.
Left: Geest-Möwe monoplane at Berlin Johannisthal.

advanced features such as enclosed gondolas and internal gangways. Full credit has never been given to Dr Schütte, possibly because his craft emerged on the eve of war when censorship was beginning to take effect and because in many ways they were overshadowed by the dramatic evolution of Zeppelin's airships. Zeppelin incidentally later used many of Schütte's ideas and subsequently took credit for them!

In November 1912 Count von Moltke, who had become Chief of the General Staff in 1906, signed the death knell of the non-rigid airship when he issued a directive stating that only Zeppelins or other rigid airships should be procured and production of the Parseval (P) and military built semi-rigid type Ms should stop.

He also issued a directive that all future purchases should be Zeppelins, but this seems to have emanated from a pleasure trip he took in a Zeppelin rather than any military advantage he might have thought existed; fortunately such a monopoly was never observed by the War Office who continued to use their limited funds on a variety of dirigibles.

These funds were indeed very limited and it can be argued that the small amount of money allocated resulted in poor development of the airship leading to them being grossly oversized, and lacking in speed and useful carrying capacity when war eventually put them to the test. Many hoped that the good points of the Schütte-Lanz and Zeppelin designs would lead to. the advancement of efficiency of both, but this was not to be so, and in the end they were not ready for use in warfare either in terms of design or knowledge of application. The Zeppelin became the accepted military craft and both the Army and Navy used considerable quantities, but hindsight shows them not to have made any major contribution to the development of German military aviation, either in terms of operational equipment or the gaining of long-term useful knowledge.

The army's experimental use of balloons brought pressure on the navy to reopen their own investigations which had been abandoned in 1890 after tests at Wilhelmshaven and Helgoland had shown that instability was a problem. As in the army the advocates of progress were initially outnumbered by those who could see no future in the use of the air in military situations. The navy relied on forward reconnaissance to detect mines, submarines and other threats to the fleet; this was achieved in the traditional way by using destroyers and high-speed launches, so the very idea of a forward air scout costing less and therefore enabling the navy's budget to be spent better, should have had great appeal. This was not so and many obstacles were raised despite the prophesy of General von Bernhardi who commented in relation to the naval use of air power: 'The numerical superiority of the English cruisers is so great that we shall probably only be able to guarantee rapid and trustworthy "scouting" by the help of an air-fleet. The importance of the air-fleet must not therefore be under-valued.'

Interest was revived following the success of the kite balloon and in 1897 a detachment was sent to Kiel to assess operations. These proved to be a disaster, not because of the failure of the balloon, but as a result of associated equipment and human error.

The kite balloon was attached to a torpedo-boat which then put to sea as it was felt that the main advantage would come from ships underway operating the device. Failure of the telephone link between the man aloft in the kite and the ship, saw the observer attempt to send his messages down in a small pouch via the balloon's mooring cables; this jammed and resulted in no further messages being passed in this way, so an attempt was made to drop the reports on to the deck, this too proved a failure due to the small size of the area involved. Not surprisingly the cruise was called off and subsequent efforts never overcame the bad impression that had been created by the vital first one. Soon after this the navy terminated the experiment supposedly for lack of finance.

Despite the advantages to be gained by the use of the balloon in off-shore gun ranging – ably demonstrated by the Italians in 1911 at Tripoli – and in the direction of naval gun fire from shore installations, the navy took no further interest in ballooning and dropped all thought of aerial scouting until the airplane appeared in 1911. During the developing period of the airship attempts were made to revive naval interest but despite attempts to hide his prejudice against them, it was apparent that Admiral von Tirpitz totally opposed the use of dirigibles.

Below: Anthony Fokker, the famous Dutch designer, photographed in 1911 aboard a Spin monoplane.

The matter may well have rested there if it had not been for the enthusiasm of the Kaiser's brother, Prince Heinrich of Prussia, and the intervention of the British navy.

The Prince had long been an advocate of naval aviation and when the navy received 100,000 Marks for research into seaplanes in 1911, decided that it was time he learned to fly. Consequently he went to the flying school at Döberitz and became the first German naval officer to receive pilot training. Prince Heinrich was in reality the patron saint of German aeronautics, he supported both the army and navy and was never overawed by von Tirpitz who steadfastly refused to consider airships claiming that they were a form of defense whereas a navy's prime objective should be its strength in attack. He also made it quite clear on several occasions that if money was spent on defensive equipment – not necessarily airships – he would resign. Despite this threat, Prince Heinrich was instrumental in establishing a permanent naval representative at the Zeppelin factory in Friedrichshafen. In 1912 the factory received an enquiry about the purchase of a Zeppelin from the British Admiralty whom it was known had been interested in a British-built airship constructed by Vickers along similar lines to that of the German design. Failure of the Vickers design to live up to expectations appeared to result in the British abandoning interest, but this was not the case and in September 1912 the British Naval Airship Section was reconstituted and recommendations made that foreign equipment should be purchased until the British could build their own, hence the enquiry to Zeppelin.

As a direct result of this interest, Alfred Colsman, Zeppelin's business manager, visited von Tirpitz in an attempt to make him change his mind, but the Admiral remained unmoved despite Colsman's comment that unless orders were forthcoming Zeppelin would go out of business, and to prevent that, he would accept any orders from the British. The embarrassing questions that might be asked at the Reichstag eventually persuaded von Tirpitz to send a naval delegation to look at the Zeppelin proposal, and this, as well as astute pressure from representatives of the company in Berlin who continually quoted the implications of a British order, brought about the purchase of the first naval Zeppelin. Known as the L 1 this was ready in October 1912 and as the navy had no facilities, was housed at Johannistal for acceptance tests. These proved successful and on 8 May 1913 the Navy Airship Detachment under the command of Kapitänleutnant Metzing was established. The craft performed well during fleet maneuvers but on 9 September 1913 it was hit by high winds and forced into the sea. This brought about the first deaths of naval aviators and among the 15 killed was Metzing.

This unfortunate accident gave ammunition to those who still opposed the naval use of the airship, but by this time the L 2, which incorporated many improvements had been ordered and was delivered in October 1913 for acceptance trials. On the 17th of the month disaster struck again. This time an engine fault led to the airship being left in the unusually hot sun (for October) which caused the gas to expand to above maximum capacity and 'bleed off.' When repairs had been concluded the engines were started and the craft rose majestically to 1500 feet when a flash back from the forward engine ignited the escaping gas, causing the airship to disintegrate in a ball of flame. Everyone on board including the Naval Board of Acceptance and the navy's representative from the Zeppelin works, died in the crash, thus dealing a devastating blow to the navy and Zeppelin.

Arguments as to where responsibility for the crash lay raged back and forth; the navy blaming Zeppelin and they blaming the navy. The head of the Airship Detachment, Peter Strasser, made a wise move in acting swiftly to counter the affect on his personnel. He chartered the privately owned *Hansa* and immediately got his key personnel back into the air, and soon had their confidence back on an even keel.

The enquiry into the loss of the L 2 placed much of the blame on a poorly designed return valve; the type used on the Schütte-Lanz was better but covered by patents preventing Zeppelin from using it. The Count could not tolerate criticism, and feeling that his own supporters were now turning against him, took less and less interest in the craft that carried his name into history.

The third naval airship, L 3, was obtained in May 1914, and was in fact smaller and less powerful than the L 2, whose fate had halted certain improvements in Zeppelin design mainly due to the company's reluctance to accept some of the innovations included on the rival Schütte-Lanz craft. However, it was soon in operation at Fühlsbüttel from where it carried out training flights over the sea and maneuvers with the fleet. The L 3 was the only airship in service with the navy on the outbreak of war at which time it also boasted a most modern hangar fitted with dual turntables located at Nordholz near Cuxhaven.

The purchase of the nine aircraft mentioned earlier meant that the army had to carry out some re-organization to their structure to take account of the new equipment. The original balloons and airships had been the responsibility of the Verkehrstruppen (Transport Troops); this was extended on 1 April 1911 to become the Generalinspektion des Militärverkehrswesens under whose control came the Inspektion des Militär Luft und Kraftfahrwesens (Inspectorate of Military Aviation and Transport). Although the importance of military aviation was becoming very evident it was still not considered worthy of its own budget so financial requirements were met from those of the unit from which personnel and equipment were drawn. However, a commission of officers from the General Staff and War Office was set up to take a close look at the requirements of the army, and this resulted in an additional allowance being made of 500,000 Marks.

During the remaining months of 1911 a further 37 aircraft were purchased and by the end of the year 30 officer pilots had been trained and were operational. Some of them flew the newly acquired machines in the 1911 military maneuvers which provided very useful material in relation to the use of aircraft in conjunction with troops in the field.

Eight aircraft took part in these operations, four on each side, those in the 'Red' army were monoplanes and those in the 'Blue' were biplanes. Weather conditions proved to be ideal and simulated battle situations tended to be unrealistic, so the end results did not really give an honest appraisal of what the airplane could do in actual war conditions. Although the commanders had been told to use the aircraft for reconnaissance, they did in fact tend to stick to the old fashioned method of scouting cavalry but failed to mention this in reports, therefore

Left: Oberleutnant Erler and Leutnant Mackenthun at the start of a 720km cross country flight from Döberitz to Hamburg on 28 March 1911. During the flight they landed 14 times.
Below: Count von Zeppelin in white hat, Kapitän Hackner and Dr Eckner in the gondola of LZ 10 in 1911.

implying that all results had been gathered from the air. Detailed analysis quickly indicated this and the War Office, which still had to be convinced of the value of aircraft, continued to hesitate although the General Staff was well convinced that aircraft and not airships were where the future lay. However, the War Office view tended to filter through all levels of the army so it is not too surprising that when war eventually started the heavier-than-air machine was still looked on with suspicion.

There can be little doubt that 1911 was the make or break year as far as the setting up of a firm foundation on which a strong German air force could be built. Much credit for the General Staff being very much in favor of an air arm must go to the work of Major Hermann von der Leith-Thomsen, who was responsible for the majority of tactical analysis used by Oberst Ludendorff in pushing his arguments and quite rightly this work is duly acknowledged in Ludendorff's Memoirs.

Hesitancy still prevailed during 1912 but such was the rate of progress that some pilots had to be trained under contract at civilian flying schools where they received their basic licence before going on to the military training establishments at Strassburg and Metz. The original establishment of a military chain of command was very much based on that used by the French whom General von Moltke (the Chief of the General Staff) saw as the most serious threat to Germany. Despite opposition from the expected sources he submitted a plan in September 1912 outlining the aviation units and the organization that would be required should war break out.

It is necessary to oversimplify the proposals, and counter proposals, as well as the various paths followed, and the reader is recommended to the Bibliography for source material which explains this in great detail, but the following paragraphs provide an outline of what was in fact a very complex development.

Basically von Moltke proposed that each army command should include two or three aviation units supported by a supply and communications unit. This organization could be expanded to provide every army corps with an attached aviation unit in the event of war. His recommendations also included the provision of an artillery co-operation unit for every corps, as well as a proposal – not very well received – that the air units be divorced from the overall control of the former Verkehrstruppen and its inspectorate, and be established as a separate branch of the service. Although these far reaching proposals were not generally approved by the War Office, who could see in them too great a measure of independence for an untried arm, they were gradually infiltrated and by the autumn of 1912 formed the basis of reorganization.

1 October 1912 saw the first moves in molding the existing flying units of the German army into a structure that would eventually become the army air service. The establishment at Döberitz was brought into line with the training schools at Strassburg and Metz and a fourth was added at Darmstadt; at this time the first Fliegertruppe, which was in fact The Royal Prussian Flying Troop, came into existence and was attached to the Gardekorps its strength being 21 officers and 306 men. A revised budget requirement was placed before the Reichstag and additional financial assets were provided from a fund under the patronage of the indefatigable Prince Heinrich which had produced over 7 million Marks from a public appeal.

This fund was known as the Nationalflugspende (National Fund for the Promotion of Aviation) and a lot of the money subscribed was used to further civilian flying as well as finance research and the embryo German aviation industry. The trend toward integrating flying units into army corps continued throughout 1913 and on 1 October the proposed Inspektion der Fliegertruppen came into existence with Oberst von Eberhardt as its head. Flying units were still very much subservient to the army who directed their operational usage. Their role was still considered to be primarily artillery spotting and reconnaissance. Experimental work in the fitting of guns and bomb sights was being carried out at this time but, it must be stated, without any conclusive results. Strategic bombing was still considered to be a role to be carried out by airships and plans were afoot to have fifteen in service.

Twelve companies forming Flieger Bataillone were established at eleven airfields located at Döberitz, Grossenhain, Posen, Graudenz, Königsberg, Köln, Hannover, Darmstadt, Strassburg, Metz, and Freiburg, with the semi-independent Bavarian Army adding a two company unit at Scheissheim. This impressive start formed part of an overall plan to provide 57 Feldfliegerabteilungen (Flg Abt) by April 1916 with another 46 forming artillery spotting units to follow.

However, the General Staff realized that this expansion was rather too grandiose in view of the resources available, and settled for the formation of four Flg Abt from each of the 12 Fliegerkompanie by 1 April 1914. The last few months of peace saw priority being given to training and the refinement of reconnaissance methods, with special emphasis being placed on artillery spotting and methods of communication.

By the end of July 1914, 118,000,000 Marks had been spent by the Germans on military aviation in the eight years since 1906, clearly some had been wasted in pursuit of impossible dreams, but overall wise counsel had prevailed. Although it was generally considered that the French led the field in military aviation, the German army air service had many areas in which it was superior to the air force of any other nation. Mobilization came at 18.30 hours on 1 August 1914 at which time the Army possessed 12 airships, and 260 aircraft, and the Navy just one airship with its ultra modern hangar at Cuxhaven. Personnel comprised 254 pilots and 271 observers who were distributed among 34 Flg Abt, ten Festungsflieger Abteilungen whose task was defense of the fortress towns and the military bases at Boyen, Breslau and Glogau, and eight Etappen Flugzeugparke (Zone bases) to look after the supply of equipment and men.

The single and two-seat Taube accounted for about half the available aircraft, the rest being parasol monoplanes or Albatros and Aviatik B-type biplanes. Total mobilization took five days during which the various field formations were assigned to their relevant army headquarters. One Flg Abt was attached to each of eight headquarters which also had an Etappen Flugzeugparke. One Flg Abt was also assigned to each of 25 infantry corps.

So the stage was set, and the hour of reckoning was upon those who had for many years advocated a strong military aeronautical presence. In the wings ever watchful were those to whom the very thought of aircraft was abhorrent, at least in a military context. Enthusiasts and critics both awaited the outcome with considerable interest.

Right: The distinctive bird-wing shape of the Etrich Taube is perhaps the closest early designers came to reproducing a bird profile.
Below: The LZ 18, which became Marineluftschiff L 2, made its maiden flight on 9 September 1913.

An Albatros C V in January 1917. The C V was a completely new design although it followed the general pattern established by the C III and IV. Over 400 were built although it was unpopular due to its difficult handling and constant engine problems.

COMBAT ON THE WESTERN FRONT

The influence of air power on the outcome of World War I has variously been described as puny or overwhelming; the truth lies somewhere in between. Prior to the start of hostilities most nations had given more than a passing thought to the use of aircraft in war. Since at this time lines of diplomatic communications were rarely strained, much of this had been shared, so basically everyone started on a common footing. Many papers, discussions and manuals came forth from military circles as well as lay groups and suggestions ranged from liaison, through bombing, reconnaissance and aerial combat to simple artillery spotting in support of the army. A realistic appraisal of papers of the period tends to indicate that most authorities were agreed and content to consider only the reconnaissance aspect in which enemy movements prior to the commencement of land battles were passed to the ground commanders. It must be borne in mind that many of the decisions reached were due to the limitations of the aircraft then available, and very few could accurately foresee the giant steps that would be taken in the development of aircraft by the time the conflict ended. Much of this work did of course arise from experience in the field and came about as a result of experience gained, in many cases, by improvization.

It is too easy to dismiss the limited acceptance of the aircraft in military circles as a reluctance to adapt to new devices. This is true in some cases and there can be no doubt that the power of some who held such views affected the general overall thinking, but it is nearer the truth to suggest that time was needed to assess the advantages and disadvantages of fitting aircraft into the long established doctrines of warfare as known, taught and accepted by the military at that time. It was one thing to carry out aerial observation in peace time maneuvers, and theorize on the results, but quite another when the bullets were real and interpretation could result in success or total failure. The many pitfalls could only be learned by practical application and the first two years of war proved this in many ways.

It had been expected by certain elements in the German air force that the airship would play a decisive part but their confidence in this type of aircraft was soon to take a very early knock. On 4 August, as German columns under the command of General von Emmich met stubborn opposition near Liége the High Command decided to send airship Z 6 to help by bombing the fort. Aerial bombs as such were not available so the airship carried 8 artillery shells weighing 200 kg in all. It can only be assumed that the psychological aspect must have been considered as the main weapon, since such a load could easily have been delivered by conventional artillery. If this was indeed the case it came sadly unstuck, for despite the belief widely held both by military personnel and civilians that there

Right: The AGO C 1 with its twin light-weight wooden booms and pusher propeller gave the observer a clear unobstructed view from the nacelle. It was a successful reconnaissance aircraft, and a naval version was also built which was fitted with floats.
Below right and below: The LVG C VI preserved by the Shuttleworth Trust in Britain. This was one of 1000 built in 1918 which served in the reconnaissance and spotting roles.

Above: A replica of the Fokker E III Eindecker.

would be no effective counter to aerial bombing, the Belgian troops stood fast and their artillery supported by small-arms fire soon tore the envelope of the Z 6 which had been unable to ascend above 4700 feet, to shreds. The airship crashed in woods a short distance from Bonn on trying to carry out an emergency landing.

By the end of August there was a major question mark against the use of the airship in daylight reconnaissance and bombing raids, for on the 21st of the month Z 7 and Z 8 had fallen victims to ground fire while trying to carry out armed reconnaissance. The former dropped bombs on French positions, probably in the hope of gaining height rather than inflicting casualties, before it succumbed to small-arms fire, and the latter was shot down by the French after having been damaged by its own ground forces who fired on it by mistake. Seven days later Z 5 crashed and fell into Russian hands during an attempt to bomb a railway junction at Mlawa. So in less than a month four airships had been lost on operations and a decision was taken limiting them to operations at night. Bombing raids on Antwerp and Rotterdam showed that the airship could perform a vital role but again conditions had to be ideal and moonlight brought just as many dangers as daylight.

September 1914 saw the loss of another airship but this time the circumstances highlighted an aspect that was to develop to much greater effect in World War II. The British Royal Naval Air Service mounted a bombing attack by aircraft against the Zeppelin hangars from Antwerp on 22 September 1914, but thick mist obscured the target and only one aircraft dropped its three bombs, all of which failed to explode. But during the night of 8/9 October a further attempt by Flight Sub-Lieutenant R.L.G. Marix flying a Sopwith Tabloid was successful when he destroyed Z 9 in its hangar. Further efforts during November achieved little apart from forcing the Germans into strengthening their defenses, so although from the point of view of effective bombing the results can be considered poor, they did result – as similar German efforts had and were to – in a diversion of forces away from the main areas of ground combat.

Strategic bombing was considered important by the German air force and in November 1914 the first tentative but important steps were taken to initiate such a plan by the formation of the Fliegerkorps des Oberste Heeresleitung under Major Wilhelm Siegert. This unit which went under the quaint code name Brieftauben-Abteilung Ostende (literally Carrier-pigeon Unit, Ostend), was equipped with 36 aircraft mainly Aviatik B-type biplanes with a brief to attack London. Satisfactory accomplishment of the set task depended on the capture of Calais and other Channel ports since the machines did not have the required range to reach their target from Ostend.

With it becoming increasingly obvious that such an objective was a long way in the future, the unit was moved in early February to the Eastern Front to support the German offensive in Galicia. Prior to this, it had carried out a raid against Dunkirk on 23 January 1915 with 12 aircraft, inflicting little damage but losing one machine. An abortive night raid on the same target was also made later in the month. Nonetheless, it was the first unit to be fully mobile with its own rail transport making it flexible in accordance with area demand, and as such provided a lot of valuable lessons to the High Command. A second unit known in the same style as B.A.M. was formed near Metz, the location giving the M in the title, amd this was used to support units at Verdun and in attacking rail junctions and sea ports.

Bombing aside for the time being, let us look at the situation as it developed during the period 1914-1916.

Reconnaissance was the all important prime function, and the need for the enemy to foil this by counter action either by ground or air forces, gradually saw the evolution of air-to-air combat and ground attack roles by aircraft. There can be no doubt that some aspects of air reconnaissance were treated with suspicion by the army commanders, but there is no real evidence that all aerial reconnaissance was mistrusted.

Above: Typical flying kit from around 1918. The pilot is putting on his parachute harness and holding the static line that will release it from the rather primitive pack. The aircraft is a Fokker D VII.
Below: A 1914 Rumpler B 1 unarmed reconnaissance biplane.

The whole concept of military aviation at this time was based on reconnaissance and spotting, so it is foolish to suggest that all failures on the ground were as a result of poor information from the air, it just so happens that many historians have chosen to highlight such events. There was of course a natural suspicion of the aircraft, and a lack of thought given to strategic deployment coupled with problems in co-ordination and communication, helped to support those who were blinkered in their attitudes. One popular myth is that von Moltke failed to take proper note of reconnaissance reports during the Marne campaign, but there is no evidence to suggest that such reports even reached him or had any cause so to do. It will be recalled that he was one of the main advocates of air power so was unlikely to miss an opportunity to use it if he had been in a position to benefit from it.

Weather conditions are also factors that are often overlooked when assessing overall situations, an early example being when General Krafft von Dellmensingen, Chief of Staff of the German Sixth Army used air reconnaissance to discover the situation of the French army on his left flank which he believed was making a move against Saarburg and Saarbrücken. Reports on 14 August confirmed this but pointed out that French movement was very pedestrian and at the pace being followed the attack the Germans thought imminent would not take place until the following day.

A break in the weather brought all flying to a halt, so it was another four days before patrols could be flown. In the meantime the Germans had changed their plans (because of the initial air reports) in an attempt to lure the French into a trap thus turning defense into offense. These plans were so advanced, by the time the next air patrols reported on 20 August that the situation had grossly changed, that they could not be altered and so the proposed offensive failed. General von Dellmensingen put total blame on the failure of air reconnaissance claiming in a letter to the supreme command that, 'we can only create clarity by battle.' In this case he had chosen to ignore not only the elapsed time element but also facts reported from the air that he did not wish to believe. Such was the state of the art at this time that interpretation of aerial reports was open to much conjecture; later it became a far more precise occupation and from it grew the highly skilled photographic interpretation units that performed vital tasks in WWII.

Ground forces quickly learned to take cover on the approach of an aircraft, and this was the downfall of General Alexander von Kluck commanding the German First Army during the British retreat from Mons. In moving north and west of the British in an attempt to outflank them, he opened a dangerous gap between his forces and those of General Karl von Bülow's Second Army. Eventually one aerial reconnaissance report reached Kluck from which he concluded that the direction in which he was advancing was clear of troops.

From this he assumed that the road was clear, the Allied retreat was in full swing, and he could ignore the gap his advance had created. What in fact had happened was that troops on the ground had taken cover so the German observer had thought the area was clear and reported this was *likely* to be the case. But other reports suggesting caution did not reach the army, and coupled to this fog prevented flights being undertaken to update the situation, so the German First Army blundered into a full frontal counterattack by the British. Once

Above: A 1916 AEG G IVk bomber, an experimental version fitted with a 2cm Becker cannon in the nose.

Below: Oswald Boelcke, the inventor of the fighter combat techniques that resulted in the formation of Jagdstaffeln.

Below: The beautifully cowled rotary engine of the Fokker E I with Leutnant Max Immelmann in the cockpit.

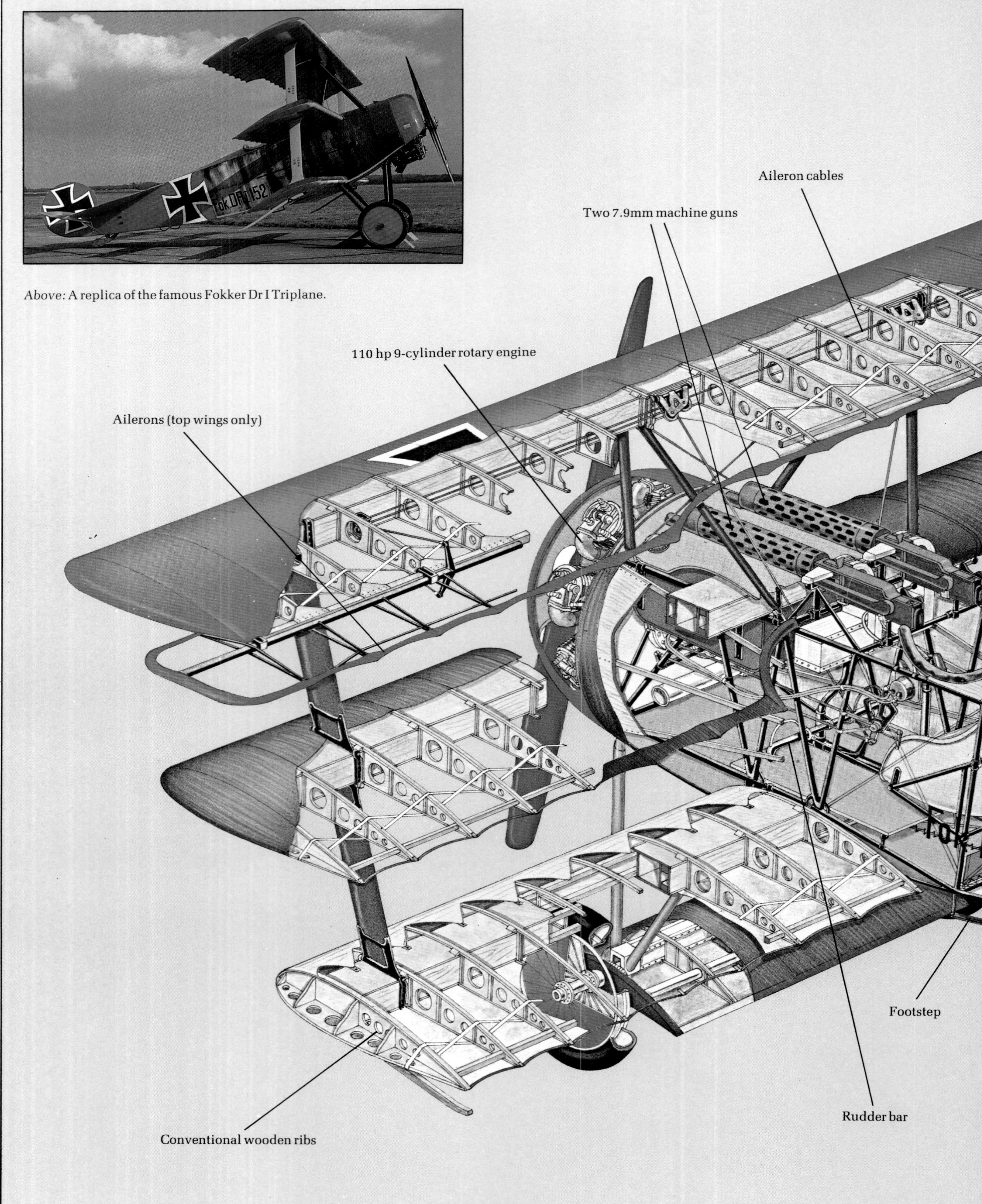

Above: A replica of the famous Fokker Dr I Triplane.

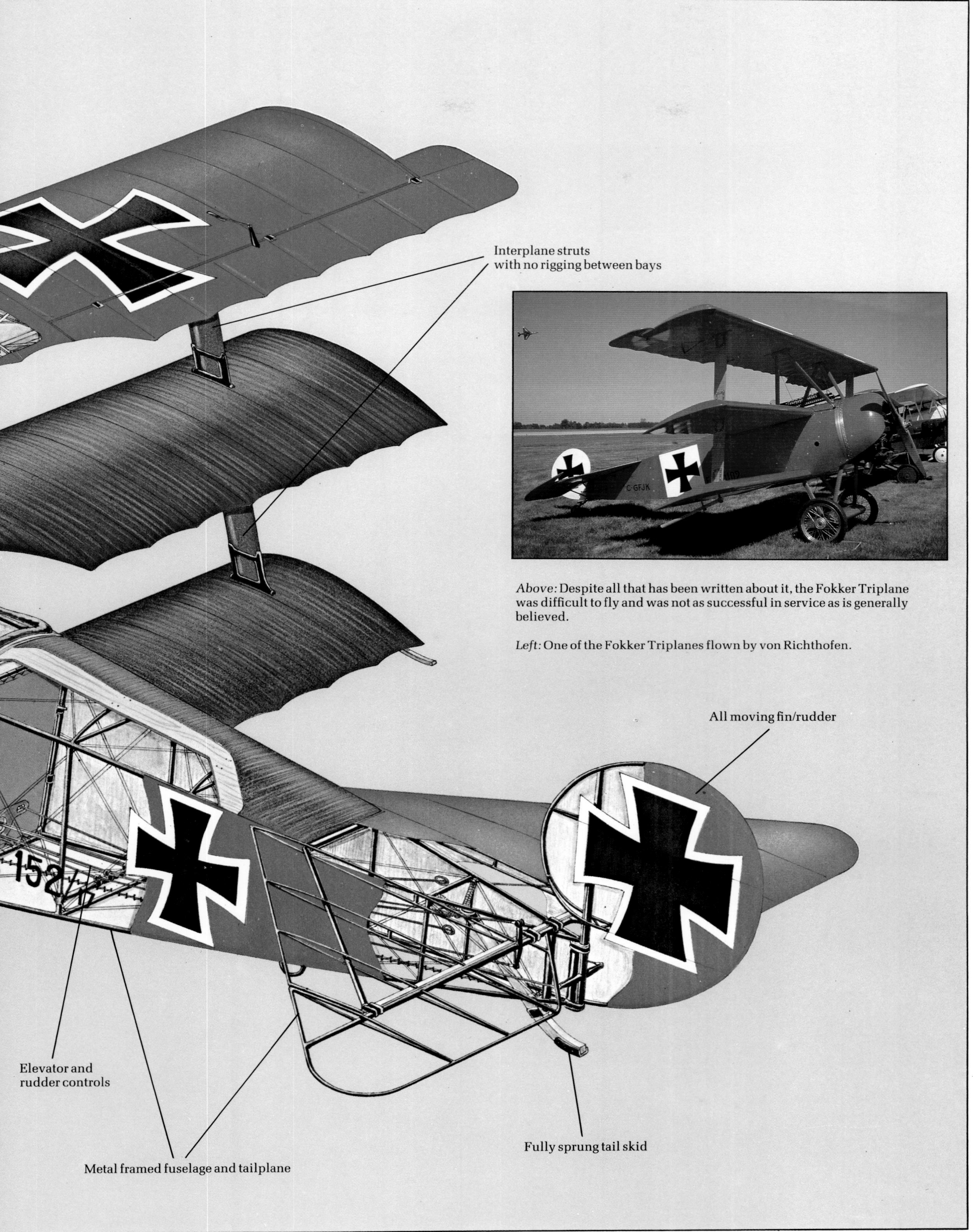

Above: Despite all that has been written about it, the Fokker Triplane was difficult to fly and was not as successful in service as is generally believed.

Left: One of the Fokker Triplanes flown by von Richthofen.

again too literal an interpretation had been placed on an isolated report. These two examples tend to support the view that it was in communication rather than actual reconnaissance that the main fault lay, but at the time it was easier to blame the aircraft.

By the end of 1914 when the development of trench warfare heralded what was to be a long period of static combat, the air weapon was established as an important reconnaissance method. However, there was no sudden shift from negative to positive, failure and success were still the two extremes with only about 50 percent of reports ever reaching the respective headquarters.

The obvious counter to aerial reconnaissance was to destroy the source of information. Static balloons and airships did not present too great a problem as both were vulnerable to ground fire, but the airplane was a rather different problem.

Almost since the beginning of hostilities crews of reconnaissance aircraft had taken pistols or rifles aloft with them, more in a gesture of defiance, than with any hope of inflicting damage to an unsuspecting enemy. But the thought of mounting machine guns on aircraft had long been in the minds of many, and there is a popular belief that most French machines were so equipped from very early days. Like most generalizations this is a dangerous one, and can be disputed by the fact that the first aerial victory of the French ace Jean Navarre on 1 April 1915 was gained when his observer, Lieutenant Robert, shot down a German aircraft with a carbine.

The same day saw another questionable 'first' which has been made much of over the years. This was the shooting down of a German machine by Roland Garros flying a Morane Saulnier Monoplane which had plates fitted to the propeller to deflect shells from a machine gun arranged to fire through its arc. In fact much more sophisticated interrupter gear enabling the propeller to be synchronized with the firing of a forward facing machine gun had been in the course of development by the French, British and Swiss, and it was just that Garros' more primitive device went into service sooner and accelerated development when it fell into German hands on 18 April 1915 when Garros was forced down by engine trouble behind enemy lines.

Above left: A Taube monoplane built by Germania Flugzeugwerke of Leipzig in 1914.
Left: An observer demonstrates the use of his Parabellum machine gun. The 'secondary' armament is a standard infantry rifle.
Below: The Albatros C III was largely based on the B III.

Above: Leutnant Werner Voss in the cockpit of his Fokker Dr I Triplane. Voss gained 48 victories before his death in September 1917.

Above left: Pilots of a Jagdstaffel prepare for an offensive patrol in 1918.
Above: The observer of a ground attack aircraft is handed grenades before taking off on a raid against enemy infantry.
Right: A replica of the Fokker D VIII. It was dogged by structural problems and only 85 had been delivered by November 1918.

Garros achieved only three victories with his device before his capture, and the fact that only two days later the well-known Fokker synchronization gear was ready for test, puts into true perspective the situation regarding the primitive deflector plates. They certainly helped from the point of view of pushing the urgency for Fokker to get his working properly, but did not influence the fighter war to the degree often claimed. It is more likely that the Nieuport with a machine gun mounted above the mainplane and firing forward over the propeller arc, was of greater influence than the Saulnier device. Incidentally, technically it is incorrect to refer to the Fokker equipment as interrupter gear since operation of the trigger fired the guns during moments of safety and did not cut-out the mechanism on the passage of the propeller.

First victory to a German pilot using the forward firing machine gun on a Fokker Eindecker was on 1 July 1915 when Kurt Wintgens' victim fell into French territory. The Germans were very particular about aerial victory claims and only usually allowed them on examination of the wreckage, so the first confirmed success had to wait until 1 August when Max Immelmann shot down a British aircraft over Douai. This heralded the start of the much publicized era known as the 'Fokker Scourge.'

Although the arrival in April 1915 of the armed C-type biplane, used mainly to escort the unarmed B-type reconnaissance machines, had restored some balance to air power, it is generally considered that in the overall pattern of events the Allies held supremacy until the advent of the Fokker toward the end of the year. Once again this has been claimed as an almost overnight success story, but again the truth is far from this. Following Immelmann's success in August, there was much demand for the fighter, but it was basically unstable and its rotary engine made it rather tricky for the average squadron pilot. A series of fatal crashes at Döberitz saw the aircraft grounded and it was not until late October that the Inspector of Aviation, under pressure from front line units, allowed training to recommence.

The exploits of Immelmann and Boelcke who were to become the first household names in relation to aerial successes as far as the German propaganda and publicity machine was concerned, brought a much needed boost to morale. Aerial combats increased in frequency as both sides sought to protect their reconnaissance machines and balloons, and losses to RFC aircraft mounted alarmingly. Questions were raised in the British Parliament about the standard of aircraft and training; and morale among reconnaissance crews floundered as every German scout encountered was a 'Fokker.'

A directive was issued that every RFC recce aircraft had to be escorted by at least three fighters, and a climax was reached in early February 1916 when on one occasion 12 escorts covered one reconnaissance aircraft observing a railway junction.

The reaction caused was out of all proportion to the threat, for at the end of 1915 only 40 Fokkers had reached the front-line and most of these were concentrated opposite the French at Verdun. The situation is perhaps best summed up by an RFC pilot who wrote at the time: 'Early in 1916 Fokker was the menace of the RFC. Hearsay and a few lucky encounters had made the machines respected, not to say dreaded by the slow unwieldy machines then used by us.'

In April 1916 a captured Fokker was pitted against a Morane Saulnier Monoplane which easily outmaneuvered it, thus helping to restore some perspective to the situation which had shown grave danger of becoming totally out of hand. A further

Left: General Ernst von Höppner (left) C in C of the German Air Service and his Chief of Staff Oberst Hermann Thomsen.
Right: A beautifully constructed replica Fokker D VII, generally regarded as the best German fighter of WWI.

Leergewicht ... 567 Kg
Nutzlast ...... 200 Kg
Vollgewicht ... 763 Kg
Fok. E V 157/18
40!

indication of the actual impact of the Fokker can be gauged by the fact that at the time of Immelmann's death on 18 June 1916, five of his fifteen victories had been achieved before the Fokker legend came into being.

The exploits of Immelmann and Boelcke captured the imagination of the German public although to a certain degree they were unheard of at the front. They led to the glorification of the individual ace system that by the end of the war had made many flyers in all combatant air forces, very much public figures. It was primarily at Boelcke's suggestion that specialist fighter units were established, and from these grew the Jagdstaffeln that were eventually to become part of Jagdgeschwadern and in some collective cases gave birth to the so called 'Flying Circus.'

The menace of the Fokker as seen through the eyes of the allies, was countered not only by the introduction of new aircraft like the British Fe2b and DH 2, but also the adoption of formation tactics in which the combined fire from the gunners of two-seat scouts or reconnaissance aircraft, provided an effective defensive barrier. This again is an example of a lesson that was carried forward to WWII but proved far from successful in that war mainly due to greater advances in technology which produced a far greater differential between fighter and bomber performances. Nonetheless the build-up to the Somme offensive saw the Allies once again in the ascendancy.

The advances in aircraft design were such that those reaching the front line in late 1915 and early 1916, were not so much better in terms of speed or ceiling, but had greatly improved armament and maneuverability. The limiting factor was in fact aircraft production, which was like most of the other factors dictating progress in the field of aviation, a new art that had to be learned.

The start of the Allied offensive on the Somme on 1 July 1916 brought greatly concentrated attacks on observation balloons and German ground forces. The pendulum had swung away from the Germans, who were finding that superior tactics and numbers were causing morale sapping drains on their air elements. At the start of the campaign the British had 185 aircraft available in the Somme sector and the French 201; the

Above: A Rumpler B 1 and crew ready for action. The B series were unarmed reconnaissance biplanes.
Top: A LVG C I of Feldflieger Abteilung 23 in the early summer of 1915. Note the absence of a fuselage cross.
Top right: An impressive line-up of Albatros D IIIs. This was probably the most successful of the D series of Albatros Scouts and entered service in 1917.
Below: Aviatik B 1 type aircraft at the Aviatik Training School Habsheim, 1915.

Below: A cutaway view of the Albatros D Va.

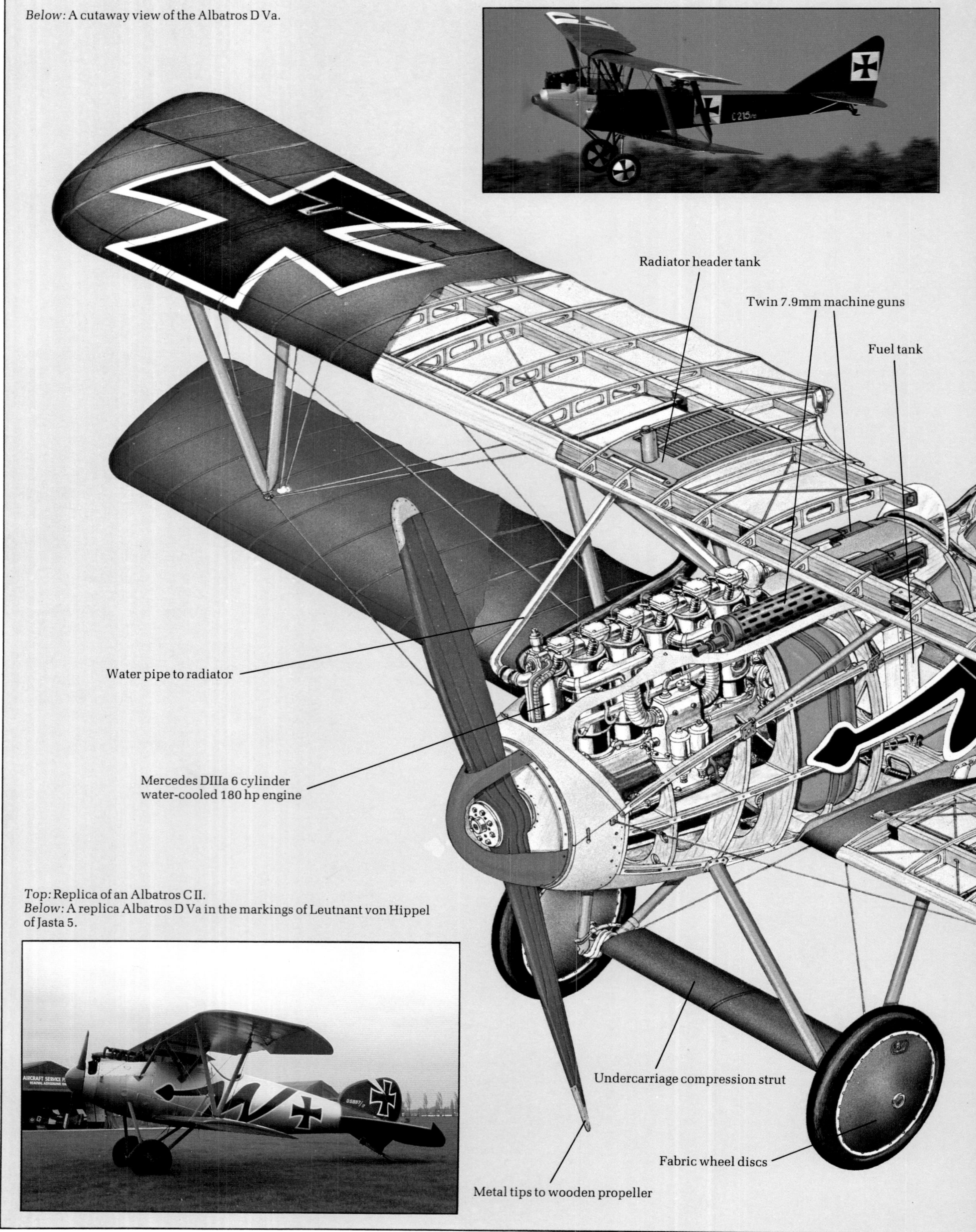

Top: Replica of an Albatros C II.
Below: A replica Albatros D Va in the markings of Leutnant von Hippel of Jasta 5.

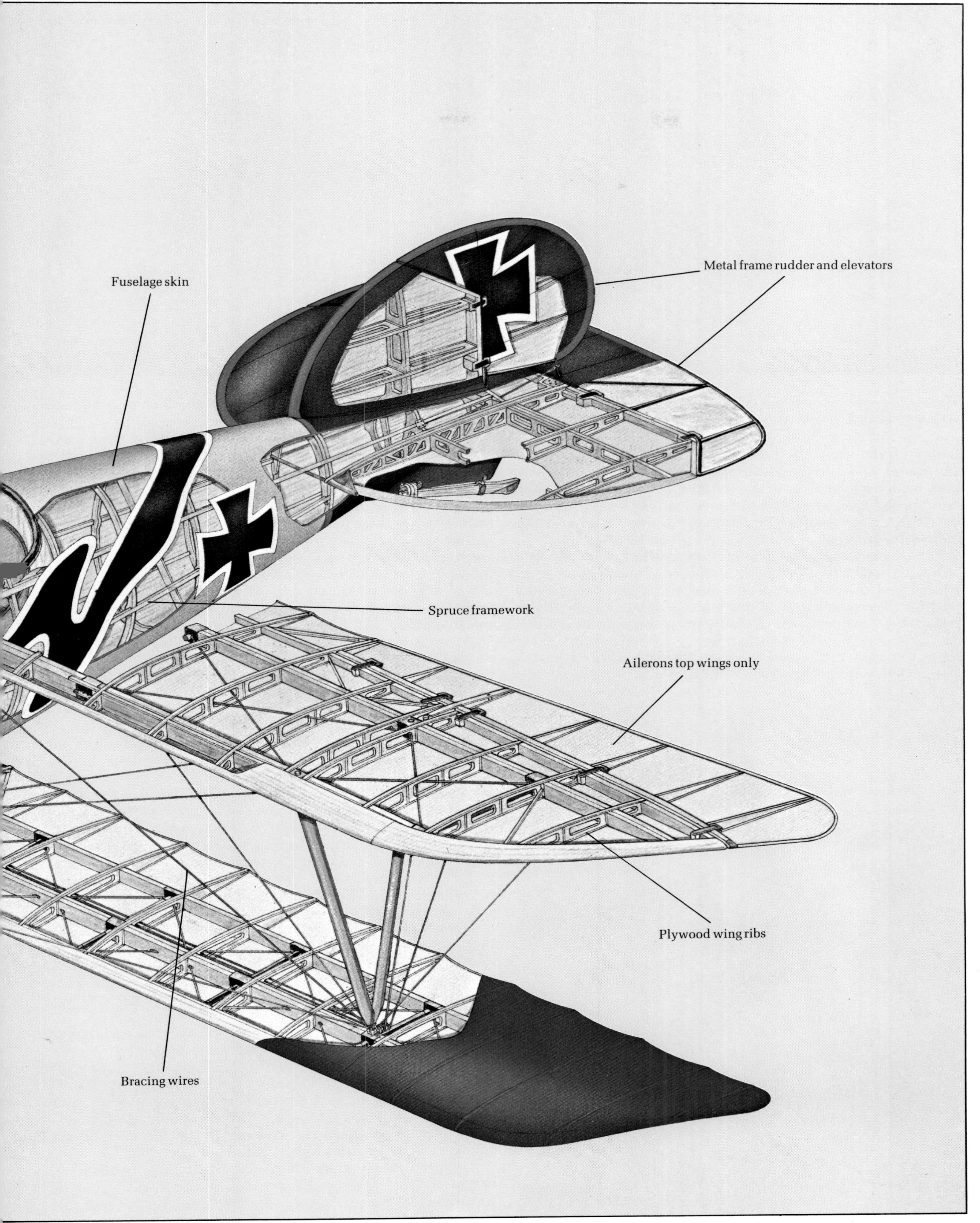
Fuselage skin
Metal frame rudder and elevators
Spruce framework
Ailerons top wings only
Plywood wing ribs
Bracing wires

Above: A typical German airfield somewhere on the Western Front. The tents are in fact hangars for the aircraft.

German force was 129, thus they were outnumbered by 3-1, and found this a tremendous disadvantage in every respect. Most of all it was evident to the troops on the ground that Allied artillery spotting appeared to be accomplished without too much interference, so the German air force came in for increasing criticism.

The German strategy came in for total reappraisal at the end of August and on the 28th of the month von Falkenhayn resigned as Chief of the General Staff and was replaced by Field Marshal Paul von Hindenburg with General Ludendorff as First Quarter Master General. One of the new commanders' first actions was to halt all offensive operations, which immediately released aircraft from the Verdun front to strengthen the units engaged on the Somme. Consequently a new British offensive on 15 September was countered by a mixture of C- and D-type aircraft totalling close to 350. The first fighter unit Jasta (Jagdstaffel) 2 under Oswald Boelcke also became operational, and justified itself by destroying 76 enemy aircraft for the loss of only 7 of its own number during the period September to November. Total losses in the German air force over the Somme were only 12 for the month of October against 27 the previous month when the battle was at a peak.

Below: A mechanic works on the wooden propeller of an Albatros D V. Note the veneers which make up the propeller.

One of the most significant and far reaching appointments however, came in October when a 56 year old former cavalry officer and Chief of Staff of the Third Army, General Ernst von Höppner, became Commanding General of the Air Service. Up to then the air force had been divided into small units each the responsibility of a higher army command, its tactical and equipment requirements being handled by lower ranking staff officers such as Siegert and Thomsen. The latter, now an Oberstleutnant, became von Höppner's Chief of Staff. The air force although still not autonomous, was at last a true air service under one overall commander, and he was not only an accomplished administrator but also very enthusiastic about air power and its uses.

Little time was wasted in introducing changes to the structure of the air force, and these were primarily aimed at integrating many small units into more easily managed larger ones. The Feldflieger Abteilungen became simply Flieger Abteilungen and incorporated the former Artillerie Flieger Abteilungen now identified as Flieger Abt. (A). The Kagohls (Battle Wings) were reduced to three and started to be totally equipped with long range G-type aircraft. Surplus units within this organization were redesignated Schutzstaffeln, their prime task being to escort the two seater reconnaissance aircraft of the Flg.Abt. (A). The Jasta remained unchanged but received immediate priority in expansion and re-equipping with the latest D-type biplanes.

The flying units were not the only subjects for wholesale change and the supporting control sections also came in for reappraisal. The changes which became effective during the opening months of 1917 certainly brought the much desired change in fortunes, and coupled with the arrival in some quantity of the Albatros D III, enabled the Germans once again to retrieve the initiative during the spring of 1917. These changes brought about a hidden disadvantage in that increased demands created a severe drain on raw materials, and this had not totally been overcome before the United States entered the war in 1917. The huge resources of the new enemy presented many problems for the Germans, for although they were by no

Above: NCO pilot Weckbrodt served on the Eastern Front. He scored two victories before being killed in action on 13 October 1917.
Above right: A Rumpler D 1 with Herr Rumpler the designer (right) in deep conversation with the test pilot.

means immediately evident, it was clear to many that ultimately there was no way in which the rich resources of such a vast country could be matched or countered. So, the situation in late 1917 was very much akin to that which was to face Germany some 25 years later under similar circumstances.

Organization and politics aside, the newly formed air arm soon exercised its new found freedom and began to assert its authority on the battlefields of Europe. The sterling work carried out by German reconnaissance aircraft crews often takes second place to the exploits of the fighter aces, but it must be remembered that they carried out vital tasks while suffering high casualty rates but were not beyond giving a good account of themselves when necessary.

In the autumn of 1917 the C-types used for this work were supplemented by the improved CL machines which were initially the Halberstadt CL II and Hannover CL II and III. Their prime role was to escort the reconnaissance aircraft and in this they formed the basis of the Schutzstaffeln, but they were also used to carry out attacks with small bombs on ground forces and their contribution certainly cannot be lightly dismissed as they played a far more offensive role than any other part of the German air force. Ground attack had featured prominently in German strategy and the heavily armored J-types with greatly improved protection for crews and fuel tanks were first seen in action at low-level at Verdun. The initial types which were modified C machines were primarily the Albatros and AEG J Is, and these were followed by aircraft specifically built for the purpose, the most successful of which was the Junkers J I with its completely armored nose section and an ability to absorb a tremendous amount of punishment.

The increasing effectiveness of anti-aircraft weapons and fighters gradually forced both sides into defining strategies that were in the broadest sense to become the basic parameters for aerial warfare. Control of the air brought control of the battlefield, and ground attack aircraft could only operate in any force and degree of safety if opposing fighters were kept at bay, or

Below: The Halberstadt D III, shown with its pilot and ground crew, began to replace the Fokker Eindecker in 1916. It was robust and popular but never achieved the status of the Albatros scouts.

Above: Pilots of JG.1 Left to right, Wüsthoff (27 victories) Reinhard (20), von Richthofen (80), Löwenhardt (53) and Lothar von Richthofen (40).

better still wiped out. So the fighter, whose task was to clear the way for the reconnaissance and supporting ground attack aircraft, came into its own and with it brought a rather special breed of pilot, who over the years has always typified every schoolboy's hero.

The advent of the Jasta in September 1916 was instrumental in changing the face of air-to-air combat. The new force gradually grew in stature and by April 1917 the Albatros D III was the major equipment of the 37 units then formed. At this time the main tactic was to lie in wait for the Allied two-seaters to cross the line on reconnaissance flights, whereupon the fighters would descend from the sun and create havoc. Faced with similar problems the previous year the Germans had opted to abandon such flights. The Allies pushed on with mounting losses but dogged determination, each piece of information obtained being bought with high loss of life. This period became known as 'Bloody April' and in some ways can be looked upon as a victory for the Allies rather than the defeat often associated with it.

The reason for this is that although German fighter aircraft were still numerically less strong than the French and British, the latter had not yet perfected the operation of the Spad, Sopwith Triplane and Camel, and SE 5 then coming into service, so were not able to give the close protection needed. The Germans always tried to avoid contact with the Allied fighters, their prime objective quite rightly being the destruction of reconnaissance aircraft. They were also operating over their own territory which gave them a better than even chance of returning to their units in the event of being shot down or making a forced landing.

The introduction of the Spad and Camel saw the balance once again moving towards the Allies, but this was again countered by the Albatros D V and Va, although overall there was not much to choose between the aircraft and in the end a great deal depended on the respective skills of the pilots. This period of the war brought the massed fights between Allied and German aircraft which could last for up to an hour, and range from ground level to the aircraft's ceiling. These became known as 'Dogfights' and are how most people with no more than a passing interest see the air war of 1914-18. The arrival of the fabulous Fokker D VII in 1918 certainly gave the Jastas a major advantage, and there can really be little doubt that this was one of the most effective aircraft to come out of the conflict, this being supported by it being specifically banned by the Treaty of Versailles.

The effectiveness of a Jagdgeschwader owed a great deal to training and the ability of its commander, the first being formed on 23 June 1917 by placing Jasta 4, 6, 10 and 11 under the command of the famous Baron Manfred von Richthofen, but it was later felt that the acute shortage of well qualified regular officers with sufficient experience, made an overall change in such matters rather impractical. Nonetheless, the Jastas did operate in conjunction with each other in what might be termed big wings each of which was self-supporting and could be moved along the front to areas where they could be used to gain the greatest superiority.

Below: The Junkers CL I was of all-metal construction and powered by a Mercedes six-cylinder 180hp engine. It was too late to see any effective service and only 47 were built.

The movement of these wings along the front brought about the coining of the well-known phrase 'Flying Circus' which gradually became applied to all fighter units whether or not they formed part of a Jagdgeschwader. Their use more-or-less saw the end of the individualist fighter pilot who operated alone looking for targets of opportunity, nevertheless they were the breeding grounds of many of the names now associated with the Great War, and in ending this necessarily brief look it is worth considering the factors taken into account in the making of an ace.

The Germans were very strict in their crediting of victories to individuals, and usually demanded confirmation from ground forces, which tended to be fairly easy since most combats took place over German occupied territory. It can be reasonably assumed therefore that the victories credited to the top three aces, von Richthofen 80, Ernst Udet 62, and Erich Loewenhardt 53, are accurate. Acclamation by decoration was used by the Germans as a powerful propaganda weapon and recipients of medals tended to be fêted and encouraged to flaunt their ability to an admiring public. The ultimate accolade was the Pour le Mérite, more commonly known as the Blue Max, this being awarded only to officers. During the period of WWI 363 German pilots had become aces using the commonly accepted standard of 5 victories – the Germans themselves used 10 as the criterion – Britain and the British Empire counted 784, and the French 158.

The air war in the west has been concentrated on because it

Above: This Albatros D V is the aircraft flown by the ace Hauptmann Ritter von Schleich who flew with Jasta 32.

had the greatest influence on the development of the German air force. Most other campaigns were confined very much to reconnaissance and co-operation in attacking ground forces; this does not mean they were of no consequence to the outcome of the conflict, but were secondary to the development of air power. Space prevents a detailed look at these but in an attempt to give some balance a brief outline will be given in the next chapter.

In the context of the overall evolution of air power, the strategy and tactics of providing an air umbrella and blockade flying which gained Allied supremacy at the beginning of 1916 especially in the Somme campaign, were in essence not a great deal different to the plans behind the air offensive mounted over Germany in 1944. Tactical support of the army was eventually fundamentally the same in both wars, and isolation of the battlefield by the use of air power was a concept that originated in WWI. At the conclusion of the Somme campaign it was quite clear that aerial superiority was essential if land operations were to be successful, but this lesson had still not been digested and totally accepted by some commanders until well into World War II.

Below: The popular Fokker D VII. This particular aircraft was built under license by the Albatros Werke in 1918.

STRATEGIC BOMBING

One of the giant class DFW R I heavy bombers seen with the much smaller single-seater SSW D I.

From the earliest time that man took up arms against his fellow man, combat was a straightforward event with the objective being to defeat the opposition in the field or at sea. It was fairly easy to differentiate between legitimate combatants and non-combatants, and the capture of supply dumps, lines of communications and seats of government was very rare, defeat in the field usually resulting in total surrender of all such properties. The blockade of supplies in sieges or control of vital sea lanes thus cutting off ports, was the closest early commanders ever came to what might loosely be termed a strategic objective.

It is not surprising therefore that when a third dimension, in the form of air power, was introduced into warfare, most of the generals and admirals found it difficult to change habits that had been indoctrinated into them from the dawn of their own military service. Some far-sighted leaders could see that the versatility of the aircraft could change the whole concept of warfare, others saw and expected far too much too soon, while others believed that the involvement of civilians in the bombing of cities, would quickly bring capitulation from the governments of those concerned. As early as 1899 the legitimacy of bombardment from the air, albeit from balloons, had been discussed at the first Hague Convention, when an attempt was made to reach agreement between the 26 nations present as to the laws of air warfare.

Of the three declarations accepted, one prevented the discharge of projectiles from balloons, this later being modified at Geneva to cover release from airplanes or airships, although the modification was not totally accepted. This resulted in some confusion since the Germans took a literal translation that the agreement extended only to objects being released from balloons, whilst the French and British felt there was a moral obligation only to attack strictly military targets. No one accepted total prohibition so it is to be concluded that all felt that any future air war would include some form of bombing.

The definition of a legitimate target is of course another difficult area. It was generally thought that any city, town, or area containing centers that were vital to the enemy war effort, that came within the area of combat by ground forces, was a good military target. Any civilians present could be evacuated or remain at their own risk, the question of the difference in

involving civilians by the use of artillery from a range of say 10 miles, or an aeroplane that was dropping bombs having travelled a greater distance so to do, was something that was not taken too seriously into consideration during the moral aspects of the argument. But generally speaking it is perhaps best to use the yardstick that defined strategic bombing as attacks on objectives outside the zone of operations without direct relation to any particular ground operation.

So the early so called strategic bombing raids by the Z 6, Z 7 and Z 8 mentioned in the previous chapter, were not strategic in the true sense of the interpretation as they were supporting planned military ground objectives.

However, the long-range reconnaissance by the Schütte-Lanz (SL 2) which flew nearly 300 miles into Russian territory on 22 August 1914, and returned with reports on army build-ups miles away from the front, is a good example of strategic use although in this case not bombing. Similarly, the attacks made on the Zeppelin works at Friedrichshafen and the one against the installation at Cuxhaven on 25 December 1914, are good examples of strategic bombing, as they involved long penetrative flights into territory where those on the ground might well have considered themselves to be well clear of danger. Incidentally, the 25 December raid was the first ever offensive strike carried out by aircraft from a ship in the history of air warfare. Although little was achieved in the way of lasting or effective damage, plans were immediately put in hand to strengthen defenses, so effort that could have been directed at strengthening front line positions was diluted to cover areas previously considered safe. Britain and France were forced to carry out the same spread of effort following German raids so strategic bombing was beginning to achieve one of its objectives which was to force the enemy into a previously unthought of dispersal of military forces.

In September 1914 airships were used to drop small bombs and propaganda leaflets over Antwerp and Warsaw, and on 30 August four bombs fell on Paris having been released from an aircraft. The leaflets probably had more effect on the civilian

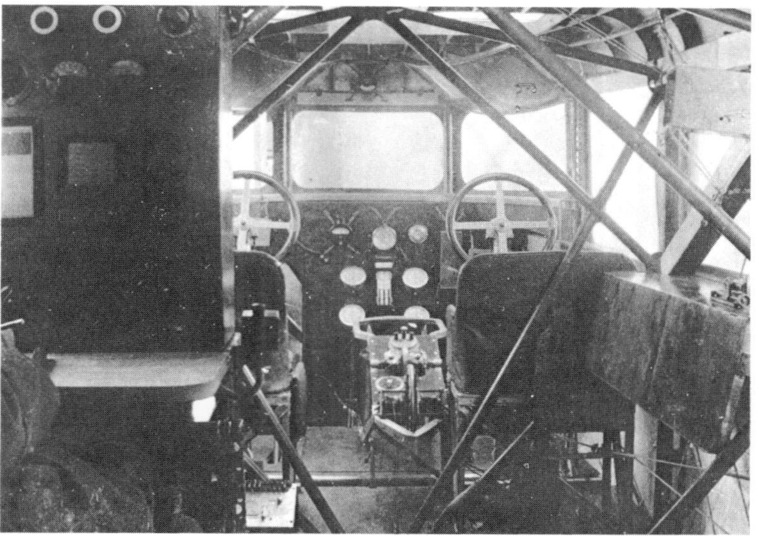

Left: The huge Friedrichshafen G III (illustrated) and the Gotha G V, formed the backbone of the strategic bombing force in 1917/18.
Below left: The LZ 107 in winter camouflage setting off to raid Boulogne.
Right: The cockpit of the giant Zeppelin Staaken R VI long-range heavy bomber.
Below: An artist's impression of London under aerial bombardment by naval airships.

Below: A Zeppelin Staaken R VI long-range bomber. The wing-span of this aircraft was nearly 140 feet; the modern A300 Airbus is 147 feet.

Above: Major Wilhelm Siegert, architect of German strategic bombing.
Left: A Zeppelin is carefully maneuvered into its shed, clearly a tricky and time-consuming operation.

population than the bombs, but it was a start in involving civilians in front-line situations.

The formation of Major Wilhelm Siegert's Fliegerkorps des Obersten Heeresleitung in November, with the sole objective of bombing London with aircraft, was a little premature, but it serves to illustrate that more than a passing thought had been given to this method of carrying the war to the enemy.

In the event the first bomb to fall on British soil came down harmlessly near Dover on 24 December 1914, having been carried across the Channel by a C-type biplane. The first Zeppelin raid followed on 19 January 1915 when two airships dropped bombs in East Anglia killing two civilians in Great Yarmouth and two elsewhere, as well as injuring sixteen. Several other raids followed but created little in terms of damage but a lot in terms of public feeling. The raids highlighted that the defenses were quite inadequate; casualties among British pilots trying to intercept the airships were quite high, not because of any form of resistance offered by the airship crews, but simply that night flying was a skilled art that

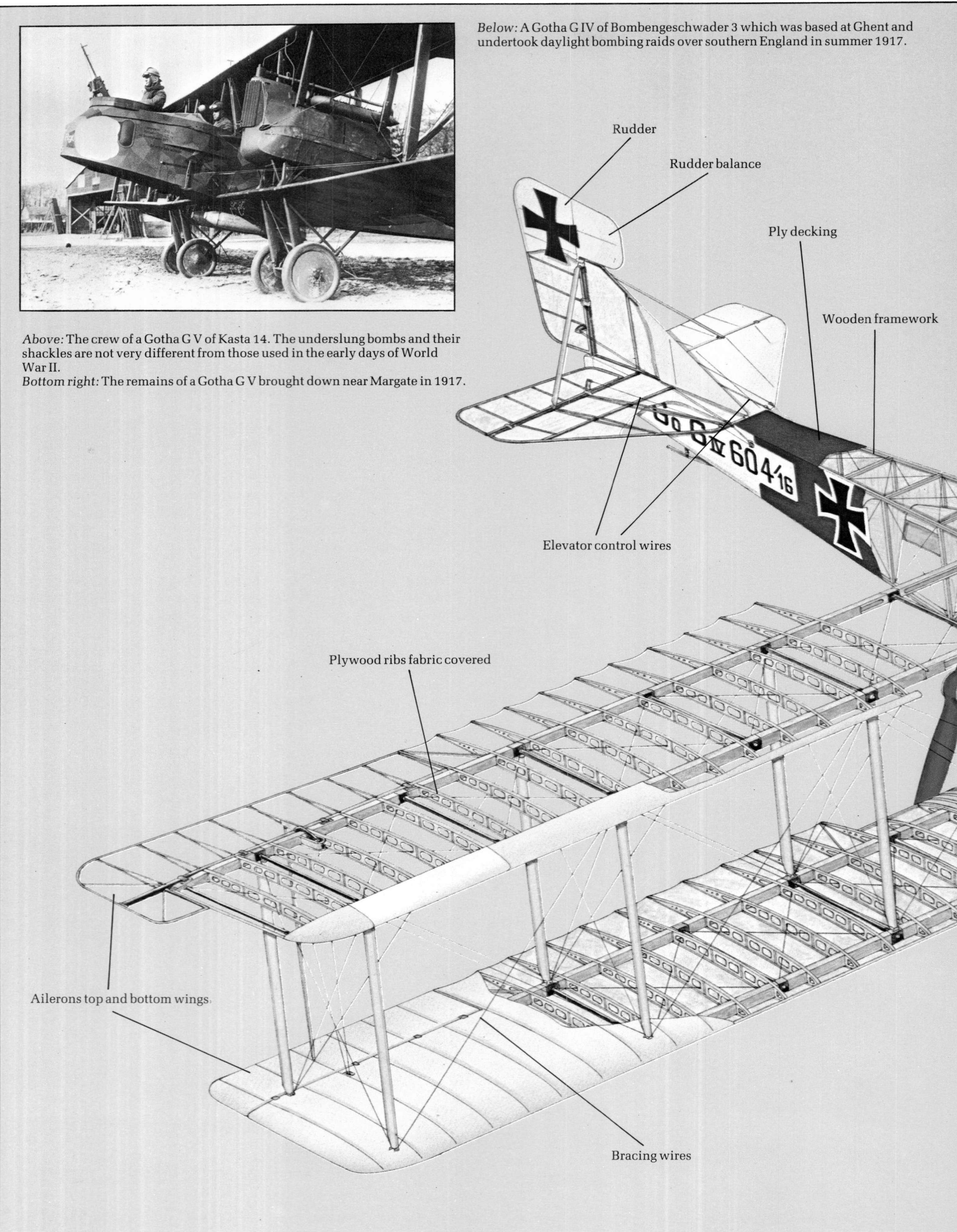

Below: A Gotha G IV of Bombengeschwader 3 which was based at Ghent and undertook daylight bombing raids over southern England in summer 1917.

Above: The crew of a Gotha G V of Kasta 14. The underslung bombs and their shackles are not very different from those used in the early days of World War II.
Bottom right: The remains of a Gotha G V brought down near Margate in 1917.

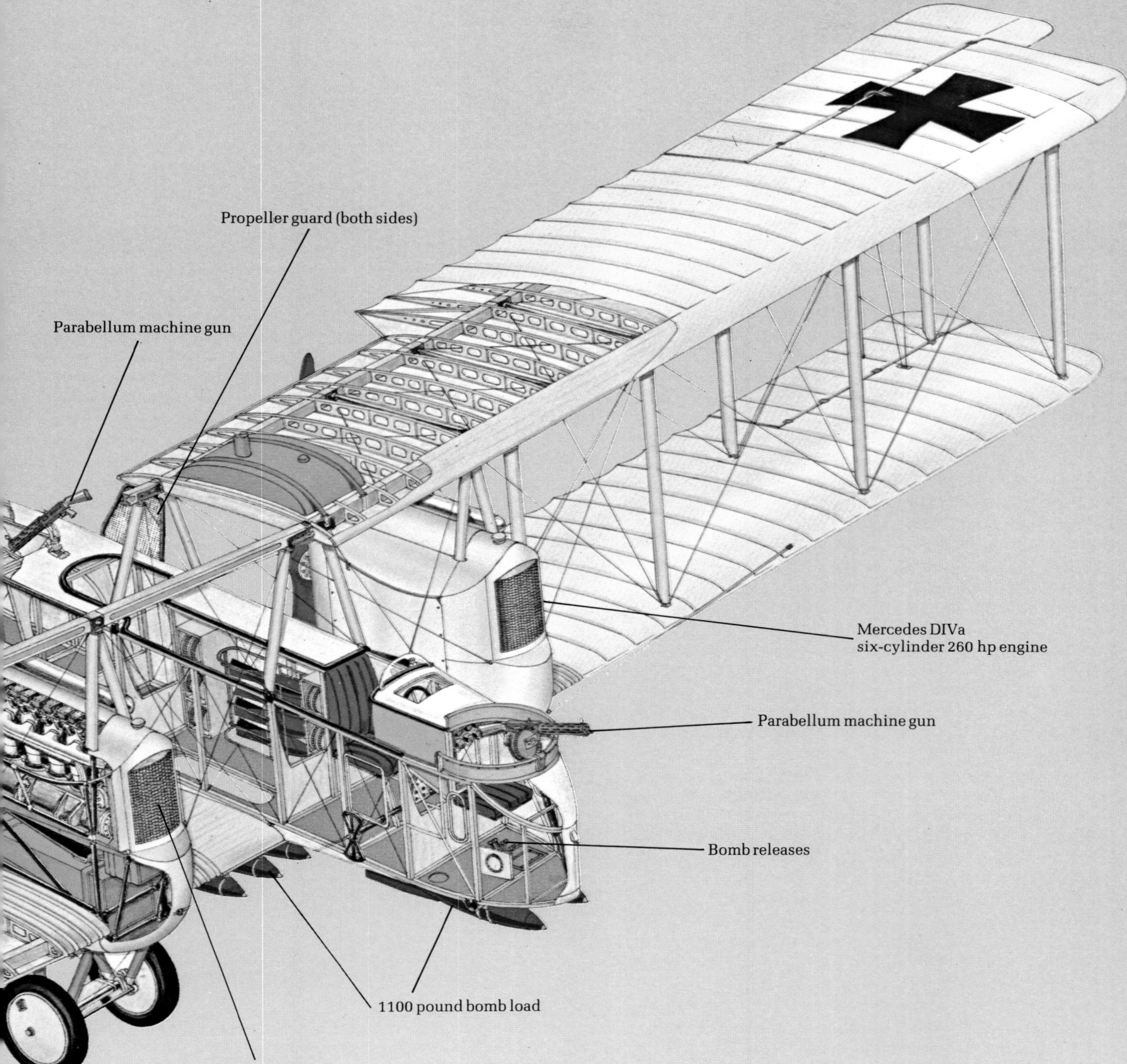

Propeller guard (both sides)

Parabellum machine gun

Mercedes DIVa
six-cylinder 260 hp engine

Parabellum machine gun

Bomb releases

1100 pound bomb load

Coolant radiator

few had ever undertaken at that stage in the development of aviation. Artillery was much more effective and it was in fact the guns of Dover that gained the first success when they accounted for the L 12 on 10 August 1915, this craft crashing in the sea near Ostend after being damaged.

But it was not all plain sailing for the airship crews; night navigation was very difficult, a typical example being the previously mentioned L 12 which thought it had made a landfall in Norfolk but was in fact 100 miles south over Kent.

A naval gunnery expert, Admiral Sir Percy Scott, was put in charge of British anti-aircraft defenses, but this proved beyond his capability since there was a vast difference in ranging guns at a naval target and an airship travelling at 60mph at a height of up to two miles. Nonetheless, the presence of the guns had two positive effects, one it boosted the morale of the public, and secondly it forced the airships higher. Bombing accuracy, once the target was located, was quite good, as the commander was able to slow or stop his ship directly above the objective, but the nub of the problem was finding the target. Dead reckoning navigation and radio cross bearings were the accepted norms of the day, but the guns forcing the airships higher, cloud, unpredictable and unforecast winds, made this very much a hit or miss situation. There were many occasions when crews claimed to have bombed targets in England when in fact they were nowhere near where they thought they were, and similarly there were raids which went unnoticed by the British simply because the airships had been miles out in their navigation. But once again the propaganda machine proved to be a powerful weapon and the exploits of the airship crews were repeated by the media across Germany where they were greeted by the public with great enthusiasm. In an attempt to overcome the problem of position and target identification, a Köln engineer, Herr Hagan, designed a capsule that could be lowered beneath the airship to guide it while it remained above or concealed by cloud.

The L 12 was fitted with this device and on 17 March 1915 used it for the first time during a raid on the east coast. Weather was bad and the country was shrouded in cloud. Kapitän-zur-See Ernst Lehmann totally lost track of his position and so, after turning south hoping to locate the Thames estuary, he lowered Leutnant Max von Gemmingen – a nephew of Count Zeppelin – 2500 feet into clear air. The cable carrying the capsule also incorporated a telephone line through which the observer could contact the main control bridge of the mother ship, and this was used by the intrepid Leutnant to advise Lehmann that the craft was in fact over Calais. This device proved reasonably workable and was later extensively used by the airship fleet.

The bombing offensive of Britain continued with the army using their shorter ranged craft and the navy opening a wider range of targets with their longer ranged airships operating from more distant bases. This attention resulted in greater efforts being made to strengthen defenses by increasing searchlight coverage, the quantity of guns, and more important, concentration on night flying techniques for fighter aircraft.

Although ground fire had proved effective when the airship was being used for reconnaissance work over land battles, the counter was ineffective on bombing raids which of course took place at higher altitude. The first airship to be destroyed by an aircraft was L 37 which fell to Sub-Lieutenant R Warneford who dropped bombs on it over Ghent on 7 June 1915, but it was to be another fifteen months before a similar success was recorded over England.

The ease with which airships began regularly to appear over England and the apparent ineffectiveness of the defenses, was beginning to rouse considerable public feeling, when on the night of 2/3 September 1916, Second Lieutenant William Leefe Robinson flying a BE 2c shot down the Schütte-Lanz SL 11 over Cuffley, Hertfordshire. The SL 11 was one of a force of 14 which had crossed the coast heading for the capital, this turning out to be the biggest airship raid (in terms of numbers) during the war. None of the craft reached the objective, and Leefe-Robinson's victory which was achieved with tracer ammunition was seen

by many hundreds watching from the ground. The airship fell in a ball of flames from 13,000 feet, and its funeral pyre heralded not only a boost to the flagging morale of the public, but the beginning of the end of long-range airship raids over England.

Six nights later L 13 inflicted over £500,000 damage to London in a raid which saw the first 300kg bomb dropped, but gradually as the defenses became stronger, the raids petered out as the airships had to seek higher safe altitudes, which coupled to the lasting navigational problems, a more effective black-out and a vast improvement in fighters and night flying methods, made bombing less and less accurate. By the end of 1916 five more airships had been lost and although the final such raid did not occur until 5 August 1918, the feared threat was over. Of the 1100 airship crewmen lost in action during the war, approximately 270 were killed, wounded or taken prisoner in raids against England.

The German navy used the airship extensively as the eyes of the fleet, but once again the same problems were encountered by the aviators as those met by their brethren over the trenches.

Above: The construction of a Zeppelin. Each bay is 3 meters; note the strengthening on the ring of every third bay.
Right: LZ 38 commanded by Major Linnarz was the first Zeppelin to bomb London, on 31 May 1915, killing seven and wounding 35.

The airship proved an ideal craft for shadowing the fleet, and monitoring movement of submarines. But in general terms communication was in its infancy and sometimes reports which could have had a bearing on deployment of warships were received too late or not totally believed. In the great sea battle of Jutland on 31 May/1 June 1916, the German navy deployed five airships, but they were hampered by bad weather conditions and only L 11 managed to submit a report on the location of the British fleet, and this was not accepted in its entirety by Admiral Scheer. The seaplane gradually took over the role of the airship and to the Germans went the distinction of damaging the first battleship with bombs when they hit the Russian ship *Slava*, from seaplanes operating off the converted freighter *Santa Elena* in the Gulf of Riga.

German maritime aircraft harassed ports and shipping but at sea it was the U-Boat that was seen as the weapon of the future, and by the end of the war it had the biggest military budget allocated to it, although new aircraft for the flying services were a close second.

The advent of the Gotha twin-engined long-range bomber brought a revival in 1917 of strategic bombing. The G I prototype first flew in January 1915 and during the next two years the Gothas, together with the AEG G IV, Friedrichshafen G III and Zeppelin Staaken types, were introduced first in bombing on the Western Front, and then to look again towards civilian objectives. The Gotha was the most widely produced of these types and thirty of them were used to form Bombengeschwader 3, which was established specifically on the orders of General Ludendorff with the prime objective of bombing London. This was to be a dual effort to undermine the determination of the public, the other element being the increasing use of U-Boats to attack shipping in the hope of cutting supplies to Britain.

Operations were scheduled to start in February 1917, but it was not until 25 May that the bombers were ready to attempt their part of the task. Twenty-three Gotha G IVs led by Hauptmann Ernst Brandenburg set out for London, but encountered deteriorating weather conditions and were forced to turn back when they reached Gravesend. Bombs were dropped on Folkestone and the defenders mounted 74 individual aircraft sorties, only one of which, flown by a RNAS aircraft, engaged the bombers and shot one into the sea. Two weeks later on 13 June twenty aircraft set out and this time fourteen reached their objective dropping 72 bombs on the City of London. This resulted in the deaths of 162 civilians, one observer in a Bristol Fighter and injuries to 432. The result was far reaching in terms of public reaction which now reached a pitch well beyond that provoked by the airship night raids. The appearance of bomber aircraft over London forced another detailed look at the defenses and this resulted in the setting-up of three day-fighter squadrons with Camel and Pup aircraft, and the re-organization of anti-aircraft guns and searchlights into a command known as the Home Defence Brigade.

The last daylight raid on London took place on 7 July after which the effectiveness of the defenses forced the Germans into looking for the cover of darkness. The Gotha daylight raids had killed over 400 civilians and injured a further 878, for an expenditure of twenty tons of bombs.

The night campaign started on 3 September 1917 with the bombers leaving their bases individually at five minute intervals, thus highlighting the limitations of night navigation, and to a certain degree pre-empting the effect of massed formations, at this time not so much from the point of view of combined fire power in defense, but the achievement of a more concentrated bombing pattern. Twenty raids followed during the next few months, the last being on the night of 19/20 March 1918. Of these raids 15 were aimed against London and just over 50 tons of bombs were dropped inflicting 1432 casualties of which 435 were fatal. Disruption of work in the London area was certainly achieved, and with greater efforts the power of strategic bombing might have been proved. But on the other hand, the cost to the German air forces was high, 48 bombers were lost, of which only 8 fell to fighters, twelve were brought down by AA fire and the rest suffered mechanical problems, some of which were no doubt caused by ground fire. The air defenses were, therefore, not too effective. One important lesson had been learned from the use of the bomber, and it was that the defenders were forced into tying up considerable numbers of aircraft, guns and troops which could have been employed elsewhere.

This is illustrated by the fact that by March 1918 the London Air Defence Area had eleven fighter squadrons at its disposal with a total of 400 first line aircraft and 350 pilots. This was backed by ten training squadrons involving another 220 aircraft and 165 pilots, and the use of 174 landing grounds.

For the last six months of the war there were no further bombing raids on England, partly because of the increased defenses and partly because many of the airfields from which the Germans were operating were themselves coming under heavy attack by the British equivalent of the strategic bombing force using Handley Page 0/100 aircraft. Five airships had a final fling on the night of 5 August 1918 but they withdrew before reaching the British coast when L 70 fell to the guns of a defending DH 4. When Russia finally went out of the war in early 1918, Germany withdrew all its efforts to the west, and priority, second only to the already mentioned U-Boat force, was given to fighter aircraft. The French, British and Belgian air forces had all matured in men, machines and experience. The British and French in particular had turned their attention to bomber aircraft on a more or less equal footing to that of fighters. This resulted in greatly increased activity in the closing stages of the war with German airfields, and industrial targets receiving a great deal of attention. In these raids the German fighter pilots acquitted themselves with honor, on one occasion accounting for eight from a total of nine DH 9s that were attacking Mainz. In this case the German fighters were flown by reserve second-line pilots.

The single biggest losses on one day were encountered on 8 August 1918 when in the face of the new Allied offensive that was in fact to lead to the end of the war, major air battles raged along every front. The Allies lost 83 machines and the Germans 49, but such was the power of the Allied air force by this time that they could afford to sustain such a loss rate and in fact had mounted attacks by massed formations of fighters in attempts to keep the German air force on the ground. This failed as far as fighter operations were concerned and in September 1918 773 Allied aircraft were lost. By the end of the war German claims mounted to just under 7500 machines for the loss of 3000 of their own. Of the claims made by Germany only some 360 were on the Eastern Front.

There can be little doubt that at the time of the armistice, the

Below: Friedrichshafen G IVB 1429/18 on display in London, 1918.

German air forces were a strong and powerful fighting unit, and it would be grossly unfair to claim that they were defeated. The tactics evolved both by their bombers and fighter units, had in most cases led the field in the development of the third dimension in warfare. The combined strength of the Allied air forces which in the end were able to withstand a greater rate of attrition, had proved decisive in combination with ground and naval forces, in forcing Germany to surrender, but the contribution made by Germany's airmen is reflected in the total ban on an air force which was a condition of the Treaty of Versailles that was to follow.

The German navy was committed to a defensive policy since although in many ways it was powerful, it could in no way be compared with the British fleet which was still in the heyday of its glory. Naval aircraft did get involved in raids against shipping and coastal targets, but their prime role and that of the airship was reconnaissance. Starting the war with only 12 seaplanes, split between Helgoland (6) Kiel (4) and Putzig (2), 30 officers and 3 NCO pilots and no trained observers, the naval air arm was very much the poor relation. Reconnaissance and limited attacks on shipping, especially submarines, were carried out but this was a very minor activity, especially the latter with only one definite sinking of a submarine (the German UB-32) being achieved by either side throughout the war. In the overall context of the development of German aviation, the navy played a very small part in World War I, and to a certain extent this legacy of the poor relation was carried on to World War II.

The German high command hoped for a decisive victory in the west before they would need to send strong forces against the Russians whom the Germans expected would invade to create pressure in the east. Much of the early work carried out in the field of reconnaissance by the Germans has been greatly exaggerated in relation to the outcome of early battles against the Russians.

Above: A Gotha G IV's crew pause for the camera during preparations for a raid over England.

Air reconnaissance certainly warned the Germans of a threat from the south during the actions at Tannenberg and Gumbinnen, but this was poorly interpreted on the ground and there is a lot of doubt as to how much of the resulting success was directly attributable to the air element. The comments attributed to General von Hindenburg in which he is alleged to have told Major Siegert that the success was totally due to air power, must be viewed with a lot of suspicion. It is likely they were made to Italian journalists and simply advised that the airmen had made a considerable contribution but certainly not to the exclusion of everything else. On the Eastern front aerial opposition was not nearly as effective as that on the west, so the history is primarily one of improving reconnaissance techniques and support of ground troops. Weather presented many difficulties to both sides, but the German aircraft were much superior to their opposite numbers and the crews better equipped. This led to a much greater air of confidence, and in turn a greater understanding and co-operation with ground forces. In 1917 the Russian Revolution brought a new slant to the situation regarding the war against Germany and the Austro-Hungarians, and in the overall general narrative of this work, has little bearing on the development of the German air forces.

Similarly the campaigns in Serbia, Italy, the Balkans, Rumania, the cooperation with the Turks in Mesopotamia and Palestine, placed certain demands on the German air force and its leaders, but only in the same way as it did on the French and British. The overall influence of air warfare, its future use, tactics, and aircraft, were very much decided on the Western Front with the rest making mainly minor and to a degree fairly insignificant contributions, at least as far as Germany was concerned.

REBIRTH OF AN AIR FORCE

A trio of Junkers Ju 86D-1 bombers on an air exercise in July 1938. This type served with K/88 in the Legion Kondor.

When the armistice came on 11 November 1918, the German Air Service had a first line strength of 2570 bombers, fighters and reconnaissance aircraft, with some 4500 aircrew involved in operations. Total aircraft strength on the German inventory was in the order of 20,000 machines, although many of these were in fact wrecks or existed only on paper, as losses during the last six months of the war took some little time to collate. The result was that during the later part of 1919 and early 1920, just over 15,000 aircraft and close to 30,000 aero-engines were surrendered to the Allied Control Commission under the terms of the Treaty of Versailles, which had been signed in June 1919 and effectively ended the war with Germany.

Such had been the rise of air power during the Great War, that one part of the Treaty specifically forbade Germany from having a peace-time air force although it allowed an army of 100,000 regulars and a small navy. Another imposition was the cessation of manufacture of military aircraft by the German aircraft industry. There were of course many weaknesses within the Treaty and most of these are outside the overall objective of this book, but one of the fundamental ones was that the basic legacy of World War I was that it destroyed the European balance of power. In defeat Germany still remained the most powerful nation in Europe, the war having shown that the combined efforts of Britain, France, Italy, Russia and other minor states had been inadequate to bring Germany to her knees; final victory only being achieved when the European powers had the vast resources of the United States and Pershing's armies behind them.

The post-war settlement was determined by the total effort of many countries, but following the refusal of Britain and the USA to enter any binding commitments with France, the settlement could only be maintained if France was in a position of superiority over Germany, and from a long term point of view, this was impossible. There could never be any doubt that many Germans never accepted the reality of defeat and harbored a strong desire to reverse the outcome of WWI. It was only a question of time before leadership on the political front generated enough national fervor to make moves in this direction. It is perhaps not surprising that against a background of war weariness in Britain and France and growing economic problems world wide it did not prove too difficult for those who sought to restore Germany to what they considered her

Above: Ernst Udet poses on his 40th birthday with his personal glider that bore his name.
Below: The prototype of the Heinkel He 46E (D-ILHE), which was an intended export version powered by a British Panther X engine.

Above: Flak batteries demonstrate their firepower at a Nazi Party Rally in Nürnberg in 1936.
Right: Erhard Milch became Secretary of State for Aviation in 1933 and played an important part in creating the German aircraft industry.

rightful level of leadership, to make initially clandestine but later quite open moves to do so.

The Air Clause of the Treaty of Versailles omitted to ban the production of civil aircraft, and although in 1922 limitations on the size and performance of such aircraft were imposed, these were withdrawn four years later under the terms of the Paris Air Agreement, which also incidentally restricted the number of German service personnel who were allowed to fly as part of their duty.

Like many other countries during this period Germany saw the growth of air transport through small airlines, and an increasing interest in air-mindedness through flying and gliding clubs. The manufacture of light aircraft and civil machines for use by such airlines and clubs, saw the German aircraft industry develop through companies whose products were to become household words within a few years. Such people as Heinkel, Dornier, Messerschmitt and Junkers kept in tune with aeronautical developments and, although in the main their companies were small and under financed, despite considerable help from the Reichsverkehrsministerium (Transport Ministry), they were able to produce designs that in the majority of cases were very thinly disguised military aircraft.

A typical example was the Heinkel He 70 Blitz which followed on from the He 64 which had been victorious in the Europa Rundflug (Round-Europe Race) of 1932. Ernst Heinkel had seen the single-engined Lockheed Orion mailplane of 1931 and recognized the potential of such a small fast mailplane. It did not go unnoticed by Dipl.Ing.Schatzki, who at that time was the head of technical matters with Lufthansa. Schatzki, who was a Jew and later suffered under the 1933 Nazi purge, met Heinkel and the two men discussed the possibility of a similar German designed and built mailplane. At this time Erhard Milch had placed an order with Junkers for an aircraft to match the Orion, but Junkers encountered severe financial

Above: One of the earliest versions of the Messerschmitt Bf 109, the B model, which began to enter service in April 1937.

problems which led to the business being taken over by the State. Although Heinkel had not previously built aircraft for Lufthansa, he had an ally in Ministerialrat Brandenburg, the former commander of Bombengeschwader 3 that had raided London during the war. Brandenburg was aware of the thinly disguised military aircraft Heinkel had built in contravention of the Treaty of Versailles, and invited Heinkel to meet him and Milch to discuss a rival to the Orion.

At a meeting held on 12 February 1932 Lufthansa placed an order with Heinkel for a fast mail carrying aircraft with a crew of two and a passenger capability of four. This machine was the Heinkel He 70 which proved to be far better than even Heinkel's initial design study had indicated, and went on to capture several records previously held by France and America. Among these was the carrying at 222mph of payloads of 500 and 1000kg over a distance of 1000km, at a time when the world air speed record – achieved by a purpose-built machine – stood at a mere 259mph. The significance of the technical achievement in getting a standard Lufthansa in service mail plane to get so close to such a record, was not lost on the aviation world, and among the accolades that came Heinkel's way was one from Reginald Mitchell of Supermarine Aviation, whose Spitfire was to tangle some seven years later with Heinkel's He 111 bomber which was developed from the He 70. It is of interest to compare the planforms of the He 70 with the Spitfire, when the origin of the latter's elliptical wing becomes evident.

The He 70 also had a remarkable effect on those officers then rebuilding the new German Air Force. Until its advent they, like many others in different countries, thought the biplane to be the supreme fighting machine, but the performance of the Heinkel monoplane was so far in excess of any fighter they could then foresee that Oberst Wimmer, then head of the Technical Department of the Luftfahrtkommissariat, which later became the Reichsluftfahrtministerium (RLM) or State Aviation Ministry, issued a requirement for a single-seat monoplane fighter with retractable undercarriage and a top speed of 280mph. This eventually led to the Fw 159, He 112 and 100 and ultimately the Bf 109.

Parallel to such developments in the embryo aircraft industry, were plans to provide training facilities for pilots who would be required in considerable numbers for the new air force. Several former officers of the Imperial Flying Corps, who continued to serve in the German Army after WWI, maintained their interest in aviation and were supported by General Hans von Seeckt the Chief of the General Staff who made sure that there were very close links between the Army and the Civil Aviation Department of the Ministry of Transport.

An agreement with Russia was initiated in 1923 which enabled those officers interested in flying to be trained at Russian flying schools, and by 1926 establishments at Lipezk near Moscow and in the Ukraine, were turning out pilots and

Below: The aesthetically pleasing lines of the Focke-Wulf Fw 44 Stieglitz trainer would not be out of place today.

Above left: Hermann Goering (center) and the Italian Fascist dictator Benito Mussolini (left).
Above: The second prototype Henschel Hs 123 V2 broke up at Rechlin in a terminal velocity dive. However, the Hs 123 served throughout the war mainly as a dive bomber and ground attack aircraft.

observers. Interest in aviation was also cultivated through private flying schools and those used by Lufthansa, as well as the Deutscher Luftsportverband (DLV), which by the end of the 1920s boasted a membership in excess of 50,000 making Germany one of the most air-minded nations in the world. Most of the officers destined to achieve high rank in the WWII Luftwaffe, passed through the Russian training schools at some stage of their careers.

In the 1928 German elections the Nazi Party totalled some 810,000 votes, small when compared with the nine million cast for the Social Democrats, but enough to give them 14 seats in the Reichstag, one of which went to Hermann Goering, a man destined to become the architect-in-chief of Hitler's Luftwaffe, and in many ways also responsible for its failure as an effective fighting force in World War II.

Goering had been a fighter pilot in World War I and for the last five months of the conflict had commanded the famous Richthofen Geschwader. Although at the time of his appointment in July 1918, Ernst Udet, with 60 victories against Goering's 20, seemed to have a greater claim for the honor. Goering's prowess was ably rewarded by the award of the Pour le Mérite, the Iron Cross, and the Order of Karl Friederich, as well as other decorations, and his nationalistic pride was shown when he revealed a foretaste of his unreasonable behavior soon after the armistice by ordering pilots of his unit deliberately to crash their aircraft in defiance of French Air Force orders. His fiercely patriotic feelings were made known to all and sundry in the weeks following the 1918 armistices, when he expressed his anger at the defeat of his beloved Germany and his commitment to the Fatherland. However, he did not return immediately to Germany and took a flying job in Denmark. In doing this he forfeited any chance he might have had of joining the post war German Army or of being given an appointment in the Defense Ministry as did his former colleagues Kesselring, Stumpff and Sperrle.

For several years he was in the wilderness but encouraged by his second wife, was active on the political scene in the early 1920s and first met Hitler in 1922, after deciding that the future Führer's opinions closely tallied with his own. A period of great personal trauma including a severe beating during a Nazi rally, when he was shot and seriously injured, an addiction to morphia, deep periods of depression and his wife's poor health, all had a lasting effect and explain some of his later irrational decisions, but he seemed to be well recovered from these when he entered the Reichstag in 1928, and started making telling speeches.

Although he concentrated mainly on aviation and transport, analysis of his political activity indicates that he was in fact deeply involved in many other subjects, so that aviation in fact only occupied about half his time. So although he was in touch with some developments, he was not totally aware of or able to appreciate some of the more important aspects. This and the fact that he was an impatient man and never willing to accept advice, accounts for some of the remarkable gaps in his planning and strategy. But the heady days of 1935-1940 were still some way off although by March 1933 when Hitler finally came to power Goering was very popular and it came as no real surprise when he was appointed Aviation Minister.

Most of the aviation planning at this time was delegated to Erhard Milch who was Deputy Air Minister and General Walther Wever who was earmarked for the position of Chief of Staff of the new German Air Force. Goering's former colleague Ernst Udet also became deeply involved with the formation of the Luftwaffe, but although a brilliant pilot, failed to achieve the same level in the hard world of commerce and politics. He became Director of the Technical Department of the Air Minis-

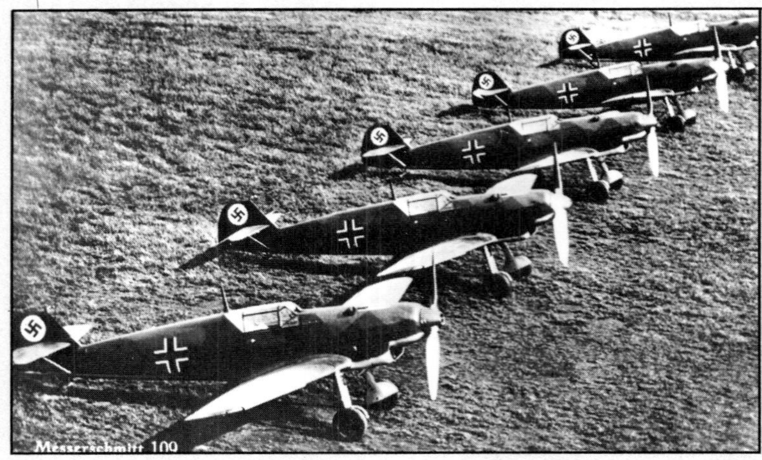

Above: Bf 109B-2s, probably of 3/JG.334 at Wiesbaden in 1938.
Above right: Heinkel He 51 of II/JG.132 'Richthofen' at Jüterborg-Damn in 1935.

try in 1936 and by 1939 was Director General of Equipment but he was unable to manage the demands made on him and on occasions found it difficult to cope with Goering's unstable character, one example being his frustration in convincing the Minister about the potential of the USA in aircraft production. Following several major blunders culminating in the failure to have adequate replacements early in the Russian campaign this superb pilot and WWI ace committed suicide, in November 1941.

On the other hand, Goering's deputy Erhard Milch, was a brilliant organizer and planner who had been responsible for making Lufthansa, of which he was Chairman, Europe's leading airline. He was able to retain this position after his appointment as Deputy Minister and in fact because of Goering's increasing political work was virtually head of the Air Ministry. Under his guidance and direction the aircraft industry was expanded to be in a position to supply the growing needs of a still officially non-existent air force. Companies involved in ship-building and the production of railway locomotives and automobiles, were all instructed to become involved in the aircraft industry either in the design of aero engines, or the undertaking of sub-contract work. There was a love-hate relationship between Goering and Milch and although in 1936 Milch became a General in the Luftwaffe, it also saw his responsibility for aircraft procurement transferred by Goering to Udet; a mistake that was to prove very costly.

Another vital aspect that affected the Luftwaffe in the long term was the death in June 1936 (the same month as Udet's appointment) of General Wever. There can be little doubt that at this time Wever was the most competent and far-sighted staff officer in the Luftwaffe, and he almost alone could foresee the value of long-range strategic bombers, and was therefore very much in favor of the development of the Dornier Do 19 and Junkers Ju 89. Oddly enough Wever was killed when he tried to take-off from Dresden-Neustadt with the aileron lock on an He 70 still in place, this aircraft being the forerunner of Heinkel's successful bomber designs, and also being used as a reconnaissance aircraft in the Spanish Civil War that was to erupt in the month following Wever's death.

General Wever was generally acknowledged as Chief of the General Staff of the Luftwaffe, and his obituary referred to him as such, but records indicate that such a position did not officially exist until 1 July 1937.

The thinking behind the officers responsible for the planning of the Luftwaffe, clearly indicates that they all, Wever apart, saw it as an extension to the Army and as providing a weapon for use in support of the land forces. This is hardly surprising in view of the military backgrounds of most of those concerned. Among the former Imperial Army officers who had a tremendous influence on the formation and subsequent role of the Luftwaffe was Generalfeldmarschall Albrecht Kesselring, who served as a General Staff officer in WWI and in 1933 became involved with the secret build-up of the Luftwaffe as head of administration in the Luftfahrtkommissariat, in which capacity he was mainly responsible for the creation of capacity for the mass production of the aircraft the Luftwaffe would need. He became a General in 1934 and for a short time held the position of Chief of the Luftwaffe General Staff. During the war he commanded Luftflotte 1 (Air Fleet 1) in Poland and then Luftflotte 2 which spearheaded the campaign in the west and subsequently the start of the Russian offensive. He later became C-in-C of all German forces in the Mediterranean.

Generalfeldmarschall Robert, Ritter von Griem, also served as an artillery officer in World War I, before transferring to the flying service in 1916. He became an ace with 28 victories, and in 1935 was appointed by Goering to the post of Inspector of Fighters and Divebombers. He commanded Fliegerdivision 5 in the early days of WWII and stayed with it through several changes of title until it became Luftflotte 6 in July 1943 by which time he was a Generaloberst. In April 1945 he became Commander-in-Chief of what then remained of the Luftwaffe.

Cousin of the famous Manfred von Richthofen, Dr Ing Wolfram Freiherr von Richthofen, served with an Hussar regiment but learned to fly in 1917 and by the end of the war had 8 aerial victories to his credit. His affinity with Goering assured him of an important role and after obtaining his doctorate in engineering he featured prominently in the ground work behind the scenes from 1933. He commanded the Legion Kondor in Spain and in the opening days of WWII enhanced his reputation as an exponent of aircraft in the close support role. He commanded Fliegerkorps VIII until July 1942 when he took over Luftflotte 4, and in 1943 was promoted to Generalfeldmarschall in command of Luftflotte 2.

Another WWI flyer favored by Goering was Hugo Sperrle who remained in the Reichswehr after the war and transferred to the Luftwaffe in 1935. He too commanded the Legion Kondor for a time and during WWII commanded Luftflotte 3 until his retirement in August 1944.

Another officer who chose to stay in the Reichswehr after the armistice, was Hans Stumpff, who became Chief of Personnel to the Luftwaffe in 1933, and Chief of the Luftwaffe General Staff between June 1937 and January 1939. After commanding Luftflotte 1 and 5, he became commander of Luftflotte Reich responsible for the defense of the Fatherland in 1944 and stayed in this important position until the cessation of hostilities. These officers, together with others such as Josef Kammhuber, Karl Koller and Werner Kreipe, all played important roles not only in the early days of the laying of the Luftwaffe's foundations but also very much as it rose to become Europe's premier air force, backed by a reputation that it started to generate in the skies of Spain.

Above: A Junkers Ju 86D-1 with ventral turret extended. This bomber was virtually obsolete by 1940 and saw little action in World War II.

Two years after gaining power Hitler felt secure enough to reveal Germany's new air force, and in so doing his true intent to form the missing third arm of his military establishment became apparent to the world.

March 1935 therefore saw Goering established as Commander-in-Chief of the Luftwaffe, which was an independent part of the armed forces with the officers previously mentioned holding controlling positions. The year also saw the setting up of a Luftwaffe staff college, an extremely efficient signals service, and its own Fliegerabwehrkanonen (Flak) or anti-aircraft arm, which unlike the similar establishment in the British armed forces, came under the control of the air force and not the army. Early organization was based on four main groups located at Berlin, Königsberg, Braunschweig and Munich. This was later expanded to six, plus ten Air Districts which were responsible for supply, administration, airfield staffing and training. The laid down aim was one of flexibility and rapid mobility of flying units and their support groups, and this

Below: The ungainly looking Focke-Wulf Fw 58 'Weihe' which was used in communication and training roles.

worked so well that in effect each Luftflotte, as the main divisions became known by the time the war started, was really an independent air force able to operate with complete autonomy. In 1938 the Luftwaffe became subordinated to the new Oberkommando der Wehrmacht (OKW – Armed Forces High Command), established by Hitler to confirm his control.

In aircraft, the March 1935 strength of 1888 of all types represented a well balanced force with the bomber arm capable of employment in strategic and tactical roles, although the former modified the original theory of General Giulio Douhet, to that of limited use of 'terror bombing.' It is of interest that although the Germans clearly took stock of Douhet's suppositions made in his 1921 work, *The Command of the Air*, in which he expounded a doctrine of attack on the enemy's will to fight by destroying his cities and terrorizing the civilian population, they did not take into account his added comment that only an air force totally independent of army or naval control could achieve this. In the belief that any war they might become involved in would be very short, the Luftwaffe chiefs could only see their aircraft being used as an extension of the artillery, and although accepting that in some cases bombing of civilian targets might be necessary, never really gave a great deal of thought to the much wider implications of strategic bombing in the destruction of the enemy's war effort. Apart from General Wever, they did not greatly concern themselves, therefore, with long- and ultra long-range bombers, that could well have paid dividends especially in the Russian campaign.

The RAF however was styled along the lines advocated by Douhet, and from the very beginning operated as an independent force and in its planned expansion, and in the plans of the US air forces, the strategic bomber formed a vital ingredient, as the German people were to discover.

Supporting the Luftwaffe's aircraft in 1935 were some 20,000 officers and men, many of them very experienced fliers or mechanics, having been serving for long periods with flying clubs, the state airline or smaller feeder airlines. Much of the preparation in long-range and blind flying techniques had been carried out under the auspices of training Lufthansa crews, and this had been supported on the technical front by large strides in the field of electronics.

Among these developments was the Lorenz system which transmitted two overlapping radio beams, one sending out dots and the other dashes. It was possible accurately to follow a given course simply by flying down the path of continuous tone where the two beams overlapped. This made the finding of airfields in difficult weather conditions a fairly simple matter, and consequently the system was in widespread use not only by civil airlines but also military air forces including the Luftwaffe and RAF by the late 1930s. More important however, was the development from this system of the long range navigation and bombing aids known as *Knickebein* and *X-Gerät*, unique to the Luftwaffe and used in the Blitz against Britain in 1940-41. But in 1936 this was still some way in the future and events in Spain were beginning to occupy Hitler and his advisers.

The Spanish general election of 1936 resulted in the Republicans gaining power and forming a government that was

Below right: A Dornier Do 18 flying boat. An aircraft of this type became the first German victim in World War II.
Below: Civil registered He 51 fighters.

Above: The Heinkel He 72 Kadett was one of the Luftwaffe's most important primary trainers. This is a line-up of production aircraft awaiting delivery.

far from popular with the very right wing army. Periods of unrest finally erupted on 18 July 1936 when revolution broke out and the country became divided into Nationalist and Republican camps. The Republicans held the whip hand as far as naval forces were concerned. They were therefore able severely to curtail the aims of the Nationalist leader General Francisco Franco in transporting his troops from Morocco to the Spanish mainland.

On 26 July 1936 Franco, who at that time commanded the Nationalist forces in the South, made an appeal through the office of the head of the Tetuan Nazi Party, Adolf Langenheim, for help in supplying aircraft to carry out an airlift of men and equipment. The response was immediate. The following day on Hitler's explicit instructions, Lufthansa pilot Flugkapitän Hanke took his Ju 52/3m from Berlin to Spanish Morocco, where two days later it made its first contribution to the war by transporting Nationalist troops from Tetuan to Jerez de la Frontera. By the end of August the 20 Ju 52s working on the task had moved 7350 troops and their equipment to Spain, work they continued to carry out until the end of October by which time 13,523 men, 36 field guns, 127 machine guns and thousands of pounds of stores had been moved in the first military airlift of any consequence in history.

This operation was commanded by Oberleutnant Rudolf von Moreau who on 14 August led a raid by Ju 52s against the Republican battleship *Jamie 1* in Malaga harbor, and disabled it with two direct hits. This switch of role by the Ju 52s serves to illustrate just how thin the difference between transport and bomber aircraft was during the clandestine build-up of the Luftwaffe. Nine of the original twenty Ju 52/3ms were used to form the first three Nationalist bomber squadrons, their transport work being undertaken by Italian built SM 81s.

To protect the transport aircraft, Hitler also supplied six Heinkel He 51 biplane fighters, 20 anti-aircraft guns and 86 Luftwaffe volunteer 'instructors' all of these arriving on 6 August in Cadiz aboard the freighter SS *Ursano*.

Among the Spanish fighter pilots who had rallied to the

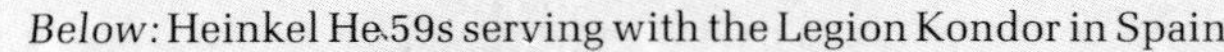
Below: Heinkel He 59s serving with the Legion Kondor in Spain.

Above: Heinkel He 70 Blitz of Lufthansa. This is a G version. The aircraft's military use was disappointing.
Above right: The 12th production version of the A1 model Ju 87 Stuka.

Nationalist cause, was Captain Joaquin Morato, a noted aerobatic ace, and it was to the guns of his licence-built Nieuport NiD 52 on 12 August, that the first Republican aircraft, a British built Vildebeeste biplane fell. At this time the Republicans also operated the NiD 52, but with the formation of the first Nationalist fighter unit at Tablada to be equipped with the He 51, the advantage of fighter superiority should have been in favor of the Nationalists. But apart from one or two pilots, including the dual commanders Captains Morato and Rambaud, few of the other Spaniards possessed the skills to get the best from the German fighter. So mid-way through August permission was given for the six German instructors, Leutnants Eberhard, Kleine, Knüppel, Trautloft, Henrici and von Houwald, to fly operationally.

This had an immediate effect with Eberhard's section recording six claims by the end of the month. It soon became clear to the Germans, however, that the rebels would need far greater help if they were to succeed, especially as France, ignoring the League of Nations attempt to prohibit outside help to the warring factions, began to pour equipment into Republican hands.

At the Nuremberg trials in 1945 Goering explained that he had urged Hitler to support the Nationalist cause to the fullest possible extent, the main reasons in his words being '. . . firstly to prevent the spread of Communism, secondly to test my young Luftwaffe in this or that technical respect.'

In the following months aid from Germany increased and on 6 November 1936 the Legion Kondor was formed at Seville under the command of Generalmajor Hugo Sperrle. Initial composition was Kampfgruppe 88 equipped with three squadrons of Ju 52/3mg4s, Jagdgruppe 88 with three He 51 equipped elements, Aufklarungsstaffel 88 with He 70F-2 reconnaissance aircraft and Aufklarungsstaffel-See 88 with He 59B and He 60E floatplanes. Supporting the flying units was Flak 88 which had some six anti-aircraft batteries, Luftnachrichten 88 with four signals companies, a repair section and the operations staff. So in essence the Legion Kondor was an autonomous air force and would give the German high command vital information on the operational and administrative requirements of such a unit, as well as confirming or otherwise their philosophy in setting up the Luftwaffe in the way they had chosen.

The initial equipment consisted of about 200 aircraft and most of these, at least as far as bombers and fighters were concerned, were virtually obsolete, as was soon proved in the closing months of 1936. However, the German aircraft industry had not been idle and new types that were to feature prominently in the coming European war, were soon winning their spurs in Spain, and the spin-off was the gathering of a great deal of information on fighting tactics, every aspect of aircraft performance and many details of techniques of operational support that was to pay dividends.

One of the first of the new types to see operational service was the He 111B-1, which began to arrive in February 1937 and was in action with 3/KGr.88 (3rd Staffel of Kampfgruppe 88) on 9 March when Republican airfields at Alcala and Barajas were bombed. The Ju 52s were also replaced by Dornier 17E-1s in the bombing role, and the Do 17F-1 reconnaissance version replaced the He 70s with A/88, the latter being transferred to the Spanish Nationalist Air Force.

The He 51s of Jagdgruppe 88 supported Franco's siege of Madrid which started in November, but by the turn of the year, with Russian built fighters and bombers beginning to join the ranks of the Republicans, the initiative in the air swung their way. The German fighters had by now been joined by Italian units equipped with the nimble CR 32 but nonetheless by the

Below: The Do 17VI, a high-speed mailplane, first flew in 1934. The lines of the Do 17 'Flying Pencil' bomber are already in evidence.

Above: A Do 17E-1 of 7/KG.255 taking part in 1938 war games. The insignia are painted out as this machine was acting as an enemy aircraft.

end of 1936 morale in the Nationalist camp was low, at least as far as air operations were concerned.

The influx of new equipment in 1937 saw a gradual change in fortunes and the arrival of the monoplane Bf 109B in April 1937 when 2/JGr.88 surrendered their He 51s for the new fighter, confirmed the state of affairs which was to prevail until the war ended.

It was over Spain that the German fighter pilots of JGr.88 devised the tactics that were to give them the initiative during the years of 1939-41.

One of the most significant of these was the evolution of the loose Schwarm 'finger four' formation. In the opening months of the campaign patrols had been flown in close wing-to-wing formation – a legacy from WWI – but the introduction of the faster Messerschmitt fighters soon proved this method to be impractical and very dangerous.

Pilots spent so much time watching each other carefully to avoid collisions that they had little opportunity to look for the enemy. It was Oberleutnant Werner Mölders who devised the new formation which introduced freedom of action and flexibility. The formation of four fighters flew in the positions shown by the tips of the fingers of the extended hand, hence the name associated with it. Every man had his tail covered by his wingman and each in turn covered the flanks of the fighters adjacent and in front of him, so there was a much reduced danger of being surprised and no need for a 'weaver' to cover the rear of all the aircraft in the formation.

Most of the fighter operations in Spain were aimed at covering the bomber formations but after such tasks were completed and providing the fighters had sufficient fuel, they would try to tempt the Republicans into the air by strafing enemy positions. Occasionally large aerial dog fights did develop but in the early months of the war these were rare, as is evidenced by the fact that Adolf Galland, an outstanding pilot of 3/JG.88, failed to achieve any aerial victories in Spain.

As the Bf 109 became available in growing quantities the He 51s were used in a close support ground attack role. Fitted with four 10kg bombs and a special detonator in the droppable fuel tank, the biplanes would attack troop concentrations and targets of opportunity at low level. Such attacks usually occurred in some strength and the effect of up to nine aircraft approaching at 500 feet and dropping their loads simultaneously on the nod of the leader's head – no radio was fitted at that time – can be imagined. Ground troops had never experienced such ferocious aerial assaults and morale quickly suffered. The Chief of Staff of the Legion Kondor at this time was Oberst Wolfram von Richthofen, and he quickly saw the

Below: Examples of the Dornier 23G of 5/KG.253 at Erfurt. By 1936 this aircraft had been relegated to training schools. Some 210 of the type were built and it was later used in experiments in aerial mine-sweeping.

Above: An early production He 111B-2. The black line outboard of the port engine is a leading-edge installed surface-coolant radiator.

advantages to be obtained by such methods and pioneered their development, a move that was to pay handsome dividends in the early stages of the war to come when other air forces were still employing the old tight formation methods that had been generally successful in World War I aircraft.

Such was the success of the close support role that in late 1937 three Ju 87A dive bombers were withdrawn from the Germany-based I/StG.162 (the first Gruppe of Stuka Geschwader 162) and attached to JG.88 to give crews experience under operational conditions. The Ju 87 crews were in much demand and although only three aircraft were used they saw action in Teruel, on the Ebro front and in the Catalonian offensive. The success of the Legion Kondor in this task was slightly colored by the fact that the Ju 87s operated in conditions of almost total air superiority, and thus generated an air of invincibility that was eventually to cost dearly. (Stuka is in fact an abbreviation of the word *Sturzkampfflugzeug* meaning dive bomber and therefore refers to any type of such aircraft. But it has generally become associated with the Ju 87 only.)

Luftwaffe thinking was also colored by the apparent success of the bomber against both tactical and strategic targets. In April 1937 He 111s and Ju 52s had been involved in the bombing of Guernica, causing many civilian casualties and destroying the center of the town. Republican propaganda wasted no time in exposing this to the world, which was shocked by the so called terror bombing of civilians. It has never been satisfactorily proved as to whether the raid was deliberately carried out by KGr.88 to test the theory of such bombing, or if it was really poor bomb aiming against what was claimed to be a genuine military target, since the only bridge in the town had great importance to the Republicans and was therefore a legitimate military target. Whatever the reason, the result was the almost immediate capitulation of Guernica, which seemed to prove that the end justified the means. Such bombing con-

Below: The Ju 52 became known as 'Iron Annie' or 'Tante Ju.' This example is towing a DFS 230 assault glider.

Above: Ju 52/3m g3es of I/KG.152 'Hindenburg' in 1936. At this time this type equipped two-thirds of the Luftwaffe bomber squadrons.

tinued throughout the war and losses of the Heinkels and Dorniers were slight. This led to the belief that speed and not heavy defensive armament could protect the bomber in daylight operations. This was to prove far from true when the speed differential between the bombers concerned in Spain and the fighters they were to meet over England in 1940, is taken into account.

Spain continued to be a proving ground not only for Luftwaffe personnel but also for aircraft flowing from the German production lines. Bf 109C-1s arrived on the scene in June 1938 and were in action early the following month when Mölders, who had taken over from Galland as leader of 3/JG.88, made his first three kills. Other aircraft used in the civil war were the Heinkel 112, one example only of which was evaluated by Günther Radusch (a man destined to become a night-fighter ace in WWII), the Henschel 123, five aircraft being operated in December 1936, six Henschel Hs 126 replacing the Hs 45 in the autumn of 1938, and five Junkers Ju 86D-1s which were tested by the Legion Kondor under operational conditions.

Below: A Heinkel He 112 – V9. The He 112 series competed with the Bf 109; it failed to reach production status but a few were exported and saw service with the Rumanian air force.

Many of the pilots who were to become household names in WWII gained invaluable experience, among these being the already mentioned Mölders, Galland, Lipfert, Tietzen, and Balthasar, to name just a few.

In March 1939 the Republicans surrendered and a restless peace returned to Spain. Many of the mercenaries, who had flown for both sides, returned to their homes, or countries where their skills would fetch living fees. The Legion Kondor returned in triumph to Germany. In the war JG.88 had claimed 314 victories and over twenty pilots had achieved five or more victories thus qualifying for the accolade of ace. The three leading aces were Mölders with 14 victories, Schellman with 12 and Harder with 11. To Leutnant Wilhelm Balthasar went the distinction of shooting down four Ratas in six minutes during one February day in 1938, and the most successful Staffel was 1/JG.88 with 91 claims.

In Central Europe a major crisis was in the making. Following Hitler's march into Austria in March 1938 and his triumph at Munich in September when he was allowed as a 'last territorial demand' to annexe a large part of western Czechoslovakia, it became obvious to most politicians that war was inevitable. In March 1939 German forces occupied the rest of that country and the humiliated British Prime Minister, the rather pathetic Neville Chamberlain, tried to cover his previous gross errors by promising support to Poland, which it was clear was Hitler's next objective.

Although ill-prepared, Britain had used the time between Munich in 1938 and the summer of 1939 to strengthen her forces and alliance with France, while Germany had forged a military alliance with Italy and a non-aggression pact with the Soviet Union. It was a time of great unease and in May 1939 Hitler informed his commanders-in-chief that it was his intention to attack Poland at the first available opportunity.

Below: A Messerschmitt Bf 109E-3, now in the RAF Battle of Britain Museum at Hendon in London. This is the only surviving E version known to have taken part in the Battle.

EUROPE AT WAR

On 23 May 1939 Hitler made it quite clear to the commanders-in-chief of his three military forces, and their chiefs-of-staff, that it was his intention to solve the 'Poland problem' by attacking the country at the first suitable opportunity.

This statement caused some concern to commanders of Luftwaffe elements nearer to the day-to-day running of the service, than it did to Goering who had, through a very efficient propaganda machine, built up an aura of invincibility around his air force. The then commander of Luftflotte 1, General Speidel, recorded in his diary that 'time and again weaknesses in training, equipment and operational readiness, were regularly reported to higher authority.'

Such warnings went unheeded, and indeed with the benefit of hindsight one may question why they should have been taken too seriously; for Hitler believed that any war would be very short and did not believe that either Britain or France would come to the aid of the other European nations to whom they had pledged support. He also believed that the forces of those countries were not strong enough in any case to withstand a campaign against the might of his war machine.

In the same month as Hitler made his intentions quite clear in Berlin, the Chief of Staff of the Luftwaffe, Generalmajor Hans Jeschonnek, had these comments to make at a meeting in Bad Salzbrunn, 'Do not let us deceive ourselves. Each country wants to outstrip the other in air armament. But we are all roughly at the same stage. In the long run a technical lead cannot be maintained.' He was of course quite right, although to say so publicly in Germany in 1939 was the mark of a very brave or foolish man. But future events whereby the German aircraft industry was seriously curtailed in developing replacements for the aircraft in service at the start of the war, and the directives received to concentrate on improbable designs and unworkable specifications, brought an echo of truth to the Generalmajor's words during the dying throes of the Luftwaffe. Jeschonnek went on to temper his words by commenting that in the field of tactics most things were new and undeveloped, and suggested that concentration in this direction would give a real advantage over the enemy. In this he was right, but to an extent German thinking had been too strongly influenced by the Spanish experience of the Legion Kondor wherein the use of dive bombers and close support aircraft had been seen as an invaluable weapon for the army.

Udet had become obsessed with the theory of dive-bombing when he witnessed a demonstration of the Curtiss Hawk biplane in America in 1933. He persuaded Goering to buy two and took them to Germany for evaluation.

Milch had not been so convinced, and after seeing the American aircraft demonstrated, decided against purchasing them in quantity for the new Luftwaffe. But the die had been cast and from these early beginnings the Ju 87 evolved, and in the views of many, vindicated itself in Spain, although only a handful of aircraft operated in that theater.

Despite instructions to the contrary from Milch, work continued on the development of this technique of waging war, and when he was relieved from his position, on the whim of Goering who was jealous of his growing reputation with Hitler, there was little to halt progress in this direction. On the outbreak of war the four men responsible for the Luftwaffe, Goering, Milch, Udet and Jeschonnek, were a quartet of misfits. Each had his own particular talent, but in the main did not see eye-to-eye with any of the others and in the overall context were unsuitable for the jobs they had. Goering was well aware of the animosity between the three pillars of his Luftwaffe, but it suited him to fuel the fires of unrest when he felt so inclined, since by so doing he was able to exercise a rule by division theory that happened to suit him.

Jeschonnek eventually took the decision that all bombers equipping the Luftwaffe must be capable of carrying out the dive bombing role. This was too late to affect the medium range Do 17 and He 111s that were then well into full-scale production, but certainly caused many headaches and much heart searching when it came to aircraft such as the Ju 88, Do 217 and ill-fated He 177.

However, the effect of these events was still very much in the future during the summer months of 1939 when the political maneuvering only succeeded in delaying Poland's fate. Despite misgivings among some leaders, there was an air of confidence during the days of August as von Bock's and von Rundstedt's Army Groups moved forward to the borders of Poland. At the same time, Luftflotte 1 under the command of Kesselring and Luftflotte 4 under Löhr also began to move to forward operational airfields. On 25 August the codeword *Ostmarkflug* signalling the start of the campaign was flashed by Goering to the Luftflotten commanders, who in turn passed it down the line to unit commanders. One of these was General der Flieger Wolfram von Richthofen whose Fliegerkorps VIII had a predominance of staff with experience of operations with the Legion Kondor which Richthofen had commanded.

Above: A Dornier Do 17Z-2 of 9/KG.2 heads toward England in 1940.
Right: A Dornier Do 217K-I. The Do 217 was developed from the earlier Do 17 and carried an increased bomb load.
Below: Dornier Do 17s prepare to take off from France, August 1940.

As previously mentioned, Richthofen had been a great supporter and advocate of close ground support and dive bombing, and was now ready to prove his point on a much larger canvas. He was however frustrated because he felt that his main strike units were too far back from the front line. His intention was therefore to move forward as quickly as possible to ground he felt sure would be in German possession by the following dawn. His main worry was the situation regarding communications, for although big steps had been taken, and the Luftwaffe did in fact have an efficient – for the period – signals network, he did not have total confidence in it.

This lack of confidence was justified later the same day, when the original order signalling the opening of the Polish campaign was cancelled on the personal instructions of Hitler and this only just reached von Richthofen in time to halt his

planned air operations. It was in fact only the Luftwaffe communications network that saved the army commanders acute embarrassment for they had received no cancellation of the order and von Richthofen's insistence that a check be made with Berlin via his network, confirmed to them that the plan had indeed been delayed.

Fortunately there were only two areas where the message did not get through: in one a patrol of 30 men of the 46th Infantry Division was decimated by the Poles they attacked, and in the other a unit of the Fourteenth Army captured a rail tunnel which they had to abandon when the withdrawal message reached them. Ironically this was situated on a major supply route and would have been an asset to the Germans, but soon after the Poles took repossession, and now having no doubts that a German assault would materialize in the not too distant future, they blew it up and made the line impassable.

The frustration felt by the army and air commanders was short lived, for barely a week later on 1 September the invasion of Poland began in earnest. The morning of 1 September 1939 dawned with fog hanging in patches over most of Poland, but it was not sufficient to stop the planned attack and this started at 0445 hours when Oberleutnant Bruno Dilley and his radio operator Oberfeldwebel Kather arrived over their target in a Ju 87B of 3/StG.1. Dilley completed his pre-attack cockpit checks, then, signalling to the other two dive bombers in his formation, rolled his aircraft into a vertical dive with its nose aligned on the Dirschau Bridge over the Vistula River. At 3000 feet the three Stukas released their bombs which heralded the start of what was to become a six year war that drastically altered the face of Europe.

The three bombers represented just over one percent of the type then on the strength of the Luftwaffe, which on that fateful morning was:

1505 bombers including 335 Ju 87
1125 single-engined fighters
195 twin-engined fighters
825 reconnaissance and maritime aircraft.

With reserves and training aircraft the total number of available aircraft was less than 5000. Taking serviceability into account the actual operational strength was probably less than 4500, a

Left: A consignment of bombs ready for loading onto the Ju 87's wing and fuselage racks.
Below: A Messerschmitt Bf 110 photographed over the English Channel by a Luftwaffe propaganda photographer.

Above: The Bf 110 heavy twin-engined fighter met its match against British fighters, but later had a distinguished career as a night fighter, a role in which its poor maneuverability was less disadvantageous.
Right: Willi Messerschmitt, designer of the famous fighter aircraft.

far cry from the estimates of between 7000 and 10,000 often quoted and generated from propaganda figures issued at the time.

Because of the uncertainty regarding the British and French reaction to the invasion of Poland, it was decided to retain a sizeable force in the west, thus the number of aircraft available in the two airfleets of Kesselring and Löhr was in the order of 1650. Within 30 minutes of Dilley's attack the German Panzer and infantry divisions had entered Poland initiating the technique of co-operation with the Luftwaffe that was to be given the general name of Blitzkrieg or Lightning War.

The Luftwaffe's initial objective was to put the Polish airfields out of action and to achieve this He 111 and Do 17 level bombers were employed as well as the Ju 87s. These types were also employed to great advantage in attacking troop concentrations and movements, and it is not difficult to imagine the havoc caused among the horses of the elite and proud Polish cavalry units by the screaming dive bombers. Surprise was of course a vital element and this was generally achieved, with many Polish aircraft being destroyed on the ground. But those that did get airborne were able to give a worthy account of themselves although in the main they were outclassed technically if not in piloting skills. There is a widely held belief that the Polish air force was totally destroyed on the ground during the opening few days of the short-lived campaign. This is not so, and although at the beginning of the war its strength was a mere 397 aircraft of which only 159 were fighters, they had accounted for 285 German aircraft by the time capitulation came. Of these, 67 were the new Bf 109 fighters, and 31 were the much vaunted Ju 87s. Some of the Luftwaffe's casualties which included the loss of 734 personnel, were of course caused by

ground fire, nonetheless the Polish airmen in their outdated PZL P7 and P11 fighters had fought valiantly.

Despite these brave efforts it is nonetheless true to say that after three days the Polish air force was virtually finished as a fighting force. This left the ground forces completely unprotected from the marauding Ju 87s, Do 17s and Bf 109s whose pilots delighted in their new found task of shooting up ground installations with their cannon and machine guns. General Kutrzeba who commanded the Polish Army of Poznan confirmed that this attention created a dreadful situation, with every troop movement coming in for annihilating attack from the air.

By 17 September the lines of communication, back-up support and transport on which any army must depend had all been wiped out. The Polish army therefore became a disorientated force unable to fight with any cohesion or coordinated plan, and German victory was in sight.

During the advance the Luftwaffe had attacked military targets within civilian areas. This brought immediate accusations of terror bombing, but according to an eye witness from a neutral embassy such attacks had only taken place with military objectives in mind and civilian casualties had occurred because of their proximity to such targets and not because they were the main objectives.

Below: The German ace Werner Mölders re-lives a combat for the benefit of his colleagues.

Above: A Bf 110C-1. Note the nose mounted armament and the machine gun in the rear cockpit.
Right: A pair of Bf 110E-1 night fighters of 7/NJG.4 photographed over France in 1942.
Below right: A Heinkel He 111 H-3 of KG.1 shows off its rather elegant profile.

With victory in sight some German forces were withdrawn to the west as on 3 September Britain and France had declared war on Germany and it was felt that this area must be strengthened.

Warsaw represented the last bastion of Polish defiance and it was to von Richthofen's force that the task of softening it up fell. By 25 September resistance around the city had stiffened and despite the Russian intervention (they invaded Poland from the east on the 17th) the Polish resolve to defend their capital was if anything stronger than it had ever been.

An unsuccessful leaflet campaign was mounted in an attempt to persuade the garrison to surrender, but this failed and on the 25th a powerful artillery and aerial bombardment commenced. Over 400 bombers were used in the almost continual assault and at times there was total chaos over the city as aircrews tried to bomb what they had been briefed were military targets, through the gathering smoke and gloom over the doomed city.

One interesting aspect of this bombing offensive was the use of Ju 52 transport aircraft to drop incendiary bombs. The method was primitive in that it consisted of two soldiers tasked with pushing out the bombs from the aircraft's side doors. The slow Ju 52s made easy targets for the defending forces' guns and several of them fell victims to ground fire, but in so doing they added their loads to the crews' funeral pyres and therefore contributed to the overall objective. Prevailing east winds did carry some of the bombs into German infantry lines, resulting in a demand from the Eighth Army commander that all bombing should cease. But with Warsaw ablaze from end to end and in full view of Hitler who had arrived to see the devastation, such pleas fell on deaf ears.

The 100,000 soldiers manning Warsaw's defense systems had little chance against the continual assault of the Luftwaffe. The bombers available to von Richthofen flew almost continuously thus giving the appearance of a greater force being involved than really was, which is to be understood when it is appreciated that in operating four or five sorties per day every aircraft was able to deposit a considerable tonnage on the beleaguered city. Warsaw was not an 'open city' as has often been claimed; it was heavily and bravely defended against odds that from the beginning were obviously overwhelming. But knowing this the Polish commanders chose to refuse all demands from the Germans to surrender before the attack and therefore committed their capital to destruction.

Below: A cutaway view of the Messerschmitt Bf 109E-4 is marked as the fighter flown by Oberleutnant Franz von Werra of JG.3, which was shot down over Kent in September 1940.

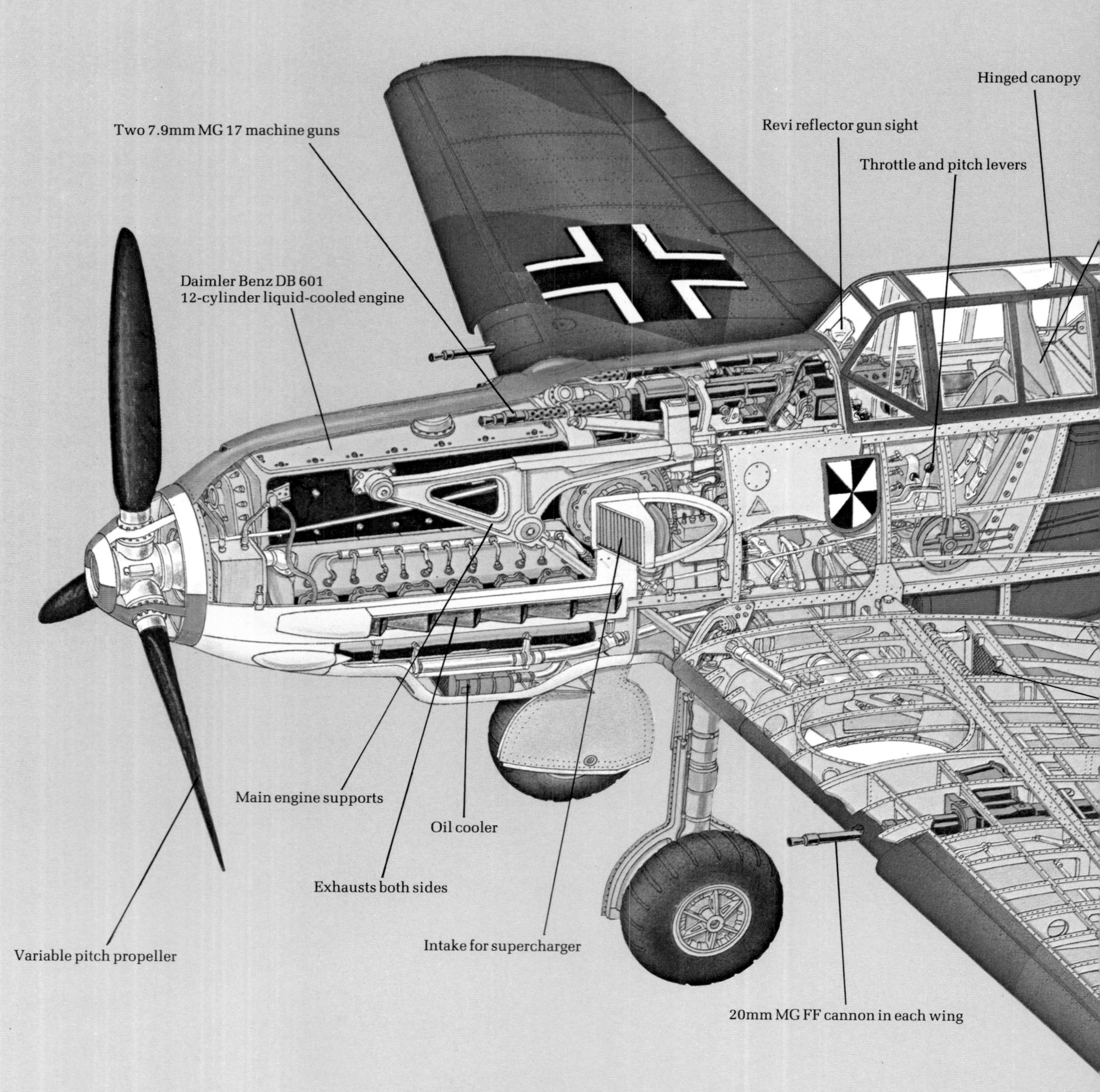

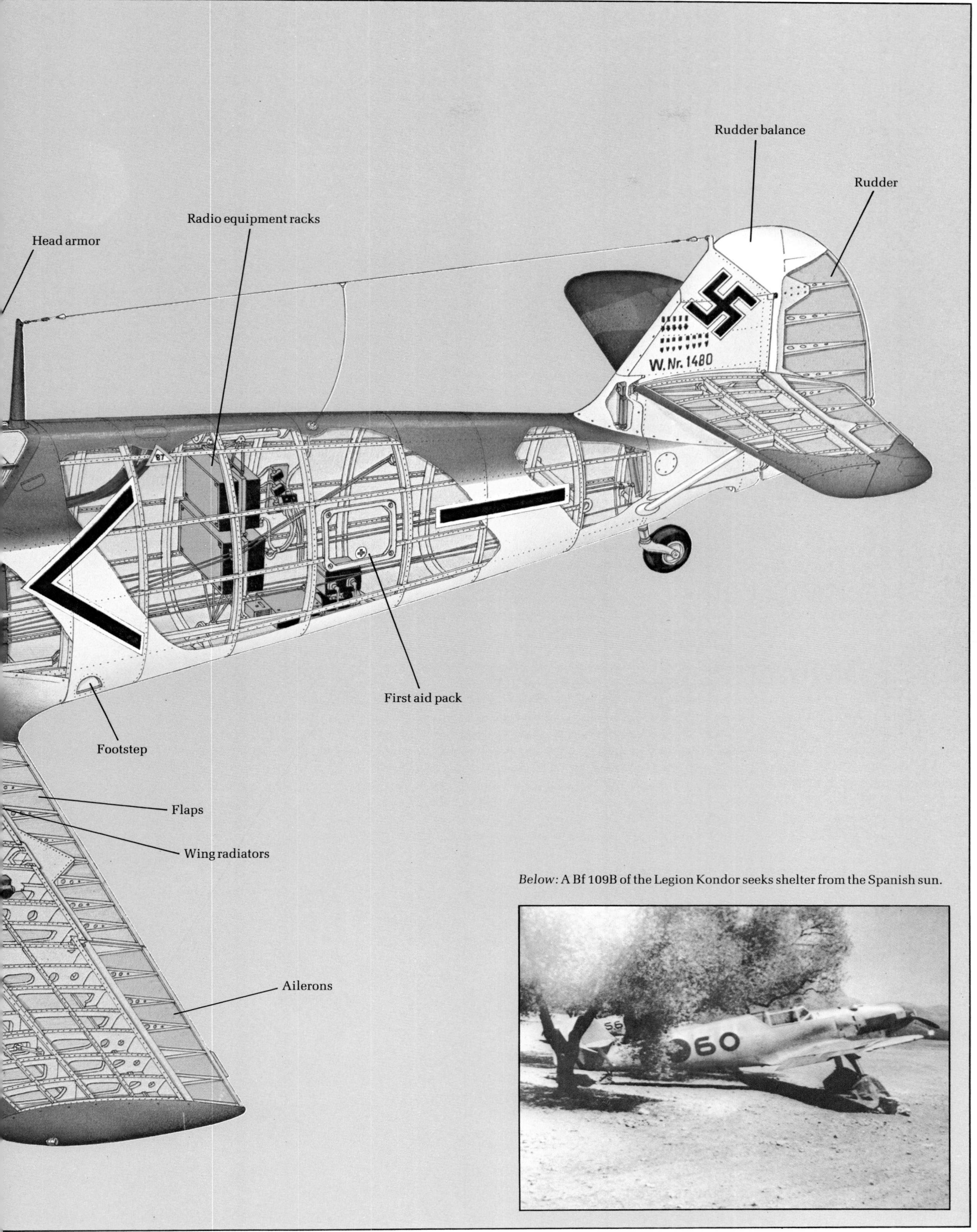

Below: A Bf 109B of the Legion Kondor seeks shelter from the Spanish sun.

On 26 September the forces defending Warsaw finally surrendered and the following day the campaign came to an end. So in less than four short weeks the Germans had demonstrated a frightening power. The co-operation between land and air forces had laid the foundations of future strategy, but a blind eye was turned to the important lessons that such success from the air could only be achieved if total air superiority was enjoyed and that, as efficient as the Luftwaffe appeared to be, it was ill-equipped to fight anything more than a short campaign in support of the army.

The successes of the Stuka crews first hinted at in Spain, and now confirmed in Poland, seemed to vindicate the ideas that those advocates of this type of bombing had been preaching. Needless to say the propaganda machine was not long in taking up the cause, and soon the fear of the so called Stuka had reached the ears of just about every infantryman who was faced with the prospect of fighting the German Army.

With the campaign in Poland over, Goering withdrew most combat units to bases in Germany where the men could rest, aircraft could be repaired and replacements integrated into the operational structure.

Although the opposing French and British armies played a waiting game with their opposite numbers in the Wehrmacht, along what was a static front, planners were already looking at Hitler's next objectives. Due to the general inactivity this period has become known as the 'phony war', but there was nothing false about the move against Denmark and Norway which came on 9 April 1940. Hitler was keen to secure his

Right: Luftwaffe air traffic controllers monitor broadcasts from bombers attacking French targets in early 1940.
Far right: Although obsolete by 1945 the He 111 fought throughout the war. Its elegant shape tended to give a false impression of efficiency. These are He 111H-2s of KG.1.

Above: The nose glazing of a Do 17.
Below: A late production Do 17P-1 with BMW 132N engines.

northern flank and the declared neutrality of both countries counted for nothing when his forces made their move.

While the German Navy secured ports and islands the first ever airborne assault by paratroopers secured the airfields at Aalborg. Copenhagen was soon also in German hands and by the end of the day the Danish government had wisely surrendered thus saving a lot of lives. The Norwegian air force harried the German machine but it was no match for the Luftwaffe and was soon completely negated. It was during the invasion of Norway that the Luftwaffe used another lesson learned in Spain, this being the transportation of large quantities of troops by air.

The ubiquitous Ju 52, or 'Tante Ju' as it was affectionately known by its crews, moved men and equipment into the country at an alarming rate. Over 500 aircraft were used, some of these being withdrawn from flying training schools specifically for the purpose. The result was that the German high command was soon able to establish Fliegerkorps X with over 700 aircraft. This was operational very quickly to harrass the allied forces attempting to re-establish themselves in Norway and it was in this theater that the reconnaissance aircraft quickly established its importance. The RAF's attempts to set up bases from which to operate their fighters were always under observation with the result that long before operations could commence, attention from the German bombers had destroyed landing grounds and aircraft.

On 10 June the combined British, French and Norwegian forces withdrew from the country thus effectively bringing organized resistance to an end. Fliegerkorps X became part of Stumpff's Luftflotte 5 whose headquarters was at Stavanger, and its objective to attack British shipping and ports.

The Luftwaffe had proved to be a decisive factor in the

Above: The Fieseler Fi 156 Storch, was used in many roles where its ability to take off and land in small spaces was an asset.

two-month Norwegian campaign. Paratroopers supported by infantry landed by the Ju 52s had secured the most important airfields and strategic positions which enabled the bombers and fighters to operate from secure bases and mount attacks against the Allied forces before they could make decisive moves. In particular communications were somewhat difficult in the Norwegian environment and command of the air gave the Germans command of the primitive rail and road systems.

With the Norwegian situation moving to a satisfactory conclusion, as far as the Germans were concerned, the thrust into France could begin. The German plan was to drive a powerful armored wedge through the center of the Allied armies thus separating them into two groups and leaving them for individual attention. Like many German plans it was simple but bold, and its success depended a great deal on the security of the supply lines as they lengthened. This security could only be maintained by the Luftwaffe. As had happened in the case of the Scandinavian countries, Hitler decided it was wise to ignore the declared neutrality of Holland and Belgium and occupy them to secure what would be the northern flank of his proposed French invasion.

During the period of the so called Phony War both the British and Germans had had salutary lessons from which they learned a lot but did not necessarily profit from the experiences.

On 16 October 1939 nine Ju 88A-1s of I/KG.30 set out from their base on the island of Sylt to bomb warships, including HMS *Hood*, which had been reported in the Firth of Forth. The Ju 88s found the *Hood* in the harbor at Rosyth so did not attack for fear that their bombs might hit land targets. They therefore directed their attention to other ships in the Firth and scored hits on the cruiser *Southampton*, but lost two of their number to Spitfires of Nos 602 and 603 Squadrons of the Auxiliary Air Force. The following day, four of KG.30's aircraft returned, again without success, but this time they managed to hit the island of Hoy, the first part of the British Isles to receive hits from German bombs during World War II.

Shipping was also a prime target for the RAF and British aircraft, mainly Blenheims and Wellingtons, carried out tentative raids against German warships and coastal installations. On 4 September 1939 14 Wellington and 15 Blenheim bombers carried out attacks against the *Admiral Scheer* and the cruiser *Emden* in Wilhelmshaven harbor. The *Admiral Scheer* was hit by three bombs which failed to explode, but the *Emden* was damaged and suffered casualties among her crew when a Blenheim, hit by anti-aircraft fire, crashed on to it.

Five Blenheims were shot down and five failed to find their targets. Of the Wellingtons which had been detailed to attack Brunsbüttel at the mouth of the Kiel canal, one managed to drop its bombs on a small Danish township, Esbjerg, located 110 miles north of the briefed target, and killed two people, and two were shot down, one by anti-aircraft fire and the other by

Below: Ju 87B-1s of II/StG.77 at Breslau-Schöngarten in August 1939, from the German magazine *Signal*.

Above: Hermann Goering with Feldmarschall List (right) and Hitler Youth Leader Baldur von Schirach (far left) in Vienna, 1940.
Right: German ground crew were called 'Black Men' because of their coveralls. This one makes carrying a belt of ammunition look easy.

Feldwebel Alfred Held of II/JG.77 flying a Bf 109. This was the first Luftwaffe fighter victory over a British bomber during World War II. The *Gneisenau* and *Scharnhorst* which had been the Wellingtons' main objectives had escaped completely unscathed, their ring of anti-aircraft protection and the fighters scrambled from Nordholz in appalling weather, being far too much for the RAF bombers.

Three months later, on 18 December, the RAF suffered its most humiliating experience of the war to date, when 24 Wellingtons were detailed to attack Wilhelmshaven. Of the 22 aircraft that reached the target area, 12 were shot down. On this occasion the aircraft had flown above 10,000 feet to avoid anti-aircraft fire, but in so doing had been picked up early by the *Freya* radar station on Wangerooge island. Leutnant Diehl, the officer in charge of the radar, calculated the bombers' position at just over 100 kilometers from the coast, adequate time in which to get fighters airborne and into an attacking position. But at this stage of the war speed of communications had not been totally mastered so it was some twenty minutes before the Geschwader commander received the message.

The delay served only to increase slightly the life span of some of the unfortunate Wellington crew members, for the Bf 109s supported by long-range Bf 110s, proved to be more than a match for the lightly armed bombers. First on the scene was Oberleutnant Joseph Steinoff's 10/JG.26, the first Wellington falling to Unteroffizier Heilmeyer's guns, closely followed by the knocking down of the second by Steinoff himself.

The German fighters harried the bombers far out to sea on

their way home, and although they lost two Bf 109s, the carnage among the bomber squadron was devastating.

The loss of five Wellingtons from a fleet of 12 on 14 December coupled with the 12 shot down on the 18th, taught the British an important lesson, but it was not totally absorbed. The theory that bombers flying in close formation in daylight would collectively generate enough fire-power to deter a fighter attack, was clearly wrong, and it would be a long time before the RAF attempted similar operations. The problem of fire created by not having self-sealing tanks was also appreciated, but what appears to have been totally overlooked was that even at night the 0.303-inch machine guns were no match for heavily armed fighters that could stand off outside the range of such weapons.

From the German point of view, there was a total failure to appreciate the value of radar or the danger of daylight bomber operations. Many months earlier Goering had dismissed radar as being unimportant, and the lesson of early warning that was to cost him dearly over the British Isles in 1940, could have been learned during December 1939. Similarly, it is hard to understand why he thought that his bombers stood a better chance of penetrating enemy airspace in daylight than the RAF ones had. The answer probably lies with his confidence – shared by the German high command – that the war would not last long, and that it would not take the Luftwaffe fighter squadrons long to knock out the RAF.

The months between September 1939 and April 1940, also saw German airspace penetrated at night by long range, Whitley, Wellington and Hampden bombers of the RAF, and although they were in the main dropping nothing more offensive than leaflets, the fact that they had ventured where Goering had assured the German people no enemy aircraft could fly, was also dismissed as being of little significance.

Left: Goering with his Pour le Mérite beneath the Iron Cross.
Above: Messerschmitt Bf 110C-1s of I/ZG.52 in 1940.
Right: The Heinkel He 177 was unusual in that each engine nacelle contained a pair of coupled engines. This is an He 177A-3/R2 model.

There was still an inherent fear that the bomber would always get through, and this had some influence on both sides in the opening months of the war when great pains were taken to avoid bombing land targets in case there were civilian casualties. But before too long such standards were to be cast aside by both sides, and the first real sign of the effect of the bombing of civilians was to come during the German advance through the low countries.

On 10 May 1940 the 'quiet' period in Europe ended as Hitler put into operation his plans for the invasion of Holland, Belgium and France. The defense of Holland was expected to be mainly along the natural lines of the Maas and Yssel rivers, and in Belgium on the Meuse River with particular emphasis being placed on the well constructed fort at Eben Emael where the Albert Canal and the Meuse met. The German plan was to

GB

attack airfields from which defensive fighters could operate, and at the same time knock out or capture the main bridges crossing the rivers as well as negating the garrison at the fort. The audacious plan devised was to mount raids by paratroopers against the bridges that were needed to be captured intact, and to land a force by troop carrying gliders within the compound of the fort. This required the Luftwaffe to carry out three vital roles: to use bombers and close support aircraft to clear enemy airfields and troop concentrations as they had in Poland; to transport large numbers of troops to their objectives as they had in Norway; and to obtain air superiority at as early a time as was possible.

To achieve these objectives there were nearly 4000 aircraft available including 475 transports, 1600 bombers, 1210 single and twin engined fighters and 47 assault gliders. These were dispersed among Kesselring's Luftflotte 2, supporting Generaloberst von Bock's Army Group B in the North, and Sperrle's Luftflotte 3 with Von Rundstedt's Army Group A in the Ardennes. Against the defenses of the Maginot Line in the south, was von Greim's Fliegerkorps V which came under the control of Luftflotte 3.

As dawn broke on 10 May massed formations of He 111s and Do 17s started their attacks against the Dutch, Belgian, French and British airfields and temporary landing grounds. At the same time bombers also ventured deep into enemy territory to make their assaults on transport and communication systems at Metz, Dijon, Romilly-sur-Seine and Lyon. In the meantime the troop carriers and gliders had made their initial landings and fierce fighting was taking place between the German paratroopers and assault infantry and the Dutch defenders. The attack on Fort Eben Emael was a success beyond the realms of the Germans' highest hopes. The audacity of the plan paid off brilliantly with just 85 German troops quickly taking command of the fortification which was manned by 750 Belgian soldiers, and holding it until reinforcements arrived. The important bridges at Moerdijk near Rotterdam, and those over the Maas in the Maastricht area, were also quickly taken, opening the path for German armor to roll into the beleaguered countries.

Below: Crews of Bf 110s being briefed in the sunshine, 1940.

In the air the Luftwaffe quickly gained control, although on the opening day their losses were very high. The Dutch air force fought well and lost 56 aircraft but, supported by elements of the RAF operating from France and England, they accounted for the destruction of 304 Luftwaffe aircraft, damage to a further 51, and the deaths of 267 German aircrew.

From 11 May the captured bridges came under heavy attack by Fairey Battles of the Belgian air force, as well as Blenheims and Battles of the RAF and French bombers. These obsolescent light bombers were no match for the Luftwaffe fighters and losses were very heavy, while the important bridges remained undamaged and firmly in the hands of the invading forces.

German fighters however had encountered RAF Hurricanes, and Luftwaffe pilots quickly realized that in this eight gunned monoplane, they were faced with more formidable opposition than they had hitherto encountered. On 13 May the Luftwaffe mounted the most intensive air bombardment of a single target so far attempted in the war when Richthofen's FlKps.VIII was called in to open the main offensive against France with attacks on French positions along the Meuse River between Sedan and Nouzonville. Once again the Ju 87s struck absolute terror into the hearts of the defenders who cowered in their fortifications and made little attempt to fight back with their anti-aircraft weapons. The French positions were quickly smashed into submission leaving the way open for Heinz Guderian's 1st Panzer Division to secure a bridgehead, from which by nightfall they had advanced and secured the Marféy Heights.

The following day the RAF and French air forces mounted an intensive effort to destroy the bridges over the Meuse near Sedan, but the Germans like the Allies, well knew that in these lay the key to the invasion of France. The Luftwaffe Flak and fighter units were well established and despite the bravery of the Allied crews in pressing home their attacks, all the French strike force and 40 from a total of 71 RAF bombers were lost.

The same afternoon the Germans had called on the commander of the Dutch garrison at Rotterdam, Colonel Scharroo, to surrender his command. Unable to make this decision without reference to higher authority at the Hague, Scharroo stalled for time. Once again communications were at fault, and the postponement of the planned bombing assault requested by the German ground commander, never reached Oberst Lackner in the lead He 111 of KG.54. While surrender negotiations were taking place, 87 He 111s droned toward the city. Each crew had a map marked with military targets and strict instructions to bomb only these areas. Despite the efforts made by HQ Luftflotte 2 to reach the aircraft by radio, the signals never got through. Plans to counter such radio failure by the use of red flares fired from the ground had been made, but such was the situation over Rotterdam that these were never seen, or if they were, they were mistaken for anti-aircraft fire. Just prior to reaching the target area the Heinkel formation split into two, Lackner leading the starboard element straight in, and Oberstleutnant Höhne leading the port in their attack from the southwest.

Just on the point of bomb release, Höhne did in fact see the red flares, and although it was too late to stop his bomb aimer, the rest of the aircraft in his flight held their bombs, and headed away from Rotterdam for the alternative target. But it was too late for the doomed city and bombs from 57 He 111s rained down. Some 97 tons of high explosive fell in the old part of the city causing widespread fires to be generated, and civilian casualties were high.

At 2030 hours on 14 May General Winkelmans, High Commander of the Dutch forces, capitulated, so in just five days, the first part of Hitler's objective had been achieved. The writing was now on the wall, and as German ground forces poured into France, the British retreated to Dunkirk to seek evacuation. During the opening days of this campaign only four Ju 87s had been lost, and the dive bombers had once again struck terror into the enemy ground forces, thus the legend of invincibility surrounding this type of weapon continued to grow.

By 20 May the German tanks had reached the Channel at Voyelles. The plan had worked beautifully with the French and British forces now split. Lines of supply to forward units were now approaching 250 miles, and the Luftwaffe fighter units were continually moving bases to protect these. However, the air battles over Dunkirk gave the Luftwaffe first sight of the Spitfire, and it was one they did not relish.

The Luftwaffe had been briefed to gain air superiority and Hitler had stopped his land forces short of the town to give Goering the opportunity of proving just what his vaunted Luftwaffe could do. The weight of FlKps.I, II, IV and VIII was thrown into action to stop the British evacuation, but so often were the Bf 109s protecting the bombers diverted from their task to counter the nimble Spitfires, that losses among the Kampfgeschwadern were very high. Most of these encounters

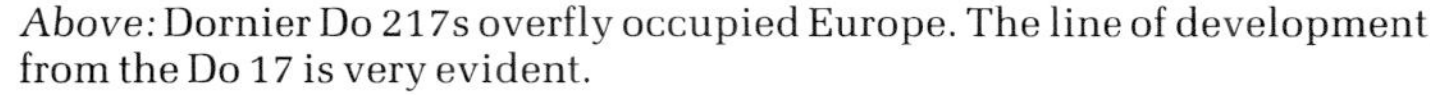

Above: Dornier Do 217s overfly occupied Europe. The line of development from the Do 17 is very evident.

took place well beyond the beaches, and on many occasions Ju 87s and level bombers penetrated the defenses giving support to the claims of the British ground forces that the RAF's contribution was negligible.

Nothing could have been further from the truth. The problem was that the British fighters operating from bases in England were at the extremes of their range and had limited time in the combat area. On the other hand, the Bf 109s were well established in France and although being drawn away from protecting the bombers, were able to dictate the terms of combat. This situation was to reverse itself a few weeks later when the Jagdgruppen were operating on the other side of the English Channel.

Below left: The Junkers Ju 88 was one of the most versatile aircraft of the war. It served as a bomber, fighter, night fighter and reconnaissance aircraft.
Below: An Fw 200 crew prepare for operations.

Above: Arguably the best German fighters of the war, these FW 190A-4s belong to 9/JG.2 and are based in France.

By 4 June what has become known as the miracle of Dunkirk was over and 338,226 men had been recovered. The Luftwaffe had suffered heavy losses, particularly in transport aircraft during the period from 10 May, but this was not to become an immediate embarrassment to them. The main concern was that they had failed to stop the evacuation which Goering had assured Hitler would not happen.

There was still opportunity for redemption and now freed of any commitment in the north, the Luftwaffe turned its attention to supporting the army as it moved toward the French capital. This was reached on 14 June and eleven days later the French surrendered, and were duly humiliated by being made to sign the instrument of surrender in the very railway coach they had used to accept the German surrender in November 1918.

The campaign in the west had taken only 46 days and only Britain now stood between Germany and total domination of Europe. Although the initial brushes with the RAF had been costly, Goering and his generals were convinced that it would not be too difficult to sweep the skies clear of British fighters, thus paving the way for a seaborne landing on British soil.

Between 27 May and 2 June, the Luftwaffe had lost 189

Below: A wrecked Polish air force fighter in 1939. Despite the overwhelming technical and numerical superiority of the Luftwaffe, the Poles fought remarkably well.

aircraft against the RAF's 99, so there was in fact a lesson to be learned in both defeat and victory, and that was that total air superiority could give freedom of operation to ground attack forces, but without this, air power could not in isolation win a land battle.

As had been the case in all theaters to that time, there was an inherent fear of the bomber on both sides, at least as far as civilian targets were concerned. The bombing of Rotterdam had only served to fuel such fires, but before the assault on England began it was still German policy not to attack civilian targets.

Since the RAF's losses were now over 1000 aircraft in the Norwegian and European theaters, it is not surprising that Goering thought the RAF only had a token force left, since he had been led to believe that total RAF strength was not far above this figure. The planned strategy was much the same as that selected in the low countries campaign, but this time the Meuse was replaced by the far more formidable Channel. In England the population steeled themselves for the coming invasion and many cast their minds back to the few minutes immediately following Prime Minister Neville Chamberlain's broadcast on 3 September 1939, when he announced that the country was at war with Germany. On that occasion air raid sirens had sounded sending people scurrying to their shelters. The alarm turned out to be a false one caused by a French aircraft heading into Croydon airport.

Its effect on the public, however, was not surprising, for during the previous decade most people had been led to believe that any future war would almost certainly start with massive air raids. Many factors contributed to this very real fear of aerial bombardment: former Prime Minister Stanley Baldwin's statement in 1932 that the bomber would always get through; the tonnage of bombs that the Luftwaffe could rain on British cities as estimated by various political commentators; as well as somewhat exaggerated stories of the Luftwaffe's activities in the Spanish War. But as in many parallel situations the truth was far from the fiction generated within political corridors.

As is well known, on the outbreak of war in 1939 the Luftwaffe was not equipped to wage a strategic bombing campaign of the type the RAF and USAAF were to launch against Germany in 1943-44. Its bomber squadrons were equipped with what were called long-range twin-engined bombers but with hindsight are better described as medium-range light bombers more suitable for the tactical role. It must also be remembered that at this time Hitler did not intend a wide-scale bombardment of the British Isles as he still hoped for a settlement between the two countries. If his intention had been to mount an aerial campaign from German bases it is very unlikely that it would have achieved the rate of bombardment feared in England, since both the He 111 and Do 17 would have needed to sacrifice at least half their designed bomb load to carry sufficient fuel reserves to allow them to get home or reach diversion airfields.

In July 1940 Kesselring's Luftflotte 2 and Sperrle's Luftflotte 3, were ranged along the Channel coast with a combined strength of 1131 'long-range' bombers, while Luftflotte 5 under Hans-Jürgen Stumpff, could muster a force of 130 bombers from its bases in Norway. Many of the crews then attached to the bomber units were experienced men who had flown with Lufthansa before the war and in many cases had previous combat experience. Although casualties mounted throughout the air battles over Britain, Luftwaffe training schools were able to keep up a flow of well trained personnel. By the beginning of 1944 the training schools had been forced to reduce their programs drastically, resulting in pilots with less than 100 hours flying time being posted to front-line units. The Kampfgeschwadern did not suffer in this respect as much as their colleagues in the Jagdgeschwadern, but as training schools closed down or reduced the length of their courses, many bomber pilots were transferred to fighter units.

The methods used in the selection of aircrew and their training were very much the same as those used by the RAF and USAAF. The exceptions were observers, who in the Luftwaffe initially trained as pilots and received about 200 hours flying time during which they received their pilot's license, before going on to specialized observer training. All aircrew spent six months in basic training, the emphasis being on drill, physical fitness, and sport. Pilots carried out initial training at an elementary flying school where they were taught aerodynamics, navigation, radio procedures, aviation law, and a host of allied subjects.

Successful completion of this course saw the tyro pilot move on to more advanced aircraft from which he would gain enough experience to receive his license. Bomber pilots then went to another school where they completed a further 60 hours flying on more advanced aircraft, and from there to a specialist school to learn the art of instrument flying. The next stage of training brought all crew members together and they flew operational aircraft on simulated sorties until they were ready to join an operational squadron. During the early part of the war the observer was usually the aircraft captain but by mid-1942 this arrangement was being phased out and the policy used by other air forces of having the pilot as captain, was generally adopted.

As pressures on training schools mounted, the phases out-

Below: Generalfeldmarschall Freiherr von Richthofen, cousin of the World War I ace, commanded the Legion Kondor and Luftflotten 2 and 4.

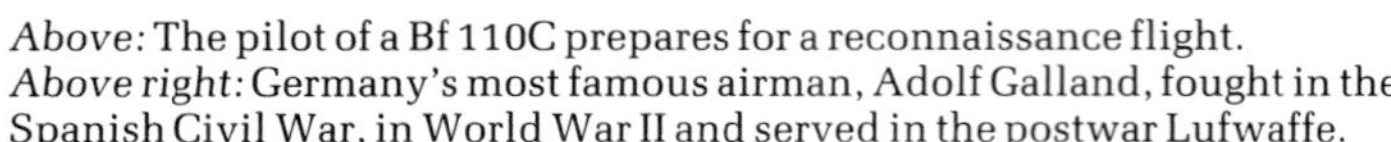

Above: The pilot of a Bf 110C prepares for a reconnaissance flight.
Above right: Germany's most famous airman, Adolf Galland, fought in the Spanish Civil War, in World War II and served in the postwar Lufwaffe.

lined were cut-down and by 1944 observers were receiving no pilot training, and completing their instruction course within six months. The usual composition of a bomber crew was pilot, observer, radio operator, flight engineer and specialist air gunner. Apart from the pilot, all other crew members also received gunnery training and manned the aircraft's defensive armament. Pilots and observers were usually commissioned or carried senior NCO status, while other members could be any rank, the policy followed by the RAF of having sergeant as the lowest aircrew rank, was not used by the Luftwaffe.

Luftwaffe uniforms followed a standard pattern throughout the war, being field blue in color. The familiar 'Eagle' emblem was carried on the right breast, this being in silver wire for officers and embroidered for enlisted personnel. Flying badges were worn on the left breast, and above them was often to be seen a clasp awarded for a number of operations.

Shoulder epaulettes denoting rank were in Luftwaffe blue with piping around the edges in Waffenfarbe; officers' badges were in silver fabric with piping and buttons in silver, and for NCOs they were in Luftwaffe blue with silver fabric edging. Collar patches together with epaulettes denoted rank, the background color being the Waffenfarbe of the particular arm of service – golden for aircrew – and wings, borders and oak leaves (the actual rank badges) were in silver. A flight jacket very similar in style to today's modern battledress was introduced in the mid 1940s.

Bomber crews often flew in a one-piece light brown flying suit on the sleeves of which were carried rank badges. The early style life jacket was a heavy ribbed kapok-filled waistcoat, but this gave way to a much lighter inflatable type. Crews were also issued with Flak helmets which were very similar to the infantry's 'coalscuttle' type but with wider brims to accommodate earphones. Unlike the practice in the RAF and USAAF, there was no set minimum of operations comprising a tour, the German crews simply carried on flying, with periods of rest and leave, until they were killed, wounded, or moved to another front with their units. Some did, of course, move to training schools, and in general there was a much more civilized approach to mental strain resulting in stressed men being rested.

The raids against British targets in the months up to July 1940 had been of a probing nature mainly against seaports ranging from Bristol to Grimsby and Hull to Liverpool. They did inflict some damage but not on the scale expected by the British Chiefs of Staff. Sporadic night raids in June caused more disruption of sleep by the widespread sounding of air-raid warnings across the whole country than they achieved in material damage.

But they did prove the inadequacy of the British night fighter force, although on the credit side, they led to the discovery of a radio beam which was being used to guide the bombers. As a result of papers found in a crashed German bomber and other intelligence, British scientists led by Dr R V Jones discovered the existence of *Knickebein*, which was a guiding beam transmitted from within enemy held-territory and used to direct bombers over their targets. Rapid work by the scientists resulted in suitable countermeasures in which a false beacon was used to confuse German aircrew who had no way of telling whether they were tuned into the original beacon or the decoy.

In July 1940 the German General Staff made their plans for the invasion of Britain and to the Luftwaffe fell the tasks of eliminating the RAF in the air and on the ground, and cutting off the supply of food and materials flooding into the country via its seaports.

The task of destroying the RAF was planned to be accomplished in two ways, the first by tempting fighters into the air and then engaging them with the Bf 109s of the Jagdgeschwadern, and the second by systematic daylight raids on RAF bases starting in the south and working northward. Opening skirmishes in July were directed at shipping, and although these achieved some success they did not affect the determination of the merchant seamen to carry on manning the convoys. These exchanges also probed the effectiveness of RAF Fighter Command, which on some occasions was able to take a fairly heavy toll of the raiders, but on others did not have sufficient warning to be in the right place at the right time. A typical example of this lack of advanced warning occurred on 4 July when 33 Ju 87s of III/StG.51 struck at shipping and installations at Portland. As no RAF fighters were patrolling the area and none could be got there in time, the only casualty suffered by the dive bombers was the loss of Leutnant Schwarze who was shot down by anti-aircraft fire from HMS *Foyle Bank*. To the Luftwaffe commanders it looked as though perhaps once again the Ju 87 was going to be a powerful weapon, but later events were to show otherwise.

Throughout the months of July, August and September 1940, a period which has generally become known as the Battle of Britain, the Luftwaffe strived to attain the objectives it had been set. But it learned to its cost that tactics whereby fighters penetrated ahead of the bombers in an attempt to lure RAF fighter squadrons into combat, thus giving the Kampfgeschwadern a relatively clear run, did not work.

Although they had some idea of the existence of an early warning system, the Luftwaffe staff did not fully understand how this operated, and broke off attacks against radar installations at a crucial (for the defenders) time. The Jagdgruppen were eventually ordered to fly close-support escort to the

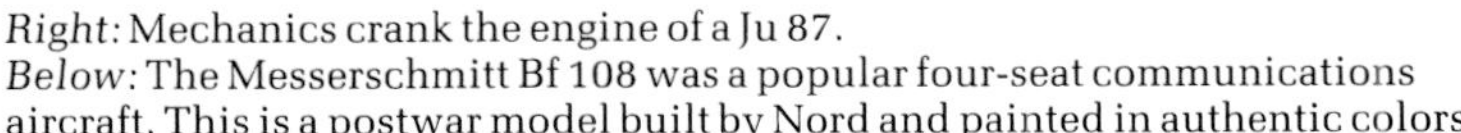

Right: Mechanics crank the engine of a Ju 87.
Below: The Messerschmitt Bf 108 was a popular four-seat communications aircraft. This is a postwar model built by Nord and painted in authentic colors.

Above: Generaloberst Hans-Jürgen Stumpff, Chief of the Luftwaffe General Staff in 1939, commander of Luftflotten 1 and 5, and in 1944 commander of Luftwaffe Reich, responsible for home defense.

bombers, a situation which brought many problems, the most serious of which was the extremely short combat radius of the Bf 109. German fighter pilots were now fighting at a similar disadvantage to those experienced by the RAF over Dunkirk, but it was in fact slightly more complicated than that, and to put things into true perspective it is once again necessary to look at previous events.

The Munich agreement of 1938 gave Britain valuable breathing space for, if she had gone to war then, RAF Fighter Command could only have matched the modern monoplane fighters of the Luftwaffe with obsolescent biplanes and the outcome would have been far different. As it was, in the two years between Munich and the Battle of Britain, British production of modern fighters had progressed at a feverish pace and by the summer of 1940 Fighter Command strength, in terms of modern equipment, was almost at parity with that of the Luftwaffe. In an endeavor to add color to the events of 1940, many writers have been guilty of perpetuating the popular myth of an outnumbered core of tired pilots fighting against a far superior enemy.

Although not detracting from the bravery and determination of the 'few', the facts are that the fighter strength of the RAF was almost identical to that of the Luftwaffe's Jagdgruppen, and there were greater numbers in reserve. The popular misconception arises because quite often the total strength of the Luftwaffe, without regard to those engaged on other fronts or in reserve, is quoted as opposing Fighter Command only. Or, in some cases where the writer has been a little more objective, he has fallen into the trap of quoting the totals of bombers and fighters ranged against the RAF. In essence the outcome of the battle depended on the ability of the Luftwaffe fighter pilots to clear the skies of British fighters thus giving their bombers freedom of operation. In the end they failed because they were restricted in their combat time over England, hampered by a directive which tied them to escort duties, unsettled by a change in tactics which involved switching their point of attack from important strategic targets to less important tactical ones, and finally thwarted by the growing strength of Fighter Command.

The Jagdgruppen were at a considerable disadvantage in that they were fighting over a hostile territory where to be shot down meant almost certain capture. The RAF obviously did not have this problem if a pilot was shot down but unhurt but they in turn were penalised by a training system that had not produced enough pilots with experience to replace those lost in combat. One major Luftwaffe advantage in this respect was the nucleus of men with experience gained in the Spanish Civil War and France.

As related earlier, experience gained in the Spanish Civil War, especially in relation to fighter tactics had seen, for example, the outdated formations of WWI replaced by the finger four system. The new ideas were passed on at training schools, and the soundness of these methods is reflected in their adoption by all air forces by the time hostilities ceased.

Tactics like this and the development of a firm belief in their equipment, were a vital part of Luftwaffe fighter pilot training, which took approximately two years, and like bomber crews once with a unit the fighter pilot stayed in almost total combat, which accounts for the ability of some to accumulate massive personal victory tallies.

Apart from the soundness of the design of the Bf 109, pilots also had first class personal equipment, including a Mauser flare pistol attached to the life-jacket by a cord, a one-man dinghy fastened to the parachute harness, and flying gear which often left a certain amount of choice open to the individual. This could include a one-piece flying suit or a leather jacket worn over, or with, normal uniform. The German fighter pilots were just as extrovert as their opposite numbers!

The Bf 109's cockpit was well protected by armor plating above and behind the pilot's head and to either side of his body, as well as a 56mm thick bullet-proof windshield. A disadvantage was the rather cramped cockpit, especially for a tall man, and the surprisingly limited radio equipment which, almost unbelievably, could not be used for direct communication with bomber crews.

With new aircraft, and the confidence brought about by successful campaigns, the Jagdgruppen of Luftflotten 2 and 3 stood poised on their airfields in France and Belgium to carry the fight across the Channel to the waiting Royal Air Force. Losses over Dunkirk indicated that the Spitfire and Hurricane would be difficult to combat, especially the former which had taken a heavy toll of Ju 87s and their escorting Bf 109s, but most of the pilots were not unduly concerned, for they believed that such RAF aircraft were few in number and would soon succumb.

At this time the strength of the two Luftflotten was 760 Bf 109Es and 220 Bf 110s, of which approximately 85 percent were serviceable and ready for combat. The RAF had 670 single-engined fighters serviceable and a further 513 in reserve, so as far as aircraft were concerned the opposing fighter forces were virtually equal. But equality cannot be judged on numbers alone, and many other factors must be considered. Important among these was radar, which had been perfected to a greater degree by the British than the German High Command appreciated, and was the key to getting defending fighters into positions where they were most needed. Initially the Luftwaffe firmly believed that the RAF was mounting costly standing patrols, thus weakening the defenders since such patrols are

Right: The Ju 188 was a development of the Ju 88. This A-2 model is getting ready for a strike at Arnhem, 1944.

Above: A Heinkel He 111 of KG.26, which was an element of Luftflotte 2 and later of Luftflotte 3.

demanding on men and machines. As far as the aircraft were concerned, the Bf 109 was a nimble and very maneuverable machine armed with two 20mm wing-mounted cannon and two 7.9mm fuselage-mounted machine guns, or similar combinations depending on the armament fit of the individual aircraft concerned.

This armament was far more effective than the eight rifle caliber 0.303-inch (7.7-mm) wing-mounted machine guns, of the Spitfire and Hurricane. Performance comparisons of the aircraft are misleading if taken out of context but it is acceptable to say that, in very general terms, the Hurricane was far inferior in performance to the Bf 109, whereas the Spitfire was about equal especially in the height band between 13,000 and 20,000 feet where most combats were fought during the summer of 1940. One big advantage the Bf 109s had was that their engines were fitted with direct fuel injection and so did not cut out if the aircraft was suddenly pushed into a dive, when a similar maneuver by the British aircraft would cause centrifugal force to upset the float operated carburetor and cause a momentary hesitation in power from the engine.

So in July 1940 the scene was set for the Luftwaffe to set about its designated task over England. Initial skirmishes began over the Channel when fighters harried convoys and bombers attacked shipping and ports. In some cases the bombers were escorted by fighters, on others the fighters flew Frei Jagd (Free Chase) patrols aimed at drawing the RAF into combat. These tactics succeeded to a degree and in the first week of July the RAF lost 18 aircraft and 13 pilots. One of the earliest large scale combats developed on the morning of 10 July when Bf 109s and Bf 110s from JG.3, 27, 51 and ZG.76 escorted bombers briefed to attack the convoy code named *Bread* off the North Foreland.

In many cases the British fighter squadrons which were scrambled to meet these early threats operated at a distinct disadvantage since they had little opportunity to gain height before the Bf 109s dived on to them. With height and speed advantage, the Luftwaffe pilots held all the aces and the British suffered accordingly. These early exchanges taught both sides a great deal and most RAF squadrons soon adopted the finger-four formation used by the Luftwaffe. But old methods die hard and even at the height of the battle on 18 August Hurricanes of 501 Sqn were caught climbing in 'vics' of three by III/JG.26. Oberleutnant Gerhard Schoepfel dived his Bf 109 from the sun and immediately shot down the Hurricanes of Pilot Officers Bland and Kozlowski who were guarding the squadron's tail. The remaining British fighters, unaware that their weavers had gone, continued to climb and Schoepfel and his wing-man accounted for two more Hurricanes before the others realized what was happening. That only one of the RAF pilots was killed, while the other three parachuted to safety illustrates the importance of operating over friendly territory for the RAF. At this time the German training schools were able to keep up the required number of replacements, but pilots in the RAF were in short supply. Nonetheless the loss of a trained and perhaps very experienced man was serious, although at this particular time the Luftwaffe's biggest headache was replacement aircraft, as in 1940 production rate of fighters in Germany was about half of that of the British.

Throughout July and August the Luftwaffe Jagdgruppen discovered to their cost that the RAF possessed more fighters than they had been led to believe, and they were flown by men whose tenacity and resolve to defend their homeland was such that the estimated numbers of fighters needed to defend the bombers had been woefully underestimated. Another painful lesson was that the twin-engined Bf 110 was no match for the British fighters, although it was not greatly outclassed by the Hurricane. On some occasions it needed a fighter escort of its own or had to rely on a far-from-effective defensive circle maneuver.

As Goering became more and more frustrated at the failure of his Luftwaffe to carry out his promise to Hitler, activity by the bombers was intensified and the fighters became more tied to them in close escort. With a combat radius of action reaching only as far as London, and sufficient fuel to allow a maximum of 15 minutes combat over England, the Bf 109 pilots became more and more inhibited.

From early July to the second week of August, the Jagdgruppen lost 106 Bf 109s and Bf 110s against a total of 148 British fighters, but among the latter were a number of Defiants which were from units which had been decimated before being withdrawn from the battle, and some obsolete twin-engined Blenheims. This rate of attrition could be sustained by the Luftwaffe, but it was losing too many of its bombers without achieving the breakthroughs expected.

A change of tactics came in mid-August when attention was turned to coastal radar installations and RAF airfields. On 11 August a large force of He 111s, Do 17s and Ju 88s, escorted by Bf 109s and Bf 110s, attacked Portland losing 11 of their number, but worse was to follow two days later when 20 bombers failed to return from 485 sorties over England. Five of these were Do 17s from KG.2 which had mounted the day's first raids on the naval base at Sheerness and RAF Eastchurch, arriving without their fighter escort which had been recalled due to bad weather, the message never reaching the bomber leader. This incident highlighted the short-comings in the communications systems between the bombers and fighters. All messages had to be passed via a third party on the ground as the radios in the fighters could not be tuned to the bombers' frequencies. Later in the war this essential necessity was put right, but by then it had cost the lives of many brave men. It also served to indicate that the hand-operated defensive machine guns of the bombers were insufficient protection against the British fighters.

The Ju 87 which had earned a reputation in other theaters, was now suffering especially on the occasions it tried to operate without an escort. The dive-bomber proved to be most vulnerable, especially as it pulled out of its dive. In the first two months of the 1940 campaign against England, Ju 87s were confined to attacks on shipping and harbors, however in early August they were assigned to the overall task of attacking inland and coastal radar targets.

The toll of Ju 87s mounted and by 13 August the end for them was in sight when one Staffel of II/StG.2 lost six of their nine aircraft; five days later I, II and III Gruppen of StG.77 lost 16 Ju 87s in attacks on the airfields at Thorney Island and Ford. Consequently the Ju 87 was withdrawn from further operations against British targets. Three Gruppen were retained in France for possible use against shipping and night raids, but they were never again used during daylight sorties where they were likely to meet RAF fighters.

With the Bf 109 now tied to close-support escort work the

Below left: Hauptman Heinz Bär, an ace with 220 victories.
Below: Major Helmuth Wick the top-scoring Luftwaffe pilot (56 victories) during the Battle of Britain.

Jagdgruppen found it impossible to make any inroads on their objective: to destroy Fighter Command in the air. Daylight bombing was proving extremely costly as was shown on 15 August when Luftflotte 5 attempted a raid on north east England with a force comprising 65 Heinkel He 111s from KG.26 and 50 Ju 88s from KG.30, escorted by Bf 110s of I/ZG.76. Sixteen bombers and seven Bf 110s fell to the guns of the defending fighters in what was almost a repeat of the situation encountered by the RAF Wellingtons in the Schilling Roads the previous December.

In the afternoon attacks were made by aircraft from ZGr.210 and KG.3 against the airfields at Martlesham, Eastchurch, Rochester, Middle Wallop, Croydon and West Malling. The German forces involved were severely mauled by RAF fighters losing 55 of their number.

In an attempt to rejuvenate the falling morale of some of his crews, Goering made several changes to the command structure of the Luftwaffe's Jagdgruppen during mid-August, introducing younger pilots with what he termed a 'more aggressive' spirit to command positions. But having done this he was not then content to allow such men as Galland, Trautloft and Lutzlow to introduce their own form of independent fighter operations. If the assault against radar and RAF airfields had continued and all other air operations been suspended, the Luftwaffe may well have achieved Goering's objective, but a switch to less important targets in early September gave the RAF much needed breathing space.

By 31 August the Luftwaffe was using up to 65 fighters to escort sometimes as few as 15 bombers. Although some fighters had been transferred from Norway to bases in the Pas de Calais area to provide even more escorts, this did nothing to solve the range problem. If the 300 litre drop tank soon to be provided had been available two months earlier than it was the fighters may well have been able to make a devastating impact. For there can be no doubt that RAF losses for August which totalled 390 fighters, against the Germans' 254 fighters and 215 bombers, were crippling the defenders. This was the closest the Luftwaffe came to defeating the RAF and clearing the way for a seaborne invasion.

A turning point in the German offensive came on 24 August when Luftwaffe aircraft accidentally bombed London, and almost immediately the civilian population was placed in the front line. A retaliatory raid by the RAF the next night against Berlin caused little damage but contributed to a 'gloves-off' policy by the Luftwaffe and cleared the way for concentrated attacks on British cities, giving the hard pressed RAF bases a welcome respite.

On 7 September London suffered its biggest assault so far when 372 bombers escorted by 642 fighters attacked the capital causing considerable damage, killing 448 civilians and injuring a further 1337. At the beginning of the attack, the RAF fighters were badly placed as they were expecting a continuation of the assault on their airfields, but during the 90 minute battle they managed to retrieve the situation and took a heavy toll of enemy aircraft, especially when the Bf 109s were forced to leave the bombers due to fuel limitations. That night a further 225 bomber sorties were mounted in the same area and the following morning shocked Londoners, some of whom had spent 12 hours in their air-raid shelters, saw the devastation bombing could cause. But far from bringing a breakdown in morale, it only served to produce hidden reserves which increased the fortitude of those concerned. The German civilian population was to respond in a similar fashion when the Allies mounted their major offensive later in the war.

If further proof of the folly of daylight bomber operations was needed it came on 15 September when the Luftwaffe lost 60 aircraft, an attrition rate that forced Operation *Seelöwe* (the invasion of Britain) to be postponed. This day heralded the climax of the Battle of Britain, and is generally regarded as the one that finally brought the Luftwaffe offensive of 1940 to an end. Of the 60 aircraft lost, 26 were fighters, and among the experienced pilots who failed to return were Oberleutnant Reumschüssel, the Staffel Kapitan of 2/JG.3, Oberleutnant Jase, the Staffel Kapitan of 3/JG.53 and Leutnant Berthol, the Adjutant of Stab I/JG.52.

Sporadic activity continued into November during which time fighter-bomber operations became a regular task for the Jagdgruppen. At this time the aircraft were modified versions of the Bf 109E adapted to carry a 250kg (550 pound) bomb on a center-line rack under the fuselage. These aircraft often formed the fourth Gruppe of a Jagdgeschwader, although in some cases a Staffel within each Gruppe might be allotted the fighter-bomber role. The advantage lay in the aircraft's speed and two methods of attack were employed. One was to approach above

20,000 feet then dive on the target and escape at low-level across the Channel, the other was to make a low-level dash across the Channel, climb sharply to altitude, bomb, then retreat at low-level. Interception of such intruders, who rarely operated above Schwarm strength, was difficult, but on the other hand they caused little damage.

When it came time to count the cost of the July to November air battles over England, the Luftwaffe Jagdgruppen found that 610 Bf 109s and 235 Bf 110s had been the price of a costly lesson which had also accounted for 888 other German aircraft. Against this the RAF had lost 915 machines and 415 pilots. In the fighter versus fighter combats the Bf 109s had shot down a total of 491 Spitfires and Hurricanes in the most intense period of fighting (24 August-6 September) which in fact gave the Germans a slight edge as far as total victories were concerned.

Right: Oberst Werner 'Vati' Mölders, the first German pilot to record 100 victories. He was killed in an accident on 22 November 1941.
Below: A DFS 230 Infantry Assault Glider.
Above: A Bf 109E-4 being taxied to its dispersal by Adolf Galland on 23 August 1940.

Both sides had lost many experienced pilots who would be difficult to replace, among these being 22 year-old Major Helmut Wick, one of only three pilots to have been awarded the Oak Leaves to the Knight's Cross, who was shot down on 28 November while leading JG.2. At the time of his death the young ace had 56 victories to his credit.

By mid-November the assault against England lay in the hands of the night bombers. This change in Lufwaffe tactics brought problems to the defenders as radar-equipped night fighters were still in their infancy, so for several months the Kampfgeschwadern were able to operate with comparative impunity. At the start of the night offensive the units involved were still basically those which had operated with Luftflotten 2, 3 and 4, and these were brought up to strength with reserves held in Germany.

The total bomber force available to Goering amounted to some 1300 aircraft of which only half could be used at any time due to the low serviceability rate. From the night of 7 September the Luftwaffe mounted raids of varying intensity on London until 14 November, a period of 67 nights during which an average of 200 bombers was over the city on each occasion. The size of the force and the capacity of each bomber was nothing like that mounted by the British and Americans over German targets later, nonetheless the duration of the German air raids was usually longer because their attacks were less concentrated, and it was a terrifying experience for those on the ground who lived through it.

No 80 Group of the RAF had, to a certain extent, negated the Luftwaffe's guiding beam *Knickebein*, resulting in large numbers of bombs falling on decoy targets or failing to hit their primary targets. But there were two other aids at the Luftwaffe's disposal, one called *X-Gerät* and the other *Y-Gerät*. The former

was operated by Heinkel He 111H-4s of KGr.100 and consisted of a beam which at three points was intercepted by other beams. The first beam crossed the guiding one some 30 miles from the target allowing the crew to set-up their aircraft for the approach; the second at a distance of 12 miles and the third at three miles. Calculations using the aircraft's ground speed enabled the automatic bomb release to be activated on receipt of the third signal. KGr.100 acted as a pathfinder force using *X-Gerät* to drop incendiaries, thus illuminating the target for the main force.

Y-Gerät was more sophisticated than *X-Gerät*, this time the release point being calculated by ground radar stations using an interrogation pulse against a response signal from the bomber. This equipment was used in He 111s of III/KG.26 but it too became ineffective once a suitable counter measure had been worked out.

Although London was the prime objective of the bombers in the early part of the night Blitz, other cities and coastal ports did not escape attention and on the night of 15 November 1940, 449 bombers guided by 13 pathfinder He 111s of KGr.100 dropped 400 tons of high explosive bombs on Coventry, devastating most of the city center and causing 1350 casualties.

During November 1940 the Luftwaffe flew more than 6000 sorties against British targets during which they lost only eight aircraft to night fighters, although of course anti-aircraft guns and the balloon barrage accounted for others. Operations were somewhat curtailed by the weather during December and January, but in February 1941 1200 sorties were flown. The 'Night Blitz', as it became known, continued until May, by which time improved radar in new night fighters began to take its toll.

Although the first German bomber shot down by a radar-equipped night fighter was a Do 17 of KG.3 which fell to the guns of a Blenheim on 23 July 1940, such successes had been few and far between and did not cause any great alarm to Luftwaffe bomber crews. The change in fortunes is graphically illustrated by the fact that in January 1941 only three bombers fell to the guns of night fighters, whereas by May of the same year the tally had risen to 96.

In September 1940 aircraft of I/NJG.2 started to operate at night against RAF Bomber Command airfields in East Anglia, using intruder tactics that were to become fairly standard practice for both sides by the end of the war. The Ju 88s would stalk returning bombers and attack them as they joined their home circuits when the flare path lights were switched on and crews began to relax their vigilance. At this time the success rate was not that high but such sorties continued until October 1941 when I/NJG.2 was moved to the Mediterranean. In the summer of 1943 Me 410s operating with the fifth Gruppe of KG.2 restarted intruder operations, but by this time the British Mosquito night fighter was fully operational and, although the German twin proved an adequate adversary, it was always in difficulties because the odds against it were so great.

Nonetheless, intruder operations were an important part of Luftwaffe operations, because they created an insecurity among bomber crews and could not be ignored. It was essential therefore to keep a certain number of defending fighters at hand to counter such operations and, while they were doing this, they could not interfere with the sporadic efforts of the Luftwaffe night bombers.

The forerunner of the Me 410 had been the Me 210 which it was hoped would be an ideal replacement for the Bf 110, but early promise proved ill-founded and although the aircraft started to equip two units in 1941 it never achieved the success hoped for. In September 1942 the Me 210 made its operational debut over the British Isles when, on the sixth of the month, two were shot down by Typhoons of No 1 Squadron.

After the hectic days of 1940 single-engined day fighters were rarely seen over England except when they chased short-of-fuel Spitfires or light bombers across the Channel, acted as escort to the nuisance raids by fighter-bombers, or were lost.

One of the most successful aircraft employed in the role of a nuisance raider was the Focke-Wulf 190 which, when first encountered over France in 1941 caused the RAF a lot of problems. A first-rate fighter able to absorb a lot of punishment, the Fw 190 was a natural for the low-level intruder role and it was not long before it was seen in varying quantities attacking coastal targets and eventually London.

Below: Generalfeldmarschall Albrecht Kesselring (center) with Luftwaffe crews in Belgium 1940. 'Smiling Albert,' as Kesselring was known, commanded Luftflotte 2 in the Battle of Britain.

Above: The long-nosed D version of the Fw 190. This is in fact a modified C airframe which in turn was built from the A-1 werke number 0055.
Right: General Kurt Student, commander of Luftwaffe airborne forces.

As early as March 1942 Hugo Sperrle had ordered JG.2 and JG.26 to form Jagdbomber or (Jabo) Staffeln within each Geschwader for the sole purpose of attacking British targets. The two Staffeln formed were initially equipped with BF 109F-4 models but these soon gave way to Fw 190A-4s, which proved far more effective. As well as harrying shipping the two fighter Geschwadern in France were always looking for stray RAF fighters, and on the evening of 23 June 1942, 7/JG.2 found such targets when they encountered Spitfires of the Exeter-based Polish wing returning from a strike against French airfields. During the ensuing combat the adjutant of III/JG.2 shot down a Spitfire then became disorientated and landed his Fw 190A-3 at RAF Pembrey. Thus Oberleutnant Arnim Faber handed to the RAF an intact aircraft for evaluation purposes, which enabled the Allies at least to appreciate the quality of fighter they were now facing.

Raids by fighters against RAF airfields brought back memories of 1940, but they were only shadows of the earlier efforts and in no way aimed at putting the RAF out of action for good, a task which was now well beyond the capabilities of the Luftwaffe.

This type of operation did however tie up large numbers of RAF aircraft, personnel and ground equipment, and the results achieved by what amounted to only a few Staffeln from two Geschwadern were out of all proportion to the minimum effort expended by the Germans.

The only way to counter the intermittent fighter sweeps and fighter/bomber strikes, was to mount standing patrols and quite often these were only able to intercept intruders on the way home across the Channel. A typical example of such a raid was the one mounted on 31 October 1942 when Fw 190s made an attack on Canterbury. Approaching at low level the raiders were across the coast before Spitfires based at Hawkinge could be scrambled, the cathedral city was attacked and damaged and civilian casualties were inflicted before the defending fighters, by this time with height advantage, despatched two of the now bombless fighter/bombers into the Kent countryside and two more into the Channel. Raids such as this were carried out by

Above: A somewhat primitive wooden frame being used to remove the Daimler engine from a Bf 110.

fighter pilots who had not received any formal training in such tactics but learned – in some cases very quickly – as they progressed.

Until June 1944 the French-based Luftwaffe fighter units, which mainly comprised components of JG.2 and JG.26, put up a gallant struggle against increasingly superior numbers and equipment and, although they had little opportunity to operate in their pure fighter role over England, they fought as hard as their opposite numbers in the RAF had during the days of 1940 when the positions were virtually reversed.

Meanwhile incensed by Bomber Command's attacks on German cities, especially the one against Lübeck on 28 March 1942, Hitler ordered a new series of night bombing attacks which have become known as the 'Baedecker' raids. These began on 23 April when Do 217s of KG.2 and Ju 88s of KG.106, led by a small force of pathfinder He 111s of I/KG.100, bombed Exeter. The following night the same target was attacked twice and on the 25th the ancient and historic city of Bath received the attention of 151 bombers in two raids. The pattern of these attacks gradually emerged as being of short duration against lightly defended targets, mainly carried out on moonlight nights. The Beaufighter and Mosquito night fighters took a steady toll of the raiders and, although Hull, Grimsby, Southampton, Bristol, Norwich, Birmingham, Ipswich and Canterbury, featured among the targets, damage was not nearly as great as it had been in the 1940 Night Blitz. Another feature of the 1942 raids was the use of very high altitude Ju 86 bombers but they were never available in sufficient quantity to cause any great problems to the defenders. The last raid of the campaign in 1942 was that already mentioned on Canterbury on the last day of October when Fw 190s by day and Do 217s at night inflicted 87 casualties.

On 17 January 1943 KG.2 and KG.6, now equipped with the latest versions of the Do 217 and Ju 88, mounted a raid of 118 aircraft against London, and on the 20th fighter-bombers visited the capital at dusk. This pattern of mixed attacks in various strengths continued throughout the year, but by now the fighter defense with its AI radar was honed to a fine edge and the skies over England were no place for German bomber crews to be.

On the other hand the fighter-bombers also operated at night when conditions were favorable, and their speed gave them a safety margin denied the bombers, so very few of them fell to the defending night fighters.

Although these raids were small in terms of numbers of aircraft involved and never lasted long they were intense inasmuch as some targets were visited twice a night, often the same bomber crews flying both missions. Therefore they managed to keep a very high proportion of manpower tied down on defense, as well as providing useful propaganda for the beleaguered German civilian population.

The losses suffered by the Luftwaffe bomber force in 1943 were severe when compared to its total strength and results achieved. However, in December Goering came under increasing pressure to mount further retaliatory raids against England in greater strength. The only way he could do this was to withdraw units from other fronts. This took time and the starting date for Operation *Steinbock*, as it was called, continued to be delayed. By the end of January 1944 the force was ready. Although the main equipment still basically consisted of improved versions of the twin-engined bombers that had carried the brunt of the Luftwaffe's efforts since 1940, there were new aircraft in the form of the Ju 188 and He 177, the latter a four-engined heavy bomber which was dogged by problems throughout its inauspicious career.

In the He 177 the Germans could have had a vital weapon, for if it had not been rushed into service and had not had very advanced features which were not given suitable development time, it could have been a superb long-range strategic bomber. Its four engines were coupled in pairs giving it the look of a

Above: A Do 17 of the Geschwader Stab of KG.3. The badge is the crest of the City of Elbing.
Right: Major Walter Nowotny scored all but three of his 255 victories on the Eastern Front.

large twin-engined machine, and this arrangement together with a fuel system that was prone to leaking and causing fires in the air, greatly contributed to its lack of popularity with crews and lack of success on operations.

On the night of 21 January a force of 227 bombers set out to raid London. The use of *Düppel*, the German equivalent to the British radar jamming aid called *Window*, confused the British radar, and Ju 88 and 188 aircraft guided the force with accurate marking. The raiders returned to their bases after bombing, where they were quickly refuelled and soon airborne, once again heading towards London. The two raids caused little damage, however, and ten percent of the raiding force was lost, a rate which could not possibly be sustained. Further attacks on London in January, March and April were mounted as were sorties against other cities. But by May more than 60 percent of the bomber force which had been available at the start of Operation *Steinbock* had been lost.

Although these could be replaced by new aircraft, trained crews were just not available, and to throw partly trained men into the cauldron over England had already proved disastrous during the mini Blitz of 1943 when heavy losses were incurred.

In June 1944 the Allies invaded Europe and gradually forward bomber and fighter bases were overrun and thus denied to the Luftwaffe. For the rest of the war manned German bomber sorties against England were practically non-existent but the unmanned V 1 missiles continued to harass the population until their launch sites were gradually captured by the advancing Allies.

The V 1 or Fieseler FZG-76 sometimes known as the Fi 103, had made its first powered flight in December 1942. It weighed a little over two tons of which 850kg of high explosive comprised the warhead, and after launching from a catapult cruised at about 400mph. Its small size made it hard to detect or intercept and for some time it caused the British serious problems. It was of course completely indiscriminating as far as targets were concerned, simply falling when the Argus pulse

Above: Kesselring congratulates Major Groth, France 1940.
Above left: Bf 110s high above the cloud over Germany.
Below left: Cockpit area and passenger entry of a DFS 230 assault glider.

jet ran out of fuel. The 'Flak' arm of the Luftwaffe was responsible for the weapon and Oberst Max Wachtel's Regiment 155 (W) was formed specifically for the purpose of using it. The first V 1s were launched on 12 June 1944, and from then until the last of the launch sites was captured some 10,500 were fired against England. Of these 7488 crossed the British coast, of which 3957 were accounted for by the defending guns and fighters. Of those that got through the defenses, 2419 fell on London, about 50 found Southampton and Portsmouth and one solitary weapon reached Manchester. The bombs caused the deaths of 6184 civilians and injured a further 17,981. Some of the V 1s were launched by He 111 and He 177 aircraft which stood off at sea, and the same aircraft also used guided bombs with some success, the latter mainly against shipping in the Mediterranean.

So it is quite in order to claim that German technology which gave the Luftwaffe the first operational jet fighter, as well as a rocket powered fighter, also produced what really was the forerunner of today's cruise missile. It also produced the A-4 rocket more commonly known as the V 2, against which there was no defense. But fortunately for the Allies most of these developments came far too late to save the cause of Hitler, and although they certainly gave the Luftwaffe a final impetus they were all too late to influence the outcome of the war.

One of the final aces played by Goering was on New Year's Day 1945 when some 900 fighters and fighter-bombers attacked Allied airfields in liberated areas of France, Belgium and Holland mainly in the Second Tactical Air Force area. The attack came at dawn and took the defenders by complete surprise. Although some Allied fighters were airborne on patrol, in the main the Germans suffered their greatest losses through anti-aircraft fire. Many of the pilots were inexperienced and the whole operation, although viewed by some German commentators as a success, was more of an embarrassment to the Allies because of the lack of vigilance revealed. Allied losses were about 150 aircraft whereas the Luftwaffe lost over 300, including 19 unit commanders, very experienced men they could not afford to lose at that time. This really signalled the end of offensive operations by the Luftwaffe in western Europe and for the remainder of the war little was seen of German air operations on the Western front.

Following the disastrous start to 1945, Hitler tried to recover the rapidly deteriorating situation in Russia by transferring six Jagdgeschwadern to the Eastern front. This created the impression among the Russians that the Allied landings in 1944 had done little to weaken the Luftwaffe's effectiveness. But all that was in fact happening was that Hitler was moving his diminishing forces to areas where, in most cases, his cause was already lost.

By May 1945 the once proud Kampfgeschwadern of the Luftwaffe had been all but wiped out. The gallant crews had set out in 1940 to prepare the way for a victorious army but had met a force that was better equipped when they came from the successes on the continent to the invasion of the British Isles.

During the Luftwaffe campaigns over Britain, 60,500 civilians were killed and 85,000 injured, the majority of these casualties – some 50,000 – occurring during the Blitz of 1940. As sad as these figures are they represent only a small proportion of those suffered by the German population during the strategic bomber offensive mounted by the RAF and USAAF in 1943 to 1945. In both cases neither bomber force achieved the breakdown in civilian morale which had been widely forecast in pre-war days as being one of the certainties of a large scale bomber offensive.

Ju 87R-2s of I/StG.3 over Trapani, Sicily, in May 1941.

MIDDLE EAST MAELSTROM

By December 1940 it was becoming increasingly obvious to the German High Command that Italian efforts to gain control of North Africa, the Mediterranean, Greece and Crete had gone seriously awry. The Allied presence in the Balkans created a serious threat to the German southern flank including the vital Rumanian oil fields.

As early as June 1940 Hitler had laid the foundations of his assault against Russia but these were now placed in jeopardy by the military failures of his Italian allies. The German successes in France had led Mussolini to believe that victory would soon be Hitler's and if he wanted to share the spoils of war he must act immediately. Consequently, on 10 June 1940 he declared war on the Allies and marched into Southern France.

Mussolini's plans to turn the Mediterranean into an area completely dominated by Italy were grandiose to say the least. His air force was numerically strong but lacked modern equipment or know-how, and his land forces were little better. Thus, there was no way he could hope to achieve the success envisaged in a long drawn out campaign, and there was not sufficient expertise to accomplish a quick victory. Initial success in southern France and the Balkans gave a false sense of achievement. However, by December 1940 mammoth losses in Libya, Greece and Egypt forced Hitler into increasing his material aid to Italy as it was vital that he protect his important southern flank which featured prominently in his Russian plans.

Since June 1940 the Luftwaffe had been helping the Italians with a liaison force under the command of General Ritter von Pohl, but this had been mainly confined to the transportation of troops. No Luftwaffe bomber or fighter squadrons appeared on the scene until December when the first elements of Generalmajor Hans Geisler's Fliegerkorps X arrived in Sicily. Geisler faced a task of massive proportions with a force totalling only some 350 aircraft, of which initially only III/ZG.76 equipped with Bf 110Cs was a fighter unit. But at this time fighters featured low in his priorities since the German plan to redress the balance was based on their previous successes with lightning strikes by dive-bombers supported by level-bombing.

Although its strategic importance was well known to the British, little effort had been made to strengthen the defense of Malta, and when Italy made its opening attack on the island on 11 June only four obsolete biplane Sea Gladiator fighters (one of which was unserviceable) were present to meet the threat.

Below: A Ju 87R of StG.1 serving in North Africa in 1941.

Above: The Luftwaffe's equivalent of the British Lysander, the Henschel Hs 126B-2. This one is from 2(H)/14.
Below: A Ju 87B of II/StG.2 code T6+EM. The empty bomb rack could signify that it is returning from a mission.

Above: Ammunition for the 37mm cannon of the Ju 87G-1.
Below: One of Germany's most celebrated aces, Hans-Joachim Marseille, with one of his victims, a Hurricane of No 213 Squadron.

Hurricanes arrived on the scene by the end of June, and supply convoys managed to run the gauntlet of the Regia Aeronautica despite the attention from Ju 87s which had been supplied by Germany and operated over the island for the first time on 2 September. The Italians were unable to make any significant impression on the island and their embarrassment was acute when Fliegerkorps X arrived on the scene.

The initial task facing Geisler was to close the Mediterranean supply route to the British and the key to this was Malta. Situated only 15 minutes' flying time from Sicily, the island was located in one of the narrowest parts of the Mediterranean in an ideal position to exert a very great degree of control over the war in North Africa. In British hands it was virtually an unsinkable aircraft carrier from which raids could be mounted against targets in North Africa as well as convoys carrying supplies to the Axis armies.

If the Germans could gain Malta the advantage to them would be tremendous, in that the already precarious sea route between Gibraltar and the Suez Canal would become impossible for British supply convoys. The advance guard of Geisler's force comprised mainly transport aircraft but, by early January 1941, Ju 88s of LG.1, He 111s of KG. 4 and 26, Bf 110s of ZG.76, and Ju 87R-1s of StG.1, 2 and 3, were established at Catania, Comiso, Palermo, Reggio Calabria and Trapania, ready for action.

Geisler set up his headquarters in the Hotel Domenico in Taormina and commenced carrying out the three major tasks his force had been assigned: first, to carry out an offensive against Malta; secondly to gain control of the straits between Tunis and Sicily; and finally to assist the Italians with air

Above: A large formation of Ju 52 transports en route to Tunis in February 1943.

support in North Africa and eventually gain air superiority to enable safe transport of supplies and men to the armies in North Africa. In addition to the main objectives, the small force available to Geisler was also expected to attack any reinforcements heading for and using the Suez canal.

Hitler did not want to become too involved at this time in the Middle East war, but he knew that the occupation of Crete by the British, which occurred as a result of the Italian advance on Greece, and the precarious position of the Italians in Albania seriously threatened his plans. Consequently, in addition to Fliegerkorps X which he hoped would retrieve the situation, he also sent two Panzer divisions to North Africa. The avoidance of a long and costly campaign was essential if his other plans were to come to fruition and the only way to ensure this was to deny the Mediterranean to the British. While Geisler formulated his plans to put Malta under siege, supplies and technicians were moved into Italy to prepare bases. The Germans were therefore committed to an air war on two fronts at a time when efforts should have been made to conserve strength for the planned assault on the Soviet Union.

The Ju 87s of StG.2 opened the Luftwaffe's campaign on 10 January when they attacked a Malta-bound convoy which had been sighted the day before and included the aircraft carrier HMS *Illustrious*. A diversionary attack by SM 79 torpedo-bombers of the Italian 32° Stormo brought the carrier's Fulmar fighters into the air, leaving the way clear for 26 Ju 87s, thirteen from each of I/StG.2 and II/StG.2, led by Major Enneccerus to carry out their attack.

Earlier in the day the carrier had escaped undamaged from an attack by He 111s of II/KG.26, but this time it was not so lucky. Starting their dives at 12,000 feet the Ju 87s successfully placed six 500kg bombs on the carrier's deck and three more close enough to cause damage. The 23,000 ton ship was now a hive of activity as her damage control parties attempted to repair the ravages of the Ju 87s. Oberfeldwebel Leesch and his

Below: The R version of the Ju 87 was basically a B with increased fuel tankage. This one is in North Africa.

Above: A Ju 88A-14 armed with a 20mm cannon, Tunis, 1943 during the last days of the North African campaign.
Below: A Ju 88A-10 of the Geschwader Stab of LG.1, North Africa, 1941.

gunner, from the 5th Staffel of II/StG.2, failed to return to their base and on this occasion were the only loss. Later the same day Ju 87s from I/StG.2 returned to harass the stricken carrier, losing one of their number to the Fulmars which had flown to Malta to refuel, then returned to escort the ship. Fourteen He 111s from II/KG.26 returned to bomb from medium level, and the following day another force of Ju 87s this time escorted by Bf 110s of ZG.76 returned. *Illustrious* was hit again but the dive bombers were unable to deliver the coup de grâce. The badly damaged carrier reached Valetta harbor to lick her wounds and carry out temporary repairs, but any thoughts her crew may have had about reaching the 'safety' of port were soon dispelled.

During the attacks on 11 January, a force of Ju 87s from II/StG.2 set out to intercept the cruisers HMS *Gloucester* and *Southampton* as they headed for Alexandria after carrying troops to Malta. Although operating at extreme range the Ju 87s were successfully guided to their targets by a pathfinder He 111, and carried out an extremely effective attack which left *Southampton* abandoned and *Gloucester* damaged. With *Illustrious* now anchored in harbor, the Luftwaffe's thoughts turned to the island itself, particular attention being paid to the carrier's berth, as well as other naval and military installations.

On 16 January the full might of Fliegerkorps X was turned against Valetta. This time the Ju 87s of I/StG.1 and I/StG.2, being supported by Ju 88s of LG.1, the bombers were escorted by Bf 110s of ZG.76 as well as Macchi MC 200s and CR 42s of the Italian air force. The luckless carrier was hit again but this time the defenders took a heavy toll, claiming the destruction of ten bombers.

On the 18th it was the turn of the airfields at Hal Far and Luqa, but *Illustrious* was a real prize for the Luftwaffe and the following day the bombers turned their attention on her again.

These attacks which heralded the arrival of the Luftwaffe in no uncertain manner, also brought home to Geisler that subduing the island, and convoys supplying it, was not going to be easy. During the three main attacks from 16-19 January over 40 aircraft were shot down and on one occasion the whole of the 2nd Staffel of StG.1, with the exception of the Staffelkapitän, failed to return to their base.

On 23 January *Illustrious* used the cover of darkness to slip her moorings and head at her best possible speed to the Suez

Canal, which she safely negotiated, then made for the US Navy repair yard at Norfolk, Virginia. Although the Royal Navy survived this struggle between the bomber and the aircraft carrier, they were in no doubt that convoys on the Malta run were going to need a lot of escorts, a lot of skilful seamanship, and a lot of luck to reach their objectives. The narrow neck of the Mediterranean between Sicily and Tunisia was firmly in control of the Luftwaffe and, on 31 January, the Ju 87s of StG.3 crossed it to join the similarly equipped 96° Gruppo which had been deployed to Africa on the 20th of the month.

Until 9 February fighter escort for the bombers was entirely in the hands of 36 Bf 110s of ZG.26 plus some Italian fighters, and the defenders were therefore able to take a heavy toll of the raiders, for the Bf 110 was no match for the Hurricane which was the island's most effective fighter aircraft at that time. This situation changed with the arrival in Sicily of 7/JG.26 under the command of Oberleutnant Müncheberg and I/JG.27 under Hauptmann Neuman, both equipped with the Bf 109E-7 which was much superior to the Hurricane and carrier borne Fulmar. Three days after these units' arrival they were in action and the first kill went to Müncheberg who downed a Hurricane on 12 February. In addition to escort duties the Bf 109s also carried out strafing attacks against land and sea targets, accounting for

Above: A DFS 230 which has come to grief in the desert.
Top: Clearly a posed picture (no propeller on the Henschel Hs 126) of a reconnaissance crew in North Africa.

Above: The famous North Africa badge of JG.27 on a Bf 109E-7.

a considerable number of Wellington, Sunderland, and reconnaissance Maryland aircraft. The object of the Ju 87s was to follow the usual pattern of close support and tactical attacks, and the Bf 110s would escort them as well as undertake a ground attack role.

Meanwhile the situation in North Africa had been deteriorating very rapidly for the Italians and by mid-January they were in full flight. On the 22nd of the month Tobruk fell and, by 6 February, both Derna and Benghazi were in British hands. The arrival of Ju 87s and Bf 110s of III/ZG.26, brought a much needed uplift to the ground forces and presented a more resolute enemy to the Allied air force whose Hurricanes and Gladiators had, in most cases, found the measure of their Italian opponents.

Throughout this period Malta was under almost constant attack. The main targets were still the airfields at Luqa, Hal Far and Takali as well as the naval dockyard at Valetta. The defenders were rarely able to put more than a handful of aircraft into the air, but these were ably supported by the anti-aircraft batteries which quickly earned the respect of the bomber crews.

Below: A Ju 87R-1 of StG.2 operating from Sicily.

The usual pattern adopted by the raiders was to mount a combined attack with Ju 87s assigned specific pin-point targets, Bf 110s or 109s making low strafing runs dropping anti-personnel bombs, and the versatile He 111s and Ju 88s saturating the area with larger bombs from medium height. The attacks against Malta can be interpreted as one of the few occasions when the twin-engined mainstays of the Luftwaffe Kampfgeschwadern were used in a truly strategic role.

The He 111 was arguably the best strategic bomber in Luftwaffe service, and is often compared with the British Wellington and later bombers used in the strategic bombing campaign against Germany. But such comparisons are unfair and invalid as the design concept of the He 111 was entirely different. It began its life as a high-speed transport for Deutsche Lufthansa and reached its peak in the 1939-40 campaigns in Poland and the Low Countries campaigns. By the opening of the Battle of Britain it was beginning to show its age, but the inability of the German aircraft industry to produce a successful replacement saw the 'H' version soldier on and on. With the failure of the He 177, the later marks of the He 111 were kept in quantity production since the few man hours required to build each aircraft made them a relatively cheap proposition; it was one of the few aircraft on either side to be reinstated after official production had ceased.

Very much a pilot's aircraft the He 111 offered excellent all-round vision from its totally glazed nose, but defensive armament until the introduction of a powered turret on the late versions, was all by hand held weapons. Both the He 111 and Ju 88 enjoyed perhaps their greatest period of immunity from enemy aircraft during the early days of the Middle East war, and it was not until the Desert Air Force was built up to full strength with modern fighters, that they encountered major problems in daylight operations. On 3 February 1941 Erwin Rommel arrived to orchestrate the failing campaign in North Africa and, despite the early set back of the fall of Benghazi three days after his arrival, started the brilliant planning that was to earn him both reputation and respect from friend and foe alike.

Meanwhile, Malta was still the center of attraction for

Fliegerkorps X which attacked it on the 1st of the month and again on the 9th. A substantial raid on 26 February brought a fleet of 70 Ju 87s, He 111s, Ju 88s and Bf 110s over the RAF airfields at Hal Far and Luqa, and while the defending Hurricanes and Fulmars engaged the fighter screen, the German bombers destroyed or damaged a total of 13 Wellington bombers and airfield installations. It says much for the fortitude of the defenders that none of Malta's military establishments was put out of action for long periods. Airfields became hostile places to be, but somehow craters were filled, fighters refuelled and rearmed and other essential services maintained. There was nowhere for the occupants of the island to seek even semi-permanent respite; the Luftwaffe was attacking a target no bigger than a large city and, although numerically superior and operating from secure bases, they were not able to bring about the total demoralization and collapse of military and civilian society as had been predicted would be the result of continuous bombing.

Supplies on the island fell to a critical level but on 23 March a convoy reached Valetta and the supplies it carried eased the situation. But even before unloading began, 30 Ju 87s escorted by Bf 109s arrived overhead and in the ensuing onslaught managed to hit two merchantmen although losing eight of their number to Hurricanes and four to the ever-effective anti-aircraft gunners.

By the end of March 1941 the RAF had been forced to remove all offensive aircraft from the island, thus preventing any further harassment of shipping and targets in North Africa from Maltese airfields; so at this stage of the campaign the Luftwaffe had achieved a major part of its objective in negating the offensive capability of the Allies' most important Mediterranean base. The raid on 23 March proved to be Fliegerkorps X's last major assault on the island fortress as its main elements were withdrawn for the forthcoming Balkans campaign, and responsibility was handed back to the Italians. One Staffel of reconnaissance Ju 88s remained but the bombers and fighters now moved to new areas. During the three month sojourn in Sicily 7/JG.26 claimed 42 victories, 20 of these going to

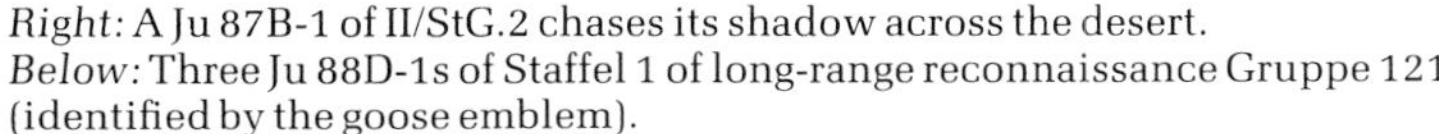

Right: A Ju 87B-1 of II/StG.2 chases its shadow across the desert.
Below: Three Ju 88D-1s of Staffel 1 of long-range reconnaissance Gruppe 121 (identified by the goose emblem).

Above: An Hs 126 observation plane in flight over Greece.

Oberleutnant Müncheberg. This element of JG.26 moved to North Africa to support the Afrika Korps, together with I/JG.27, but the Stab, II and III Gruppen of the latter, moved to Bulgarian airfields to join General Alois Löhr's Luftflotte 4.

Although shipping and land installations still came in for attention from the Italian air force, the lifting of the continuous aerial assault against Malta gave a respite which enabled the defenders to repair and re-establish military installations and the airfields. It was a respite that the Germans should never have allowed to happen, but the eyes of their High Command were on Russia and the general feeling was that once this thorn in Hitler's side had been removed, smaller entities like Malta could be dealt with.

Although the pressure was greatly relieved, the convoys and their Royal Navy escorts still had to run the gauntlet of torpedo-bomber, dive-bomber and fighter-bomber, but more and more supplies were getting through as the Regia Aeronautica proved a far less formidable opponent than the Luftwaffe which was now busily engaged elsewhere.

Below: A restored Fieseler Fi 156 Storch in typical desert camouflage.

On 26 March some 600 combat aircraft including units of KG.2, 3 and 26, StG.2, ZG.26, JG.26 and 27, were transferred from their bases in the Mediterranean, France and Germany to form the tactical support element of von Richthofen's Fliegerkorps VII whose task was to spearhead the attack on Greece and Yugoslavia, codenamed Operation Marita. Hitler had expected co-operation from the Yugoslavian government whom he expected to offer no opposition to his plans to occupy the country, but in March a *coup d'état* ousted the pro-German régime, so forcing his hand into a military campaign.

The 400 combat aircraft previously assembled in Rumania were reinforced by the 600 already mentioned; this flexibility in moving such large numbers of men and machines to bases some of which were over 1000 miles away, illustrates the mobility of the Luftwaffe and how very right its organization was. Although it had suffered a set-back against the RAF, it was still a match for any other air force in Europe as was soon to be proved once again.

Palm Sunday, 6 April 1941, was a black day for the Yugoslavian capital Belgrade, since the aerial assault opened with 150 bombers mounting an early morning attack. The defenses proved to be no match for the well trained Luftwaffe machine and by the end of the day the city was in ruins. A total of 17,000 people died in Belgrade before the Luftwaffe turned its attention to the usual targets of troop concentrations, communications and military installations.

The pattern of the campaign was similar to that successfully employed – except against Britain – in every assault so far mounted. The main assault was led by Ju 87s followed by Do 17s and He 111s, all escorted by BF 109Es and the new F models of JG.26, 27, 54 and 77, and I(J)LG.2. One of this last unit's pilots, Leutnant Giesshardt, opened his account with four Hawker Fury biplanes of the Royal Yugoslavian Air Force which he destroyed in one sortie on the opening day. In the northern sector JG.54 was engaged in a rather bizarre encounter when they were attacked by Hurricanes and Bf 109Es of the Yugoslav air force, but in their superior Bf 109Fs managed to overcome this unusual combination. The only serious loss to the Luftwaffe in this short and vicious campaign, occurred when aircraft of III/JG.27 were surprised by RAF Hurricanes of No 33 Squadron and lost five of their Bf 109s in the ensuing combat.

The simultaneous attacks on Greece started with KG.30's Ju 88s raiding Piraeus harbor where they hit the loaded ammunition ship *Clan Frazer*, the resulting explosion effectively wrecking Greece's largest port. This somewhat fortuitous incident robbed the Allied forces of the only harbor capable of handling the volume of supplies needed, and after this it was really only a question of time before evacuation took place.

Within twelve days Yugoslavia had surrendered and by 27 April 1941 German forces were entering Athens. By the following day the last of the British forces had left the Greek mainland and the country also surrendered. Once again the Luftwaffe machine had worked to perfection and had gained air superiority very quickly, although as late as 20 April RAF Hurricanes were still able to engage Ju 88s and Do 17s bombing Athens, but lost a lot of their number to the escorting Bf 109s of II/JG.27 and Bf 110s of II/ZG.26.

The end of the campaign in Yugoslavia and Greece secured Hitler's southern flank and most of the units involved were withdrawn to take part in the invasion of Russia which would no doubt have been mounted earlier if demands from the Italians had not occupied so many Luftwaffe units. In just under a year from the time Italy entered the war, the Allied armies and air forces had been forced to evacuate the whole European continent, and now only had a very tenuous hold on the island of Crete; a hold which was soon to be removed by one of the major paratroop operations of World War II.

Generaloberst Kurt Student conceived the idea of an airborne assault on Crete and convinced Goering that this would result in the capture of the island in a very short space of time and with the minimum expenditure of troops and resources. With Crete in their hands the Germans would acquire a stepping-stone to Cyprus and North Africa.

The invasion was to be carried out by a fleet of 493 Ju 52s from which the troops would jump, and these would be supported by at least 100 DFS 230 assault gliders. Air support would come from von Richthofen's Fliegerkorps VII which had a strength of 430 bombers, of which about a third were Ju 87s. Fighter cover would come from I and II/ZG.26 with Bf 110Cs and I, II and III Gruppen of JG.77 with Bf 109Es, the five Gruppen between them mustering some 180 fighters.

The landings were originally planned for 16 May, but delays in transporting troops and equipment to the embarkation airfields caused several postponements. In the meantime the air attacks comprising the first part of what had been codenamed Operation *Merkur*, commenced on 3 May when 24 Ju 88s of I and II/LG.1 raided airfields at Maleme, Retimo, and Heraklion. As the softening up process continued Bf 110s and Ju 87s joined the Ju 88s in the raids and by 19 May the airfields at Maleme and Heraklion were completely untenable for the few RAF and FAA fighters which had in fact taken quite a heavy toll of the raiders, although lacking sufficient numbers materially to affect the final outcome. By 20 May Luftwaffe fighters had reduced the defending force to just seven aircraft, four Hurricanes and three Gladiators, which were evacuated to Egypt only hours before the main assault began.

One of the most outstanding successes to come out of Crete was a series of spectacular victories for the Ju 87 over the Royal Navy. The British Mediterranean Fleet was set the task of preventing reinforcements reaching German land forces by sea and on 22 May they intercepted several small ships carrying guns and equipment to the island. But StG.2 had been based on the island of Scarpanto to foil such an operation and throughout the day Ju 87s from this unit supported by KG.2's Do 17s

Above: Ju 87B Stukas and their lethal bomb loads on a Greek airfield. Obviously there is no danger of Allied air attack with aircraft parked so close together.
Below: A pleasing study of a Ju 88 on a Sicilian airfield.

Above: Perfect side view of a Ju 87B in the mottled green and sand desert scheme.

and Ju 88s from LG.1, harassed the two battleships, five cruisers and 12 destroyers which comprised the Allied task force. During the action the cruisers HMS *Naiad* and *Carlisle* as well as the battleship *Warspite*, were damaged; but the major success came in the afternoon when the cruiser HMS *Gloucester* was caught and sent to the bottom by Ju 87s of StG.2. The *Gloucester* and her companion HMS *Fiji* had been detailed to pick up survivors from the destroyer *Greyhound* which had been sunk earlier. As the bombs rained down on *Gloucester*, setting her ablaze from end to end, the *Fiji* steamed away from the scene, but at 18.45 hours she was spotted by a lone Bf 109. Although this aircraft was at its limit of endurance, the pilot dived on the cruiser and planted his single 1000kg bomb close to the ship's side. The *Fiji* had withstood all that the Ju 87s could throw at her, but her fate was sealed by this single bomb which exploded below the waterline and took her side out. The jubilant Bf 109 pilot summoned assistance which arrived 30 minutes later and at 19.15 hours the cruiser finally slipped below the surface.

While StG.2 attacked shipping, Ju 87s of StG.3 supported the land forces on Crete which were struggling to make headway against firmly entrenched defenders, but it was at sea where more tangible signs of success were to be seen. Soon after dawn on 23 May, 24 Ju 87s of I/StG.2 led by Hauptmann Hitschold intercepted five destroyers, sinking HMS *Kelly* and *Kashmir* with direct hits. HMS *Kipling* had a charmed life when she returned to the scene, and escaped unscathed with nearly 300 survivors from her sister ships. The battered British fleet withdrew to Alexandria having suffered a truly bloodied nose from the Luftwaffe, but more was to follow. On 26 May the carrier HMS *Formidable*, which was part of a task force sent in a bid to neutralize the Ju 87s' base, was located by Major Ennecerus's II/StG.2 and damaged so severely that she had to follow in the wake of her sister carrier *Illustrious* to the USA.

When the British finally evacuated Crete the balance sheet showed that, although over 18,600 men had been evacuated, the cost had been three cruisers and six destroyers sunk, plus serious damage to two battleships, an aircraft carrier, six cruisers and seven destroyers, clearly a victory for the dive bombers on this occasion. But the German paratroopers, who were part of the Luftwaffe, also suffered heavily. Of the 13,000 involved in the land battles, over 4500 had been killed, injured or were posted missing; similarly their transport aircraft had also taken a pounding with 272 being accounted for by the defenders. The architect of the victory, Generaloberst Student claimed that Crete was 'the grave of the German paratroop regiments.' Ironically this elite force which had achieved spectacular results in Europe in 1940 was never used again in the airborne role but the successes of these airborne troops led to the formation of the British and American equivalents which were to come into their own in 1944.

While the activity in Greece, Malta and Crete had been occupying the generals and tacticians, just across the Mediterranean in North Africa other events had been following a somewhat more subdued, but nonetheless important, course. During December 1940 the British had set out with the intention of occupying all territories then in the hands of the Italians and, as has been explained, the subsequent successes brought the advance elements of Rommel's Afrika Korps to support the faltering Italians. The Germans were quick to take advantage of the stretched British supply lines and by 12 March had retaken El Agheila and mounted a major offensive causing British retreats, which by 15 April resulted in the encirclement of Tobruk.

In the opening days of the Afrika Korps' campaign aerial support had consisted of Henschel 126 reconnaissance/light bombers and some 18 Bf 110Cs of III/ZG.26 which acted as fighters and in ground attack roles. The 110s scored their first success over the RAF on 19 February when two Hurricanes of No 3 Squadron were shot down; seemingly a reversal of fortunes, for over England and France the heavy German twin had been no match for the Hurricane. But in this case the two British fighters were in the hands of new pilots who had just converted from Gladiators, and were up against Bf 110s flown by veterans. The German fighter as well as giving able support in the ground attack role, was often called upon to engage Hurricanes and Blenheims which were harassing the advancing forces. The limited forces available to Fliegerführer Afrika, as the German air commander was to be titled, also included

Below: Not the most successful fighter, the Me 410B-1 was used in limited quantities in North Africa.

some Ju 87s of StG.1 and 2 as well as Ju 88s of KG.26, and these were used in both tactical and strategic roles – harassing troops on the one hand and raiding bases from which they were obtaining supplies, on the other.

Throughout the whole of the campaign in the Middle East the Luftwaffe was never present in overwhelming numbers. It was used, therefore, with a certain amount of economy dictated not only by operational requirements but also the supply situation. There is therefore a lack of continuity with long periods of total inactivity or at best isolated incidents involving small numbers of aircraft. One of the targets that came in for somewhat more regular attention was Tobruk which had fallen into British hands in January 1941. The Afrika Korps made several determined efforts to regain the port but eventually by-passed it, although it was not ignored by the Luftwaffe. From April through to August 1941, Ju 87s, Ju 88s, He 111s and aircraft of the Regia Aeronautica mounted an almost continuous assault against the harbor and military installations. Their attention also focussed on shipping using the port and attacks were made far out to sea where the dive-bombers only had the defensive guns of their intended victims to contend with. The anti-aircraft defenses of Tobruk took a heavy toll of Luftwaffe bombers, especially the Ju 87, and claims of 289 destroyed were made between April and October.

In mid-April the Bf 110s were reinforced by the arrival of three Staffeln of I/JG.27 which was still commanded by Hauptmann Eduard Neuman, and flying tropicalized versions of the Bf 109E-4. Operating from their airfield at Ain El Gazala (which they later shared with 7/JG.26 and the Hs 126s of 2(H).14) Oberleutnant Redlich's 1 Staffel was in action on 9 April claiming four Hurricanes of which two fell to the Staffelkäpitan. But two days later when escorting Ju 87s to Tobruk JG.27 lost two Bf 109s to Hurricanes which also accounted for three Ju 87s. However, on 23 April two Blenheims and five Hurricanes fell to the 109s and among the victorious Luftwaffe pilots was Oberfähnrich Joachim Marseille, who was to become a legend in his own lifetime and the leading 'ace' in the Western desert.

Above: One of I/JG.27's Bf 109E-7s prepares for another desert sortie.

In one of the biggest air battles of the desert war up to that time, practically all of I/JG.27's 34 serviceable Bf 109s supported by ten Bf 110s of III/ZG.26, escorted 20 Ju 87s of II/StG.2 on 23 April to attack Tobruk. Four Hurricanes were shot down but two Bf 109s and four dive-bombers were lost and this total was added to later in the day when another Bf 109 was shot down. British losses in May totalled only 15, five of which were Blenheims all shot down in one action on the 21st of the month by 3/JG.27. These minimal losses were due in the main to a respite in air activity on the part of both air forces as they built up their strength to await developments and further offensives on the ground.

With a renewed British attempt in June to relieve the garrison at Tobruk the Luftwaffe was soon back in action against a much

Below: The Fi 156 Storch was used extensively for reconnaissance work for the Afrika Korps.

Above: The business end of a Ju 88. The extensive glazing afforded the crew excellent visibility.

stronger Desert Air Force which now had a strength of one Tomahawk and five Hurricane squadrons, and a useful contingent of bombers mostly Wellington, Maryland, Blenheim and Baltimore aircraft. Against this total of 150 aircraft the Luftwaffe had 41 Bf 109s and 25 Bf 110s of which an average of 35 were serviceable at any one time. Many of the Luftwaffe pilots however, were very experienced while most of the allies were young South Africans, New Zealanders, Australians and replacement RAF pilots. The action aimed at recovering Tobruk was codenamed *Battleaxe*, but it failed as British troops were decimated by the Afrika Korps' superior weapons, especially the 88mm anti-tank gun which took a devastating toll of Crusader and Valentine tanks. In the air the situation was just as bad for the Allies as the experienced German pilots accounted for 33 British fighters during the three day action. By 18 June *Battleaxe* had failed and the British had withdrawn to the borders of Egypt to reform.

Air activity in the following months continued at a less furious pace but whenever Allied aircraft appeared there always seemed to be some Bf 109s to oppose them. More often than not the nimble German fighter was in the hands of an ace pilot such as Müncheberg, Lippert or Marseille, who had achieved 23 victories by the end of September including five in one day on the 24th of the month. Rommel's aim in this period was to take Tobruk, thus leaving the way open for him to advance into Egypt. During the build up to this objective the Luftwaffe was not overlooked and, although General Hoffman von Waldau's Fliegerführer Afrika command, which had been formed in June, had only been increased by a small amount, the quality had improved. Worried by new fighters being introduced by the RAF, Luftwaffe pilots had pressed for later marks of the Bf 109 and in September were rewarded when the F versions started to filter through. The first to be re-equipped was I/JG.27 who were later joined in North Africa by II/JG.27 which had been in action in Greece and Russia before returning to Germany to convert to the Bf 109F-4.

The newly arrived Gruppe took their aircraft into action for the first time on 3 October 1941 losing one of their number but claiming three victories. To counter British night raids against supply ports, I/NJG.3 with Bf 110 night fighters had been moved from Europe to Derna, but their stay was short-lived as in October they were recalled to Germany. In early November six Ju 88C-6 night fighters of 2/NJG.2 took over the specialist role they had vacated.

On 18 November 1941 the British launched their offensive, Operation *Crusader*, and in so doing caught Rommel by surprise before his own offensive was ready. In the following weeks the 190 aircraft of Fliegerführer Afrika were to come in for a lot of hard work, a great deal of it falling on the shoulders of the Jagdgruppen. The first objective was to achieve air superiority over the battlegrounds and, although the opening days of the campaign brought bad weather which curtailed air operations, they only had to wait until 22 November to meet the revitalized RAF in a battle the outcome of which would

Below: A Ju 88A, with underwing racks bombed up for operations, moves into position for take off from a desert airstrip.

decide the whole strategy of the future fighter war in the desert campaign.

During this action the German pilots found that a well-handled Tomahawk was a much tougher proposition than a Hurricane. However, at the end of the day, JG.27 claimed 13 fighters and eight bombers for the loss of five Bf 109s, a rate very much in favor of the numerically inferior Luftwaffe, but one they could not afford to withstand on a regular basis. The following day nine more British fighters were claimed as well as one bomber, making the total haul in two days 22 fighters and nine bombers, figures which were later substantiated as ten fighters and four bombers. During the fighting on the 23rd, JG.27 lost one more Bf 109, a loss they felt very keenly as the pilot was Hauptmann Lippert, Kommandeur of II/JG.27. Lippert managed to bale out of his aircraft but succumbed to his injuries in an Egyptian hospital on 3 December 1941. The difficulties now facing the German pilots in trying to match a numerically superior force, were underlined in the two November battles. They had to take a close look at their tactics since they realized that the Luftwaffe could not survive long at the attrition rate suffered.

The new tactics centered on pilots using the superior speed of the Bf 109F to break up fighter escorts while diving through to engage the bombers. This meant avoiding air-to-air combat with fighters whenever possible but it was essential if a halt was to be called to the hammering the Afrika Korps was receiving from the air. Although the fighters continued to take a heavy toll of Allied aircraft, analysis of the desert war clearly shows that it was in late 1941 that the Luftwaffe fighter units started to concede superiority to the Allied air force.

In late 1941 Feldmarschall Kesselring, who had been moved from Russia to Sicily to take command of Luftflotte 2 which was in the process of reforming after heavy losses in the Russian campaign, once again turned the spotlight on Malta. Several minor attacks were mounted in the opening two months of 1942, but in March a major assault was launched and this lasted for two months. Once again airfields and ports were the objectives as it was essential to stop strike aircraft from hitting at Rommel's supply convoys as well as the fuel and weapons they needed to do this from reaching them via the sea routes. By this time the island's garrison had been greatly strengthened, even so the defending fighters found themselves in something of a quandary; if they ventured too far to sea they left the island protected only by anti-aircraft guns, but if they remained too tied to the island, then the convoys suffered. The danger the convoys found in running the gauntlet is illustrated by the fact that in March 1942 the Royal Navy was having to use a task force comprising one anti-aircraft ship, four cruisers and 18 destroyers to escort four merchantmen. In this particular example, one merchantman was sunk, and another went aground before reaching the comparative sanctuary of Valetta harbor. In mid-May 1942 Kesselring called off his offensive having lost about 500 aircraft of all types during the five month's action. Tentative thought was given to an airborne assault on the island along the lines of the Crete invasion but on this occasion Hitler had learned the lesson and digested it, and eventually the plan was abandoned despite the obvious importance of Malta as an Allied base.

In North Africa the Allied Crusader offensive had made gains but Rommel had fought back and now proposed new offensives. These and the resumption of the offensive in Russia emphasized the impossibility of trying to fight an air war on three fronts with limited resources, which was now becoming increasingly evident to the Luftwaffe staff officers. Rommel opened his new offensive on 26 May 1942 and by 11 June had retaken Bir Hacheim, followed ten days later by Tobruk. During the fighting JG.53 and JG.27 had supported the Ju 87s and Ju 88s some of which operated from Crete. It was during this time that the increasing strength of the Allied air force really began to tell.

Above: The Bf 110F-3 was also a reconnaissance version. This one is fitted with a dummy nose armament.

Below: A Bf 110 of ZG.2 camouflaged for operations in the desert.

The Allied Desert Air Force was receiving new equipment in some quantity, Luftwaffe bases were being subjected to constant raids by day and night, and personnel were becoming very tired. There is also strong evidence of disagreement between the air commanders and Rommel as well as a marked lack of enthusiasm among the Ju 87 crews to face an ever increasingly hostile sky. The lessons learned over the British Isles in 1940 were now being taught in Libya; and the results were the same. In a situation where air superiority could be guaranteed the Ju 87 was a superb support weapon, but when hostile fighters broke through the defending screen or met unescorted dive bombers, the diving eagle became the spent crow.

Despite the falling fortunes of the Luftwaffe in 1942, it must be recorded that there were many remarkable achievements. At the height of Rommel's counter offensive in January 1942, serviceability among Luftwaffe units was very poor and the ground forces received little support. For example, in January JG.27 could only put 24 aircraft into the air so the sortie rate deteriorated and remained at a low level for nearly three months. Despite this, those pilots who flew continued to achieve success, no more so than Marseille, who by now had been commissioned and in April was made Staffelkapitän of 3/JG.27.

This remarkable man, well supported by his wingman quite often Leutnant Karl Kugelbauer (later killed in action), continued to claim victim after victim. His score stood at 91 on 4 June 1942 when he was awarded the Knight's Cross and Oakleaves, and 12 days later he passed his century before taking a well-earned leave in Germany. On his return to the arena he was to achieve a remarkable feat which was supported by eye-witness accounts from both sides and substantiated by official British loss records. On 1 September Marseille took off for his first action at 07.30 hours; by 17.55 hours he had flown three sorties and personally shot down 17 Allied aircraft, an achievement unmatched in the annals of aerial combat.

Naturally enough two days later Marseille received his country's highest award – the Knight's Cross and Oakleaves, Swords and Diamonds – but by the end of the month he was dead. His end came on the last day of September when after a successful patrol he was returning to base and his Bf 109F-4 was seen to catch fire. Eventually the flames spread forcing the 23 year-old ace to bale out of the stricken aircraft; whether or not he struck the tail and knocked himself out is not known, but his parachute did not open and Germany lost one of her most successful fighter pilots. All but seven of his 158 victories were achieved in the Western Desert and they typified the skill and spirit of not only Marseille but all fighter pilots who fought against superior numbers but knew every trick of their chosen trade.

Rommel's attacks were halted in the summer of 1942 and by the time the British launched their counter-offensive at El Alamein on 23 October 1942, the RAF had a numerical superiority of about 3 to 1 and reigned supreme. As the *Afrika Korps* retreated they left behind a trail of wrecked and abandoned aircraft. By 15 November only about 100 German fighters of JG.27 and JG.77 remained in the area, and the lack of fuel, ammunition and spares curtailed the support they could give.

Operation *Torch*, the Allied landings in North Africa, commenced on 8 November 1942, and from then on the German High Command poured supplies into the theater, but it was all too late. Among the units moved to strengthen Luftflotte 2 (soon renamed Fliegerkorps Tunis) were several from Russia and France including II/JG.2, II/JG.26, II/JG.51, I/JG.53 and Stab and III/JG.77; of these II/JG.2 was equipped with Fw 190A-4s, the rest retaining various versions of the Bf 109. Apart from the radial-engined FW 190 another newcomer was the Me 210 which was operated by a Staffel of III/ZG.1. Hurricanes, Spitfires, and Beaufighters took a terrible toll of transports and bombers, despite losses inflicted upon them by the small but efficient German fighter force which had now also started to encounter American aircraft as B-17s, P-40s and P-38s joined with their RAF counterparts.

The B-17s started raiding Tunis on 16 November and were escorted by P-38 Lightnings, which in the main were flown by inexperienced pilots. Although the American twin-tailed fighter was faster and more heavily armed than the Bf 109, the

Below: German personnel inspect a downed British transport aircraft during the North African campaign.

Above: Bf 109G-5s, probably in Greece.
Right: This mechanic seems to be making tentative adjustments to the bomb rack of a Ju 87R, which is in one of the many desert camouflage schemes.

experienced German pilots soon worked out efficient tactics, and in the early encounters the Americans lost heavily, especially to II/JG.51. In December 1942 both sides suffered heavy losses in the air, the honors going marginally to the Luftwaffe who in one action on the 4th shot down all 11 Bisley bombers attacking forward Luftwaffe airfields.

The New Year started with the Germans fighting a rearguard action on the ground but oddly enough the Luftwaffe could still command a large amount of air superiority, a typical example being the practically unmolested roamings of Fw 190s and Bf 109s over the area containing the American airfield at The-

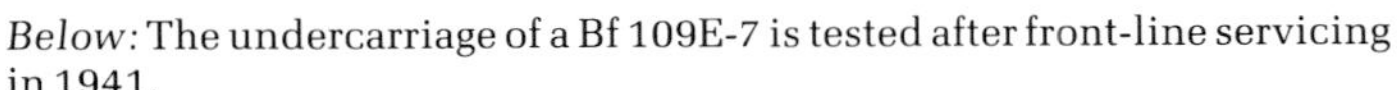

Below: The undercarriage of a Bf 109E-7 is tested after front-line servicing in 1941.

Above: A KG.26 Heinkel He 111H-5 heads for home during the North African campaign. Note the exposed position of the dorsal gunner.
Below: The 'Star of Africa' H-J Marseille and his famous Bf 109F-4 'Yellow 14.'

lepte. However, over the whole front, attrition was high and among those killed was Major Müncheberg of JG.77; to replace men of his experience was very difficult indeed. In February 1943 Fliegerkorps Tunis could muster about 370 aircraft to back Rommel's new offensive. A good start to the campaign built up hopes but in face of the growing Allied air superiority the Luftwaffe gradually crumbled and by mid-April operations became impossible as the Allied air forces pounded Luftwaffe bases and mounted standing patrols over them. As the situation in Tunisia deteriorated the Luftwaffe withdrew to Sicily from where I and II/JG.53 continued to give air cover for as long as they could. On 8 May the last Luftwaffe fighter unit, elements of JG.77, left Tunisia and by 12 May all units were safe in Sicily or had been completely wiped out. The following day the Germans surrendered and 250,000 men became prisoners of war.

Luftflotte 2 now assumed responsibility for Sardinia, Sicily and Italy and a new command, Luftwaffenkommando Süd Ost, looked after the interests of Crete, Greece and the Balkans. To counter the growing Allied air superiority, priority was given to the build-up of fighter units, and of the 400 aircraft received in the area after the evacuation of Tunisia, more than half were fighters. But although by mid-1943 the total strength of the Luftwaffe in the Mediterranean had risen to over 1200 aircraft, the exodus from North Africa had put an unacceptable strain on the mainland and Sicilian bases from which these aircraft operated.

The Germans were at a loss as to the likely site of the first Allied landings and when these occurred in Sicily on 10 June there was little aerial opposition. The bases on the island had been virtually bombed out of use and the Fw 190s withdrawn to Naples, from where they harried the Allied advance up the Italian peninsula. He 111s, Ju 88s and Do 217s carried out raids by day and night against Allied troops and installations, but the defending fighter force was by now so superior that many experienced bomber crews were lost without achieving any real success. There were occasions like that on 1 August when Ju 88s of KG.26 and Do 217s of KG.100 caught the defenders unawares and temporarily put the port of Palermo out of action, but such events became fewer and fewer.

Allied bombing had reduced Luftwaffe fighter serviceability to a frightening level and only a handful of Fw 190s and Bf 109s attempted to interfere with the landing by Montgomery's and Patton's forces. In August they conceded air superiority to the Allies by withdrawing four fighter Gruppen from the Mediterranean for the defense of the Reich. During the advance up Italy there were occasions when JG.3, 53 and 77 took advantage of Allied lapses to carry out ground attack duties, these usually being against bridgeheads and targets of opportunity, when the usual procedure was for one unit to act as top cover. Following the Allied landings at Anzio the overall situation continued to deteriorate very quickly. The Jagdgruppen within Luftflotte 2 used their Fw 190s and Bf 109s more and more as fighter-bombers but by the middle of 1944 the Spitfires, P-51s, P-47s and P-38s, controlled the skies over Italy and as far as the Luftwaffe was concerned the Mediterranean was a lost cause. Units were withdrawn to bolster those already engaged in the defense of the Reich, and by July 1944 the total strength in the theater was down to 300 aircraft.

When the Italians surrendered in early September 1943, the Luftwaffe demonstrated its prowess at providing the unexpected even in adverse circumstances. Anticipating that the Italian battlefleet would sail to Malta to surrender, Major Bernhard Jope's III/KG.100 had been standing by at Istres to blood a new weapon. The unit's Do 217s took off with 1400kg radio-controlled bombs under their starboard wings; the nine aircraft caught the fleet between Sardinia and Corsica and soon the battleship *Roma* was floundering after taking two hits; the *Italia* was also hit but made Malta albeit in a damaged condition. The first use of the Fritz-X stand-off bomb was a huge success and more was to follow when Jope's aircraft again used the weapon to attack and damage the battleship *Warspite* and two USN cruisers taking part in the Salerno landings.

In defeat in the Mediterranean theater the Luftwaffe was able to look back on some worthwhile and victorious actions; the small force which operated in the area achieved much more than it is often credited with, and the crews who continuously raided Malta and Mediterranean shipping came very close to achieving what would have been a victory brought about by strategic bombing. At the end of the day the men of the Luftwaffe gave of their best in the Mediterranean and no commander can ask for more than that.

Right: This propaganda photograph shows Bf 110 crews enjoying the sun in North Africa.
Below: The camouflage of this Do 217 highlights rather than conceals it against the blue of the Mediterranean.

THE EASTERN FRONT

From the early 1920s Hitler had considered Russia to be Germany's prime enemy. However, he could do little to secure the land he needed to create *Lebensraum* (living space), for his new Germany, until such time as his forces were strong enough to overcome the numerically superior but poorly equipped Soviet army and air force.

To offer some form of security to his eastern boundaries, Hitler entered into a Russo-German pact in 1939, an agreement he had no intention of honoring, but one which would give him time to plan what he expected to be a successful onslaught on an unsuspecting ally. Despite mounting misgivings among the German General Staff, Hitler started to make his invasion plans as early as October 1940, the basis of these being the establishment in occupied Poland of airfields and other bases.

The General Staff feared a war on two fronts as they realized that this was beyond their capabilities, but such was Hitler's obsession to crush Communism that he would not listen to reason. Hermann Goering tried desperately to sway the Führer from his plan but, by the autumn of 1940 when the Luftwaffe chiefs were advised of the proposed operation against Russia, he appeared to have abandoned his attempts and predictably sided with Hitler. A clear indication of Goering's change of attitude came when Generaloberst Alfred Keller – the commander of Luftflotte 1 whose task was the assault of Leningrad – remarked that Germany had a treaty with Russia, only to be told to leave politics to the Führer.

With hindsight it is easy to see that a move against Russia while Britain remained undefeated in the west, although bringing fresh glories to Germany in the short term, was ultimately to lead to defeat. Hampered by bad weather the Luftwaffe moved men, materials and aircraft to airfields from which they could mount Operation *Barbarossa*, the codename for the invasion of Russia. The security measures undertaken were such that very few people apart from those directly concerned were aware of the build-up of forces which began in earnest in early June, already a delay of three weeks caused by a very late thaw. Nearly two-thirds of the Luftwaffe's total front-line strength was moved into position ready for the assault; units came from the Mediterranean, France and Germany leaving these areas very weak but admittedly unlikely to come under serious attack from Britain.

Prior to the Russian assault Luftwaffe and army chiefs had argued about the tactics to be used to begin the campaign. The army wanted to mount a dawn attack against Russian troop concentrations, but needed assurance of complete air cover to protect them from the Soviet air force. The Luftwaffe experts pointed out that the best policy was to destroy Russian aircraft on the ground, but if they delayed their attacks until dawn it would be a full hour before they could reach forward enemy bases, by which time the news of the invasion would have caused the enemy aircraft to be dispersed. There seemed to be little chance of compromise, since the army pointed out that, if the Luftwaffe crossed the front in darkness to be in position to attack Russian bases when the ground forces opened their assault, their passing over the border might well alert the defenders. In the end if was decided that hand-picked crews – experienced men with many hours of blind-flying behind them – would take off early, climb to high altitude before crossing the Russian frontier, and open the attack at precisely 03.15.

In 1941 when the German offensive was planned, the Luftwaffe had an available strength of 2005 aircraft of which 1085 were bombers. Many of the crews were very experienced with combat skills obtained in the West and the Middle East. Ranged against them was the world's largest air force, over 8000 combat machines in 23 air divisions. But in this case numerical strength is misleading, and it must be remembered that the Great Purge had robbed the Soviet Air Force of many of its leaders, replacing them with inexperienced officers or, worse still, men appointed for political reasons. The rapid expansion of the Russian air divisions had brought a hurried training program resulting in many aircrew being far from fully trained when they took their places in front line squadrons. Nonetheless, the 4000 aircraft which were ranged along the expected front of the German attack, although mainly obsolete biplane and obsolescent monoplane designs, did have a sprinkling of more modern designs such as the Yak-1, MiG 3 and LaGG 3 among them.

Although warned by various agencies that a German attack was imminent, the Russians took no steps to disperse their forces, consequently the Luftwaffe's initial strike at dawn on 22 June 1941 resulted in row upon row of Russian aircraft, ranged as though for inspection on 31 forward airfields, being destroyed. The opening phase was undertaken by He 111s of KG.53 and Ju 88s of KG.3, both units from Fliegerkorps II of Kesselring's Luftflotte 2. They were supported by large formations of Ju 87s, Do 17s and Bf 109s and 110s in support of the army. The targets had previously been well reconnoitered by reconnaissance flights made when Germany and Russia were still ostensibly at peace by Oberst Rowehl's Aufklärungsgruppen, and personnel on the airfields had a rude awakening to their Sunday morning when the advance guard of the Luftwaffe descended upon them.

Luftwaffe crews returning from the opening round, hardly had time to relive their triumphs before they were back in the

Previous pages: A Ju 88A-5 of II/KG.1 beside a wrecked Russian fighter.
Below: The unusual configuration of the Fw 189 was purely for good all-round vision for reconnaissance sorties.

Above: The asymmetric Blohm und Voss Bv 141 reconnaissance aircraft.

air returning to the fray. The second wave of sorties did encounter some opposition in the form of Soviet fighters, which numerically seemed to be as plentiful as ever, despite the huge numbers destroyed on the ground. The I-153, I-15 and I-16 fighters were all inferior in performance to the Bf 109 which equipped all the Luftwaffe single-engined fighter Gruppen, but at low level they were much more maneuverable and presented problems to the German pilots.

Leutnant Schiess of JG.53, for example, found himself well placed to open his account in Russia, but just as he was about to open fire, the I-16 in his gunsight was pulled into a full 180° degree turn and was heading for his Bf 109 with all guns blazing. The quality of some of the Russian pilots may have been lacking in some respects, but their courage was never in doubt as one unfortunate crew of a ZG.26 Bf 110 found out when their aircraft was rammed by Senior Lieutenant Kokorev of the 124th Fighter Regiment when the guns of his I-16 jammed.

The Luftwaffe bomber crews encountered a problem of their own which did not help their confidence. It was noticed that several Ju 88s and Do 17s had exploded in the air for no apparent reason, the absence of Russian fighters or anti-aircraft fire only serving to deepen the mystery. It was eventually traced to the SD 2 and SD 10 fragmentation bombs that the aircraft had been carrying. These were new weapons being used for the first time and comprised a three-inch diameter cylinder weighing 1.75kg housed in containers whose capacity depended on the type of aircraft involved. Machines such as the Ju 88 and He 111 could carry 360 SD 2s while Ju 87s and Bf 109s managed 96. The bombs were dropped in rapid succession and, after release from the aircraft, opened to form a pair of wings which rotated them to the ground where they exploded on impact. Dispersion over a wide area was practically guaranteed by this method of delivery, and the shrapnel generated by the explosion was very effective against parked aircraft, soft-skinned vehicles and troops. But there was a disadvantage with the SD 2 and the larger SD 10 (9.00kg); they

Below left: A Bf 109F of 3/JG.54 with its nose protected from the elements, Eastern Front, 1942.
Below: In muddy conditions wheel spats on aircraft like the Hs 126 and Ju 87 were removed to prevent clogging.

For at least the first two years of the campaign the Germans enjoyed total air superiority as far as equipment was concerned. At the start of *Barbarossa* all Jagdgruppen using single-engined fighters had the ubiquitous Bf 109, the majority of which were 'F' versions. Aerodynamically the 'F' was cleaner than the 'E' but the early models were fitted with only two 7.9mm MG 17 machine guns and a rather odd caliber (15mm) MG 151 cannon. Although the fire rate of the cannon was relatively high it did not produce the firepower needed, consequently pilots used to the heavier armament of the 'E' often felt dissatisfied with the new aircraft and at one time there was danger of this affecting morale. The arrival of the F-4 version in August 1941 redressed the balance since the aircraft used a 20mm MG 151 which, although firing at a slower rate, packed a greater punch. Later of course the Fw 190 and Bf 109G arrived and these were generally superior to anything the Russians had, including fighters supplied to them on Lend/Lease arrangements by the Western Allies.

Most of the German pilots engaged had experience in combat gained in the West and the majority of their leaders were veterans from the Spanish Civil War; similarly they were using tactics that had been developed and perfected against more formidable opposition than the Russians were able to offer at that stage. Another important factor was that once a pilot joined his unit he stayed with it for the whole of his service life; breaks came with official leave, or the whole unit being withdrawn for rest or to re-equip. There was no set number of

Left: Hans Rudel signing Stuka pictures in Russia. It is interesting that the picture is in fact one currently in the Bundesarchiv.
Right: The ever faithful Ju 52, affectionately known by its crews as 'Iron Annie.' This model 3mg6e is with a parachute unit.
Below: A winter camouflaged Ju 88A-4 of AufklGr.122 in 1943.

were liable to 'hold-up' in the aircraft and, with live fuses, likely to explode tearing holes in the structure, and it was this that had caused the mysterious explosions seen on 22 June. As a result of this shortcoming, Kesselring banned horizontal bombers from operating with the fragmentation device and limited them to the Ju 87s and fighter bombers such as the Hs 123 where they were carried on wing racks and could be more easily cleared if they failed to release. In fact, the SD 2 bomb had a very short operational career in Russia as far as the horizontal bomber was concerned because just prior to Kesselring's directive the Russian defenses became more effective forcing the bombers to operate at greater heights, which made the bombs difficult to use from their jettisonable containers, so the deadly weapon became the sole prerogative of the low level ground attack machines.

The element of total surprise, outstanding planning, and the will to push home their advantage gave the Luftwaffe an opening to the Russian campaign they could hardly have believed possible. By the end of the first day they had recorded the biggest single daily destruction of an opposing air force. A total of 1811 Russian aircraft lay in ruins and, of these, 1489 had been destroyed on the ground on their own airfields; on the debit side the Germans lost 35 aircraft. Among the Luftwaffe casualties was the Kommodore of JG.27 Major Wolfgang Schellman, who in destroying an I-16 could not avoid flying through the wreckage of his victim which so damaged his aircraft that he was forced to bale out. At this time Schellman had 25 victories to his credit and, although his descent was uneventful, it was subsequently discovered that he had been shot by his captors – a fate that was to befall many Luftwaffe aircrew who fell into Russian hands. On a different note, Oberstleutnant Werner Mölders, the popular commander of KG.51, was given an immediate award of the Swords to his Knight's Cross with Oakleaves for shooting down four Russian aircraft; a multiple claim that was not unusual on the first day of the Russian campaign. It is worthwhile digressing for a moment to look at the claims made by Luftwaffe fighter pilots and the general reason why these were so substantial.

Above: Fully armed Ju 88s stand ready while the crews receive their final instructions before a mission.
Above right: A restored Ju 52 in World War II colors.

combat hours, rests at training schools or periods behind an administration desk. It is easy to appreciate therefore, that any pilot who happened to be a skilful flyer, an average marksman, and whose unit was in the right place at the right time, stood a very good chance, if he survived, of obtaining a score higher than those associated with western aces.

In Russia fighter airfields were very much closer to the forward areas; thus time over the target was increased as was combat duration, but conversely turn around time was decreased, so it was not unusual for a pilot to carry out up to eight sorties a day and be engaged in combat during every one of them. A classic èxample of this is Leutnant Scheel of JG.54, who joined the unit in May 1943, and flew 70 sorties during which he shot down 71 aircraft, before his own death in combat on 16 July 1943.

The proximity of the fighter bases to the front also enabled quick confirmation to be obtained both from ground and air sources, thus greatly helping to reduce overclaiming and double claims which tend to be a gray area on other fronts. The Soviets, apart from the elite guards units, were nowhere nearly as well trained as the Luftwaffe pilots and certainly did not have the tactical awareness. Another important point to remember, was that the Soviet Air Force was fighting very much in a tactical role, so the onus of interception, bringing with it height, speed and sun position advantage, became more or less the exclusive right of the Jagdgruppen. It is advisable to keep this overall picture in mind when analyzing the Russian campaign, especially in relation to German fighter pilots' tallies of victories.

During the first week of *Barbarossa* 4017 Russian aircraft were destroyed for a cost of 179 Luftwaffe machines and many fighter pilots were getting the impression that they were at a

Below: A postwar Swiss version of the Ju 52 refurbished to World War II status.

Turkey Shoot, and the race was on to see who would be the first to reach what was then the magic total of 100 victories. On 30 June, as the German army's armored columns closed a pincer movement around the Russian stronghold of Minsk, the Soviet Air Force mounted a massive air raid in an attempt to prevent the impending disaster. The Jagdgruppen of Kesselring's Luftflotte 2 had a field day, especially the pilots of JG.51, and the unescorted Russian SB-2s and DB-3s were decimated. At the end of the day JG.51 had become the first unit to achieve 1000 victories since the opening days of the war in September 1939, and of the 114 Russian bombers shot down, the redoubtable Mölders claimed five bringing his personal total to 82. Hauptmann Joppien and Leutnant Heinz Bär, two names which were to become household words in Germany, also recorded five kills each in the action and kept themselves well in the hunt to be first to 100. Joppien never reached the target as two months later he was killed with his score at 78, of which 28 had been achieved in Russia. Somewhat predictably the first man to reach his century was Mölders and he did this on 15 July with his 33rd Russian victory which took his overall total to 101, plus 14 in the Spanish Civil War.

In support of the Army Group North, Major Trautloft's JG.54, which was part of Keller's Luftflotte 1, saw little of the early

Below: The giant Me 323 was a six-engined development of the Me 321 glider. It was used only as a transport aircraft.

Above: The Hs 129B-2/R2 was a tough ground attack aircraft. This one is from IV(Pz)/SG.9 at Czernovitz in May 1944.

action but by the end of June was well into the fray as the Russians attempted to cut off the 4th Panzer Group's line of advance by bombing the Düna bridges. The Grünherz Geschwader, as it was known, continued to support the advance of the Army Group right to the gates of Leningrad, becoming the third unit to reach 1000 victories on 1 August, having just been beaten to second place by JG.53. Later the same month Major Günther Lutzlow's JG.3, operating with Luftflotte 4, also reached the 1000 kill mark, thus spreading the successes equally over the Luftflotten.

The momentum of the opening days continued but the incredible losses suffered by the Russians, who in addition to facing the Germans were also confronted by units of the Finnish, Rumanian, Hungarian, Slovakian and Italian air forces, did not appear to have any great effect on morale or supply and it soon became very evident that the German armies supported by the Luftwaffe, would have to fight every inch of the way to a victory they had believed was theirs for the asking.

Production of replacement aircraft was not adversely affected by the Germans, who lacked a strategic bombing plan, and even if they had had one, could not have carried it out as they had no bomber capable of reaching the production factories situated in the Urals. Consequently, by the end of 1941 replacement aircraft were reaching the front at a rate of four times that of June 1941 when the invasion began. Among these replacements were LaGG 3 and Yak-1 fighters, both of which were now coming off the lines in sufficient numbers to cause the Luftwaffe serious problems. Alongside them was flowing the formidable Il-2 ground attack aircraft which was so hard to shoot down and destined to take a devastating toll of German tanks. The fact that the Russian factories were able to boost their output to three times the pre-war rate in under 12 months, serves to underline how the lack of a strategic bomber probably cost the Germans the war in Russia.

Such production rates were not of course confined only to aircraft, and it is worth considering that later in the Russian campaign one day's output of T.34 tanks was equal to the number destroyed in combat in one week. A vital factor was also that the military training of crews for the tanks and aircraft could proceed unhindered well out of reach of the attention of German bombers. So gradually a formidable force was built up in the sanctuary of peace-like conditions, in much the same way as Allied aircrew were trained in southern Africa, Canada and America. This situation was not totally understood by the rank and file member of the front-line German combat units, who daily seemed to find more and more Russian aircraft and felt he was engaged in what appeared to be a hopeless quest.

In September 1941 RAF Hurricanes of Nos 81 and 134 Squadrons arrived at Murmansk on the first Arctic convoy. The 39 aircraft were formed into 151 Wing and as Murmansk was well within reach of Luftwaffe bombers, their initial task was to provide air cover, but it was clearly on the understanding with the British that the fighters would eventually be handed over to the Russians. These few fighters formed the vanguard of a massive aid program from western nations, and were in action for the first time on 11 September when they engaged Bf 109s of JG.77. One of the Hurricanes was lost in this encounter but the German pilots now realized that in some areas combat would be on a more equal footing as far as aircraft were concerned.

Between June and September 1941, the German advance continued at pace. The Luftwaffe played an important role in two respects, first the bombers acting in close support roles were able to concentrate on troop movements, communication systems, and pockets of resistance which had been by-passed in the advance to be dealt with later by the German infantry, and secondly in the vital reconnaissance role. The latter was particularly efficient and German ground commanders were quickly able to digest the information provided and plan their tactics accordingly. One thing that the bomber crews did find, was the fortitude of the ordinary Russian soldier. Instead of running for cover when the Ju 87 or similar ground attack aircraft appeared, they would stand their ground and fire back with any available weapon. Consequently losses of both reconnaissance and bomber aircraft were high, reaching serious proportions by September by which time 1603 aircraft had been totally destroyed and 1028 damaged, the grand total being practically equivalent to the Luftwaffe strength committed at the opening of *Barbarossa*.

The failure of the German aircraft industry to achieve a production rate that would offset such losses underlined Udet's incompetence and in November 1941, no longer able to face the mounting problem, he committed suicide. He was replaced by Milch who immediately overhauled the system, but increased production was still some way off and in the long run proved too late to help in Russia.

Throughout the summer and autumn the German machine marched relentlessly on, although their advance stretched supply lines to dangerous proportions. The bomber force was particularly effective since it was again able to operate in a situation of almost total air superiority. While the Ju 87s acted in close support roles the level bombers were often used to help move pockets of strong resistance, a typical case being on 28 June when General Heinz Guderian's Panzer Group 2 was held up by the fortress of Brest-Litovsk. Despite repeated attacks by Ju 87s the walls remained intact; so seven Ju 88A-4s of KG.3 were briefed to attack using 1500kg bombs. Heavy fire from the defenders seriously upset the bombing run but two Ju 88s managed direct hits and these having breached the walls, the defenders surrendered the following morning.

By the end of September von Richthofen's Fliegerkorps VIII had again proved the worth of the ground attack aircraft, Leningrad was under siege and the army was within 290 miles of Moscow; 665,000 Russian soldiers – about one third of those available at the outbreak of *Barbarossa* – had been killed or captured, most of these in the battles of Uman and Kiev, both now in German hands. It looked very much as though Hitler's prophesy of a short war and easy victory was coming true. But there were factors which had not been taken into account, and these were now beginning to have a telling effect. It has already been noted that losses of aircraft in the Kampfgeschwadern and

Above: Armorers prepare a Ju 87D-5 for another sortie in the snow.
Below: An early version of the Do 17, a P1 still serving in Russia in 1943.

Below: A cutaway of the antitank Ju 87G.

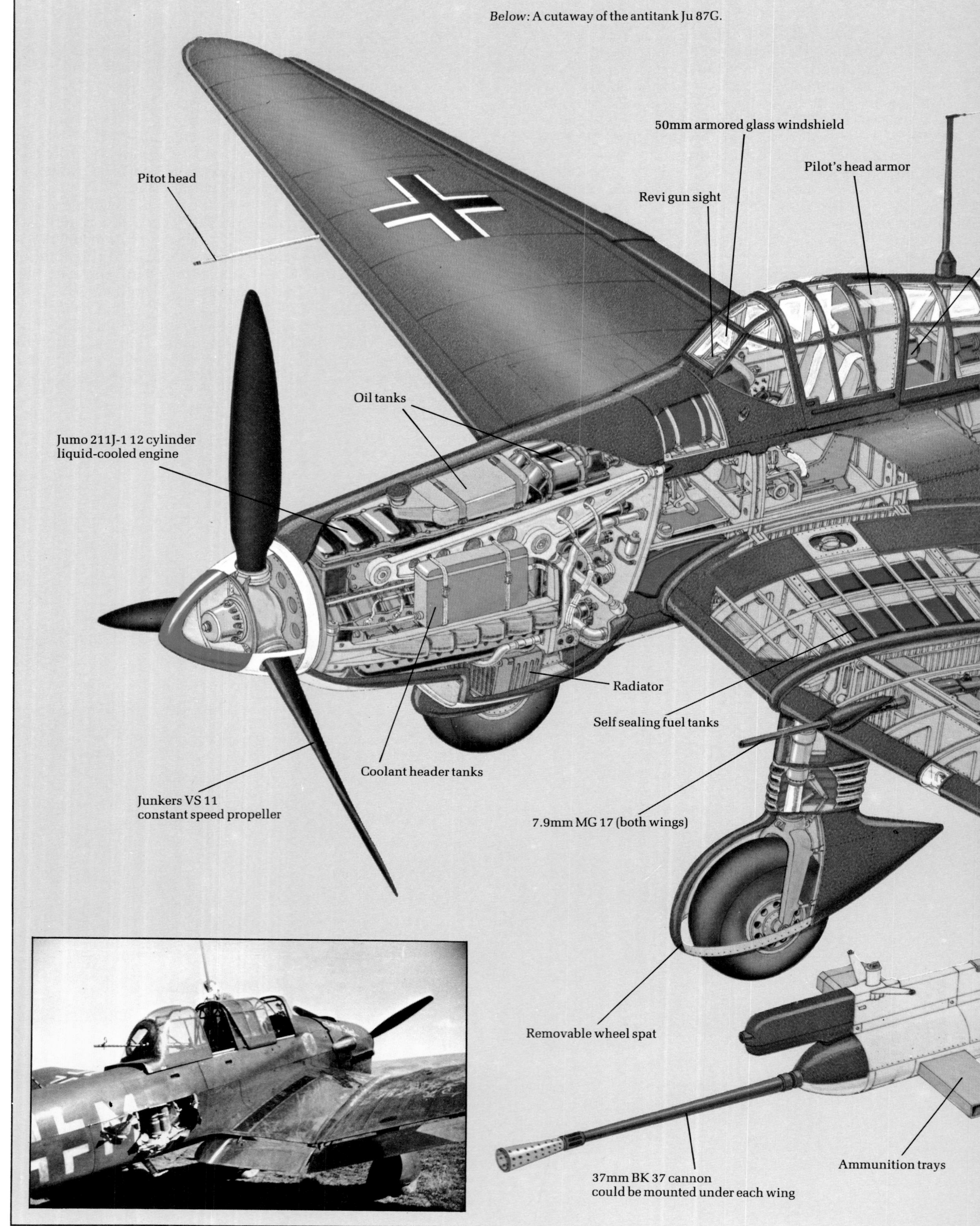

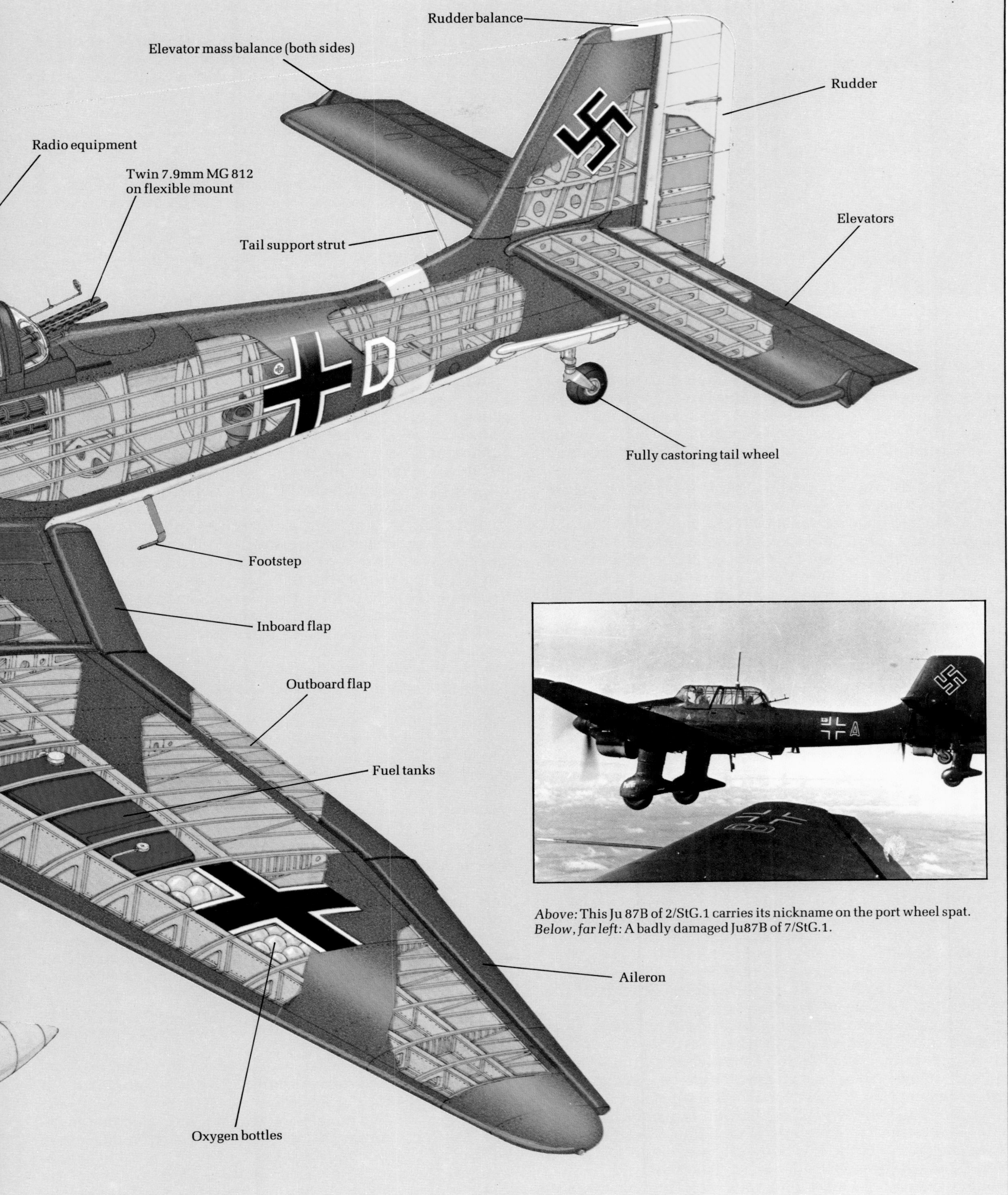

Above: This Ju 87B of 2/StG.1 carries its nickname on the port wheel spat.
Below, far left: A badly damaged Ju87B of 7/StG.1.

Above: The biplane Hs 123 carried out useful work on the Eastern Front in a ground attack role.

Stukageschwadern were becoming serious, but in addition few replacements were reaching front-line units. The onset of what was to be an unusually severe winter brought problems which neither the Luftwaffe nor the German army could overcome with the equipment then available, and morale was beginning to falter.

On 1 October, the drive against Moscow began. Since July it had been a major target for the bombers, but indifferent leadership and poor planning had resulted in little damage to the Russian capital. In early July Hitler had resolved that Goering's bombers would raze Leningrad and Moscow to the ground, but by the 15th of the month nothing had happened and the Führer was forced into goading Goering into sending his bombers into the attack. The importance of Moscow, both as a political seat and the center of military planning, should have put it at the top of the Luftwaffe's strategic targets from the first day of the campaign. The fact that it was not, simply underlines once again that the Luftwaffe was not geared to operate in a strategic role. Absence of a central policy-making command was never more apparent than in the Russian campaign, where time and again individual army commanders were able to insist on tactical help from widely dispersed bombers which themselves were part of separately commanded air fleets, instead of a centrally controlled and directed command.

On 22 July a total of 127 bombers comprising Ju 88s from KG.3 and 54, He 111s from KG.53 and 55, supported by KG.28's two pathfinder Gruppen, KGr.100 and III/KG 26, dropped over 100 tons of bombs on Moscow, but these and the 50,000 incendiaries failed to cause very much concern or damage. The Kremlin, which had been the target of II/KG.55, was hit several times but suffered little damage. The following night 115 bombers returned, and the night after 100 skirted the vast quantity of searchlights and effective anti-aircraft fire – which many a veteran bomber crew claimed was as good as London's at the height of the Blitz – but again achieved little. From then on the intensity of the raids decreased rapidly until only three or four bombers per night were being sent to the target. Of the 76 raids carried out against Moscow in 1941, 59 of them involved less than ten aircraft. The result of this puny attempt not surprisingly caused many questions to be asked about the effectiveness of the bomber force in the strategic role.

Oddly enough, in September 1941, the Luftwaffe carried out a week's strategic bombing against the Soviet Fleet, the aircraft used being Ju 87s of StG.2 which were more suited to a tactical task. None the less Oberstleutnant Dinort's I and III/StG.2, which were part of Luftflotte II, took off from Tyrkovo on the morning of 23 September to open the campaign against the Russian Baltic Fleet which was threatening the flow of raw materials from Sweden as well as supplies to the Baltic ports and Finland. Flying very high to avoid the ground defenses, the Ju 87s arrived over the target area at 15,000 feet and were faced with a dive to 4000 feet which on this occasion was their designated bombing height. The accuracy achieved by these highly skilled crews soon accounted for many small vessels as well as the 23,600 ton battleship *Marat*, the decisive blow against the latter being achieved by Oberleutnant Hans-Ulrich Rudel, who was later to become the most decorated Ju 87 pilot for his work against Russian armor. The bombers returned the same afternoon thus establishing a pattern they were to follow until 28 September. During this time they suffered heavy losses, among them being Hauptmann Steen, the popular III Gruppe commander, but they caused substantial damage to the fleet and anchorage at Kronstadt. The Ju 87s were all that the Luftwaffe had in sufficient quantities to perform this task. They achieved what they set out to do, but hardly had time to take stock of their situation before being moved to the central front to assist in the siege of Kiev.

The front along which the Germans were committed was over 2000 miles long, stretching from the North Cape to the Black Sea. To keep army units supported and supplied resulted in continuous 'juggling' of units which in the long run was doomed to failure. Requests from the ground commanders resulted in the German bomber force becoming nothing more than airborne artillery, which in many cases was how the generals saw it. At Kiev, however, the bombers achieved some success in blockading the battlefield by concentrating on communication systems. For a month the bombers systematically attacked railway installations, bridges, viaducts and train movements, achieving short-term objectives but gaining nothing in the way of long-term strategic advantages. Concentration on major junctions, marshalling yards and rail centers would have been more worthwhile objectives but neither weapons nor crews were available to do this. In the end the result was that the 6000 sorties flown against railway targets in the first six months of the Russian campaign caused an average delay of less than six hours to trains on the system!

The autumn rains turned roads into quagmires; aircraft became bogged down and the German army slithered to a halt short of Moscow. When the rain turned to snow and the winter set in, problems increased by the hour. There was no proper winter clothing for air or ground crews, no special cold weather equipment for the aircraft and spares were at a premium. At night temperatures fell to below minus 20 degrees F and crews had to leave what comfort they could find to run engines, shovel snow off wings, and check guns and bomb release mechanisms. Some of the more delicate tasks could not be carried out wearing thick gloves, so frostbite became another hazard. Many of the men had been fighting continuously for six months and were desperate for a rest; the elements now began to affect their morale very seriously.

Since the end of October there had been ominous signs that front-line units needed re-equipping and rest; serviceability rates began to fall and with them the ability of the Luftwaffe to provide the support previously usual. This is not too surprising as combat units had been involved on a daily basis since June and the dive-bomber Gruppen, to quote a typical example, had been achieving a daily sortie rate of 75 percent of their serviceable aircraft, a remarkable record and one which contributed a great deal to the many German successes in the opening rounds of *Barbarossa*.

In late November, what was to prove the final phase of Operation *Taifun* (the drive against Moscow) began, and it was then that some of the first signs of strain on the Luftwaffe started to show. Reconnaissance reports indicated that large-scale transport movements were converging on Moscow from the east, but no action was taken by any of the Kampfgeschwadern in the area. This was a mistake admitted to after the war by Kesselring who, in a letter to a friend, stated that the signi-

Above right: The white winter camouflage on this He 111H-11 was a form of soluble whitewash painted over the normal two-tone green.
Right: Rudel's Russian scoreboard, showing missions, victories and decorations.

Stolze Zahlen von den Einsätzen des
Major Rudel.

am 24.7.41 100. Feindflug
" 24.9.42 500. "
" 10.2.43 1000. "
" 1.6.44 2000. "

Flugkilometer: 530.000 Km

abgew. Bomben: 1.000.000 Kg

versch. Munition:
1000.000 Schuss MG.
150.000 " 2 cm
5.000 " 3.7 "

vernichtet: 40-45 Pakstellung.
" 45-50 Arie- "
" 35 Flak- "

vernicht. Panzer:
mit Bordwaffen 223
" Bomben 78

versenkte Schiffe:
1 Schlachtschiff
1 gr. Kreuzer
70 Übersetzboote

Brennstoff: 5.000.000 L

vernichtete LKw's:
600-700 LKw's und
bespannte Fahrzeuge

abgesch. Flugzeuge:
2 Lagg 3/1 JL-2

Auszeichnungen:

EK II:	10.11.1939
EK I:	18.7.1941
Dtsch. Kreuz:	24.4.1942
Ritterkreuz:	15.1.1942
Eichenlaub:	14.4.1943
Schwerter:	25.11.1943
Brillanten:	29.3.194

ficance of the movement was not appreciated. It seems nearer the truth that low serviceability among the units concerned prevented them from making a worthwhile strike. By the end of 1941 Luftwaffe aircraft strength on the Eastern front had fallen to 1700, and these were very hard pressed to support the 2000 mile front.

On 5 December the Russians mounted a major counter-offensive and this came at a time when Kesselring's Luftflotte 2 and Fliegerkorps II had been moved to the Mediterranean. This had been planned as early as October but was implemented at a difficult time as several units were in Germany being re-equipped. To the Germans it was incredible that the Russians could mount and support a large-scale offensive. Intelligence had reported success after success since June with over 1½ million men killed or taken prisoner, and over 15,000 aircraft destroyed, so where were all the supplies coming from? That question has already been answered, but to the ordinary German soldier or airman in the front line the size of the Russian onslaught must have been staggering. The absence of a strategic bomber was certainly costing dear not only from the point of view of disrupting production but also in the supply of raw materials. The German army was pushed back on all fronts for three months until March 1942 when the Russian advance came to a temporary halt.

In an attempt to retrieve the situation Hitler turned his attention to areas where he could strike at the Russians in depth, and his attention focussed on the oil fields of the Caucasus. The complex army plans around this spring offensive are beyond the scope of this book, but they all relied on air support which once again was predominantly in the tactical role. In the forefront was von Richthofen's Fliegerkorps VIII, now part of Luftflotte 4, whose main task at first was to give support in the Crimea.

During the raids on Sevastopol, which started on 2 June 1942, bombers from Fliegerkorps VIII – which now included the much improved Ju 87D – averaged 600 sorties per day during which they dropped 2500 tons on the beleaguered city, and this rate of bombardment was supported by artillery until the Russians surrendered on 4 July. The fortress of Sevastopol proved a tougher nut to crack than anticipated by the Germans who had allowed five days for it to be taken. It took five weeks, one of the many examples of over-confidence which come to light when the Russian campaign is studied in depth.

One of the major pockets of resistance met during the five

Above: Armorers haul an SC500 bomb towards an He 111H-6 of KG.55.
Left: A portable heater keeps a Do 17Z of III/KG.3 ready for operations on the Eastern Front. Winter 1941/2.

weeks' siege was a raft containing 164 anti-aircraft guns. This was anchored in Severnaya Bay where it commanded a large area of land, sea and air approaches. One 25 June it was decided that I/KG.51 should have a crack at removing this thorn in the Luftwaffe's side, and two Ju 88A-4s piloted by Hauptmann Fuhrhop, the Staffelkapitän of the 2nd Staffel and Oberleutnant Hinrichs, both of whom had made three previous attacks, were assigned the task. The plan was for the Oberleutnant's aircraft to suppress the flak, while the Staffelkapitän knocked out the raft, but in the event Hinrichs' bombs destroyed the raft and Fuhrhop did not have to attack. For his achievement Hinrichs was awarded the Knight's Cross. At this time many of the bomber crews were making four attacks a day

Below: Hans Rudel (left) the Stuka ace and his radio man. By the end of the war Rudel had been credited with destroying 519 Soviet tanks.

Above: The clean lines of a Bf 109G-2 of 4/JG.54 seen in typical 'summer' conditions on the Eastern Front.

on the fortress, not even leaving their aircraft while it was being rearmed. This, coupled with the hot Crimean summer and the importance of accurate flying and bombing, added to the tension mounting among the bomber crews.

Tension of a different sort was also mounting among the fighter pilots, and this was the question of who would be the first to record 150 victories. By the time the renewed summer offensive began in June 1942 fortunes had again turned Germany's way in the Mediterranean releasing units engaged in that theater to be redeployed to Russia. Among these and those coming from Germany were an increasing number of late mark Bf 109s as well as the Fw 190A which had made a disappointing debut in Russia in the winter of 1941.

The 150 target was reached in August 1942 by Major Gordon Gollob of JG.77, who was accordingly given the full treatment of publicity by the propaganda machine. In no other campaign was so much importance and publicity placed on the achievement of individual pilots and by mid-1942 a definite pattern was emerging within the Jagdgruppen. Each unit produced a handful of pilots who emerged as *Experten* (aces), reaching this status either by sheer flying ability or a combination of being in the right place at the right time and an aptitude for marksmanship. Once these men started to become established, the onus on their survival depended a great deal on the wingmen, who reaped little glory but provided most of the casualties. One exception to this rule was Oberfeldwebel Steinbaz who flew on Oberst Garf's wing. In June 1942 he received his Oak Leaves, and his score stood at 99 when he was claimed by the notorious Russian anti-aircraft guns.

The closing weeks of 1942 saw the start of one of the most epic and well documented battles of World War II: the siege of Stalingrad. Earlier in the year Goering had been given the opportunity to demonstrate the efficiency of his transport units in providing supplies from the air. Over 100,000 troops had been encircled by the Russians at Demyansk, a small town between Moscow and Leningrad. Six divisions of the Sixteenth Army urgently needed help and this came in the form of the ungainly Ju 52, 40 of which began the airlift on 20 February. There were two airfields into which they could fly by day, and by enlisting the help of flying schools, borrowing aircraft from all sources, and some careful planning, the 300 tons per day required to sustain the trapped forces were delivered. In a similar situation at Kholm supplies were parachuted or landed by glider. The siege at Demyansk was lifted on 18 May and the men at Kholm held on for three months before relief reached them from the ground. The airlift, although achieving its objectives, cost over 300 aircraft, but more importantly colored Goering's views of the operations. All the evidence pointed to a very successful outcome, but one of the most salient points overlooked was that there had been very little interference from the Soviet air force. At Stalingrad it was to be a different story though by mid-November the German army, well supported by the bomber and dive bomber squadrons, had secured most of the western bank of the Volga and it looked as though the defenders would be hard pushed to hold on.

But on the 19th of the month a counter-attack was started just outside Stalingrad whereby two Russian armies moving from the north and south carried out a pincer movement which trapped 22 divisions comprising over 300,000 men of the German Sixth Army. Generaloberst Friedrich Paulus could have attempted a break out, and would no doubt have achieved this with acceptable casualties, but Hitler ordered him to stand firm and said he would be supplied from the air. An army of this size needed supplies of food and ammunition totalling over 600 tons per day, and most Luftwaffe commanders in the area knew this was beyond the capability of the transport units, but Paulus stood firm, putting his trust in Goering's promises, which after all had been fulfilled at Kholm and Demyansk.

To increase the number of aircraft available to support the Ju 52s the Luftwaffe was milked dry on every available front. He 111s of KG.55, two Gruppen of Ju 88s, and even one Gruppe of the ill-fated He 177 were taken off bombing duties to act as transports, and operated alongside Ju 86s, Fw 200s and Ju 290s. Despite the gallantry of the crews, their determination against fearful odds, and an enormous amount of work by the ground crews, the target of 600 tons a day was never reached, and gradually the Sixth Army was starved into submission. On 2 February Paulus surrendered the remains of his army (some 91,000 men), and the Luftwaffe counted its losses. These totalled 488 aircraft, of which nearly 200 were bombers, among which were seven He 177s which at that time had not even begun to operate in their design role.

This defeat was the start of the decline of the Luftwaffe in Russia, for in addition to the bombers the fighter Gruppen had also lost a lot of aircraft and experienced men in trying to give cover to the airlift. Although forced to withdraw from the airfields close to Stalingrad, a group of pilots from JG.3 operated from Pitomnik for a six week period during which they claimed over 100 victories. But it was not so much the losses in action or the attrition which heralded the first significant signs of defeat, but events in Germany. Instructors were transferred to the Russian front, thus curtailing the training program; fuel became short and this resulted in a cut-back of all non-operational flying which of course affected training. So, although aircraft production reached its peak during 1944-45, by then there were fewer pilots to fly the new aircraft and insufficient fuel to operate them in strength.

The crushing defeat at Stalingrad and the set-backs in North Africa made Hitler more determined to seek success in Russia and in an attempt to regain the initiative he mounted Operation *Zitadelle* in the summer of 1943. This was aimed at Kursk and involved two simultaneous offensives in the northern and southern sectors. Luftflotte 4 under General Otto Desslock provided 1100 combat aircraft in the southern area and in the north Fliegerdivision I under Generalmajor Paul Deichmann contributed 700 machines, the combined force representing

Above: A Dornier Do 17 is well protected against the elements.
Below: The Fw 189 had a capacity for ground attack as well as reconnaissance; the wing bomb racks of this A-2 model can be clearly seen.

just over 50 percent of the available Luftwaffe strength in Russia. The Soviets prepared their defenses well and had over 2400 aircraft ready to meet the Luftwaffe, among these being examples of the La-5 and Yak-9 fighters.

What was to turn out to be the biggest tank battle in World War II started in the early morning of 5 July 1943 when German tanks advanced on both fronts. Prior to this the Red air force had tried to catch Luftwaffe bombers on their airfields, but radar had warned of their intentions and fighters from JG.3, 51, 52 and 54 took a heavy toll of the raiders. The ground battle in which Fw 190F fighter bombers which had started to replace the Ju 87s in ground attack roles, made a significant contribution, went against the Germans who by 23 July were forced to halt their advance and try to stabilize their line.

On that day, Leutnant Erich Hartmann of 9/JG.52 claimed his 34th victory; not perhaps an important milestone for high scoring pilots, but in this case worth recalling since Hartmann was destined to become a much feted hero. Joining JG.52 in November 1942, Hartmann achieved his first success on the 5th of the month, and by the time of his capture when the war ended in May 1945 had claimed 352 victories, one of which, a Yak II on 8 May, may well have been the last Luftwaffe claim of the war. Every theater of operations produced its aces and the legends which have developed around the exploits of Marseille in the Middle East have similarly surrounded Erich Hartmann, but in many ways to a higher degree as he is generally considered to be the highest scoring ace of all time.

His success coupled with those of his colleagues, did not influence the outcome of *Zitadelle*, and during this operation, it is worth noting that USAAF bombers mounted their first daylight raid on the German homeland. The RAF night raids had mounted in intensity and the defense of the Reich began to take priority. Fighter units were withdrawn from all fronts to strengthen those already facing the combined efforts of the RAF/USAAF, so as the Red air force increased in strength, it faced a greatly depleted adversary.

The quality of the German pilots and aircraft, which now included the G variant of the Bf 109 as well as the Fw 190, did not however deteriorate and the units left in the east continued to fight with tenacity. It is arguable whether they greatly influenced any of the 1944-45 battles, because by this time it was obvious to all that the German cause was finished. Although the German fighter pilots continued to receive much publicity from the propaganda machine, all aircrew involved suffered greatly. After a day's operations there was no question of a hot bath, a comfortable bed, and an appetizing meal: theirs was the same world of mud, snow, cold, damp, and inadequate food of the infantryman.

The courage, tenacity, and individual success can only be admired and it must be remembered that these young men were just a cross-section of a country's youth who, in the main, were involved in a war whose origins they had no clear knowledge or particular view about. The majority had become involved purely because of their love of flying, the skills they developed from this, and the inherent character which makes any flyer rather special in the context of a fighting man.

Left: The difficult weather conditions in Russia are clearly visible in this shot of a Fw 190A-4 of JG.54.
Below left: The two 300-liter wing tanks of this Fw 190G-1 ground attack fighter gave it a greatly extended range.
Below: A ground attack Fw 190F-8 of SG.2 in Hungary, January 1945.

A pair of Bf 110G-4a/R1 night fighters of NJG.6 in 1944. Aerials are for FuG 202 Lichtenstein radar.

DEFENSE OF THE REICH

Since he had been in at the birth of the German Air Force during the Great War, it is hard to understand how Goering formed some of the impressions that were to lead to his ultimate total failure as an air commander during World War II. Some of his papers indicate that he was greatly impressed by the theory of strategic bombing, and the lessons learned during the first tentative excursions during 1914-18, clearly indicated that tackled in the right way, this method of involving civilian populations not only ties up the enemy defending forces, but interrupts the manufacture and supply of vital equipment. It is likely that Goering really did believe that such was the power of the Luftwaffe coupled to the German army, that countries would capitulate before the need to undertake a long bombing campaign would occur. This was certainly proved to be correct in the case of the opening shots in the European war, but conversely it proved the major factor in the ultimate defeat of Germany and certainly cost them victory in Russia which could have changed the whole outcome of the war, not to mention the world situation as it stands today.

Goering's belief that the air forces against which his would be matched were incapable of mounting a successful bombing campaign is underlined by his often misquoted comment made during a July 1939 tour of Rhineland defenses: 'If an enemy bomber reaches German soil, my name is not Hermann Goering. You can call me Meier.' This statement must be kept in perspective, however, for when he made it he had no idea that Germany would be faced with a war of the proportions to be reached within two years. On 1 September 1939, the Luftwaffe had a strength of over 4000 aircraft and was superior to any other air force in the world. But in many ways this was illusory for it had few reserves and a number of its fighter and bomber units were well below the proposed established strengths. During 1938, the overall increase in the number of operational aircraft had been about 25 percent, the majority being attributable to the increase of transport aircraft, dive bombers and reconnaissance machines. All this clearly indicated that Goering saw the coming air war as one in which the Luftwaffe would operate mainly in a tactical support role. Failure to expand fighter units to the same extent as the rest of the force, would appear to suggest that he felt his bombers would not need fighter protection in depth, and there was little requirement for home defense fighters. Defense of the homeland was in the hands of a few day fighter units and a considerable number of anti-aircraft guns and searchlight batteries.

Nonetheless, it is hard to reconcile Goering's opinions which, on the one hand indicated that enemy bombers would not penetrate German airspace, and on the other that there was no defense against the bomber, a view he is known to have shared with other contemporary air leaders. The most likely explanation is that his own philosophy as far as air war was concerned was that aircraft were intended for use in offensive and not defensive roles, and that the coming conflict would be of short duration.

In June 1939 both Hitler and Goering attended a demonstration of radar at the Luftwaffe technical development center at Rechlin. This impressed them enough to authorize the purchase of 800 sets of the type known as Würzburg and 200 of the Freya type. However, there is little indication that the full implication of early warning radar was fully appreciated. In fact Goering left the study of its strategic importance to his signal chief, General Martini, who was unable to assess successfully the growth of parallel British developments. So in

Below: The Bf 109G-10/R3 was used extensively in home defense, as was the Fw 190 (*below right*). The aircraft shown is a Fw 190A-6/R11 with FuG 217 radar for night fighting.

1939 there were no priority plans to equip the Third Reich with any form of early warning radar although Udet did persuade Goering to experiment with a small force of single-engined fighters in the night fighter role. This scheme was not viewed with any great enthusiasm, for when General Jeschonnek, the Luftwaffe Chief of Staff, raised the matter at a meeting on 5 September 1939 he was told that night fighting would never happen. Nonetheless early warning radar played a significant part in making the daylight raids mounted by RAF Wellington bombers against German naval bases in Wilhelmshaven and Brunsbüttel in December 1939 so disastrous for the attackers. But communication between the radar controllers and the fighter squadrons was not all that it might have been, and as the fighters from I/ZG.76, II/ZG.77, III/ZG.77 and 10/JG.26 had a successful day anyway, the vital lesson appears to have gone unnoticed since no action was taken to install a similar radar warning system along all the approaches to Germany.

During the winter of 1939-40, British bombers regularly penetrated German air space – carrying out reconnaissance, dropping leaflets and occasionally trying to bomb targets of a military nature. There was usually little damage, but similarly the RAF suffered few losses to the defenses. Realizing that anti-aircraft guns and searchlights were not adequate deterrents to night bombing, Goering called on Hauptmann Wolfgang Falck, the commander of I/ZG.1 who had been using his Bf 110s as night fighters, to form the first night-fighter Geschwader at Wassenaar. On 18 June 1940, Oberst Josef Kammhuber was appointed to command the first Luftwaffe night-fighter division which comprised Falck's newly formed Geschwader and its two Gruppen: I/NJG.1 under Hauptmann Radusch and III/NJG.1, formed from IV/JG.2, under Major Blumensaat. The strength of this force was less than 50 aircraft, with some pilots still converting from the day fighter Bf 109 to the heavy Bf 110 which was eventually to become a most successful night fighter. But such was Kammhuber's skill and enthusiasm that by the end of the year, a highly efficient force of over 150 aircraft was operational and ready to face the major problem of effecting a method of interception using the equipment then available.

The first aim was the defense in a restricted zone of the German western approaches, and the first priority was to help the fighter pilots find their targets. To do this Kammhuber set-up a chain of searchlights and sound detectors along the route usually followed by the British bombers, but this was easily countered by avoiding the accepted route, so eventually the chain expanded to cover the whole approach to the industrial Ruhr. Kammhuber knew little about radar, but General

Above: Early detection of raiders was done by sound locators. This is a typical unit and crew. The equipment shown is operated by female auxiliaries. Boys almost of military age also served extensively in various duties with anti-aircraft units before going on to do the usual military training.
Below: Fw 190A-8s move out to intercept another American daylight raid.

Above: The Messerschmitt production line in 1944 with work underway on a batch of Bf 109s.

Martini assigned six companies to him and with their Würzburg equipment a system known as Helle Nachtjagd (illuminated night fighting) was evolved. This was based on the use of two radars; one controlled a master searchlight and the other tracked the movement of the night fighters which operated within a defined sector or box. Directions were passed to the night fighter by radio so that it could be vectored into a position where visual contact with the bomber could be made while the bomber was illuminated by the searchlight.

The next move was to set up ground controlled radar stations at 20 mile intervals along a line from Schleswig Holstein to Liège, each station to be equipped with a Freya for area surveillance and two Würzburgs for precision location, one tracking the bomber, the other the intercepting night fighter. Information from the two precision sets was plotted on a table from which a fighter controller was able to guide a night fighter to its target until visual contact was made. This system became known as Himmelbett and was the foundation on which all future night fighter ground control was based. Kammhuber also had plans to use his force to harass returning bombers over their home bases in long range intruder roles, but his immediate task was the perfection of Himmelbett in which he was frustrated by the shortage of suitable aircraft and crews.

Below: Aerial dish of the medium range Würzburg Reise precision radar, a key element in Kammhuber's defense plans.

The first aircraft assigned specifically to night fighter tasks were BF 110s, Ju 88s and Do 217s, none of which was designed for the role but each in its own way acquitted itself well. Special versions of the Bf 110 and Ju 88 with airborne interception radar, were later produced and formed the backbone of a very successful night fighter force. Crews were a different problem; many front-line aircrew then enjoying great success in the campaigns against the Low Countries and France, were reassigned for night fighter duties and their feelings about this can well be imagined, especially as there was every indication that the German war machine was sweeping all before it. This move by Goering does underline that he had no real depth in reserves of either aircraft or men. Fighters had not been given a particularly high priority rating as far as production was concerned and this was not rectified until it was far too late. The emphasis on quality rather than quantity was a fatal error and although production rates improved late in 1943 and throughout 1944, they never caught up with the rate of attrition. From March to June 1944, 4545 single-engined fighters were produced, but losses in the same period were 5527. The night bomber offensive by the RAF reached its zenith in 1944 by which time high priority had been given to the production of radar equipped night fighters, the figure reaching 2518 Ju 88 and 1525 Bf 110 by the year's end. The Bf 110 would also have passed the 2000 mark if nearly 500 had not been destroyed in February raids concentrated on production factories.

In June 1943 General Kammhuber had foreseen the need for quantity production of specialist night fighters and requested the supply of 2000 He 219s. This superlative fighter could well have had a great influence on the night bombing campaign of the RAF, but at this time Kammhuber was advised that conversion of existing types was quite adequate, so by the end of the war only 294 Hs 219s had rolled off the production lines. Another aircraft that might have helped if it had been developed in a proper way was the Focke-Wulf Ta 154 Moskito. Like its British namesake this was primarily a wooden aircraft and was ordered into production in November 1943. Two early production aircraft suffered structural failures – later proved to be because of faulty glue – and the production order was immediately cancelled. When the much needed fighters did reach the Luftwaffe the situation with trained crews and fuel supplies had reached a critical point, so there were more aircraft than men to fly them or fuel to enable those in use to be operated effectively.

Goering did in fact see the potential of his fighter force but firmly believed that it was mobile enough to be moved to areas where needed (shades of the WWI Flying Circus), and in some cases where he was enthusiastic about new ideas, was overruled by Hitler. A case in point was his interest and encouragement to Kammhuber, for the use of aircraft in long range intruder roles. As we know, the only machines available to Kammhuber for this task were modified bombers, and when the Führer heard that bombers were being used as fighters he ordered that the proposed force be cut in half. This role always was difficult for Hitler to accept and he constantly interfered with Luftwaffe policy, on several occasions vetoing Kammhuber's plans, and eventually ordering Goering to disband the intruder force in August 1943; this at a time when the RAF night blitz was building toward a peak and any operation to limit it would have been profitable.

Above: The unofficial crest of 7/JG.400, in which a bottle of champagne has replaced the original rocket.

In the early days of 1940-41 night fighter crews that would form the backbone of experience when the real task came in 1943-44, were gaining valuable experience. One of the first victories by a bona fide night fighter squadron, I/NJG.1, went to Leutnant Werner Streib and his radio operator Unteroffizier Lingen when they accounted for a Whitley on the night of 20 July 1940. Streib went on to become a very sucessful first generation night fighter pilot and after his seventh victory – three of which came in the space of one 40 minute sortie – he

Below: This Ju 88A-4 of AufklG.122 is in the Air Force Museum at Wright Patterson base in America.

Above: Four notable fighter pilots: (l to r) Prinz zu Sayn-Wittgenstein, Hartmann Grasser, Walter Nowotny and Gunther Rall.

was promoted to Hauptmann and given command of I/NJG.1. Pilots like Streib, Ehle, Griese, Förster and Blumensaat did not have sophisticated radar aids, but they were instrumental in getting the new force off on a sound footing and bringing it much needed publicity which helped to attract recruits from other units who still viewed night fighters with some scepticism.

Day fighter pilots had no such jaundiced views. Throughout the summer of 1940 they had been fighting the RAF over the Channel in offensive rather than defensive roles. But as 1941 progressed they found a reversal imminent as the fight was carried back over France. The ill-timed invasion of Russia left only JG.2 under Hauptmann Wilhelm Balthasar and Adolf Galland's JG.26, resident in France, with their elements well dispersed along the coast. Numerically they totalled 150 aircraft which were all sub-types of the Bf 109. These proved more than a match for the Blenheims which formed the bulk of daylight raiders then being used to put pressure on the German forces in the west in an attempt to help relieve the build-up on the Russian front.

The two German fighter units contained the RAF's efforts in France and Belgium quite adequately and achieved an average kill ratio of 2:1. The experience of the pilots and their skilful

Below: Bf 110G-4/R3 equipped for night-fighting.

use of the Bf 109F and later Fw 190 often told. August 1941, for example, saw them destroy 108 RAF fighters for the loss of only 18 of their number. The ascendancy gained by the Fw 190, which was at its height in February 1942 at the time of the Channel dash of the *Gneisenau*, *Scharnhorst* and *Prinz Eugen*, somewhat negated the hopes the RAF had for the new Boston they had introduced to replace the ageing Blenheim. The Spitfire V then in use on escort duties was no match for the Fw 190 and it was not until the Mk IX was introduced that the Luftwaffe again faced a fighter on equal terms.

The ability of comparatively few fighters to defend a fairly large area of air space, providing warning was adequate and tactics were right, was thus well illustrated by the German day fighters left to look after operations in the west. The setting up of Kammhuber's radar chain proved to be of tremendous help in this respect, and by mid 1942 the Luftwaffe was finding little difficulty in inflicting heavy losses on the RAF's daylight sorties. Freya could detect bomber formations at about 56 miles if the aircraft were above 1000 feet. As RAF policy was to form up in a spiralling climb to 7000 feet before setting course, the intention of practically every raid was known to the ground controllers. Diversionary sweeps and feints were used to try to fool the operators, but most were very experienced and quickly recognized these for what they were. The end result was that the Fw 190s and Bf 109s were in good positions to maul the attackers. In March 1942 they accounted for 32 RAF fighters and in April 104, successes almost totally due to early warning radar and the Fw 190 in very experienced and skilled hands.

However, there was a gathering cloud on the horizon and this materialized in August 1942 in a new shape that was to make a big contribution to the final defeat of Germany. The shape was the massed box formations of B-17 and B-24 bombers of the United States Army Air Force, which had been arriving in strength in England since the USA's declaration of war on Germany.

On 12 August 1942 twelve B-17Es of the 97th Bombardment Group, 8th Air Force, led by General Ira C Eaker, attacked marshalling yards at Rouen-Sotteville to open the planned daylight offensive. On this occasion the American bombers were escorted by Spitfires and returned to England without loss. But the RAF had warned their American cousins of the perils of long penetration by unescorted bombers which they had not attempted since 17 April 1942 when seven out of twelve Lancasters of 44 and 97 Squadrons were lost on a daylight attack on the MAN engine works at Augsburg. The fact that no American bombers had been lost on their first raid did not signify any loss of touch by the Germans, it was simply that they had to work out new tactics, and if anyone doubted this, their doubts were soon dispelled on 19 August when the Jagdgruppen underlined their efficiency by taking a heavy toll of RAF aircraft during the ill-fated Dieppe landings. During the day-long air battle, the longest single air engagement in World War II, the RAF lost 106 aircraft against the Luftwaffe's loss of 48. The heaviest hit unit was I/JG.2 which lost 8 Fw 190s; other Gruppen of JG.2 and JG.26 suffered losses of experienced pilots but at that time replacements were still readily available.

Above: A Bf 110G-2/R3 with Wfr 21 rocket launchers under its wings. Nose armament is a pair of 30mm cannon and the ventral pack has two MG 151 cannon.

Below: The clean lines of an Fw 190A-3 of II/JG.1 photographed in France in 1942.

Below: A cutaway of the Focke-Wulf Fw 190D-9, illustrating the unusual installation of the Junkers Jumo 213 in-line engine with an annular radiator, which gave it the appearance of a radial engine. This aircraft carries the markings of III/JG.54.

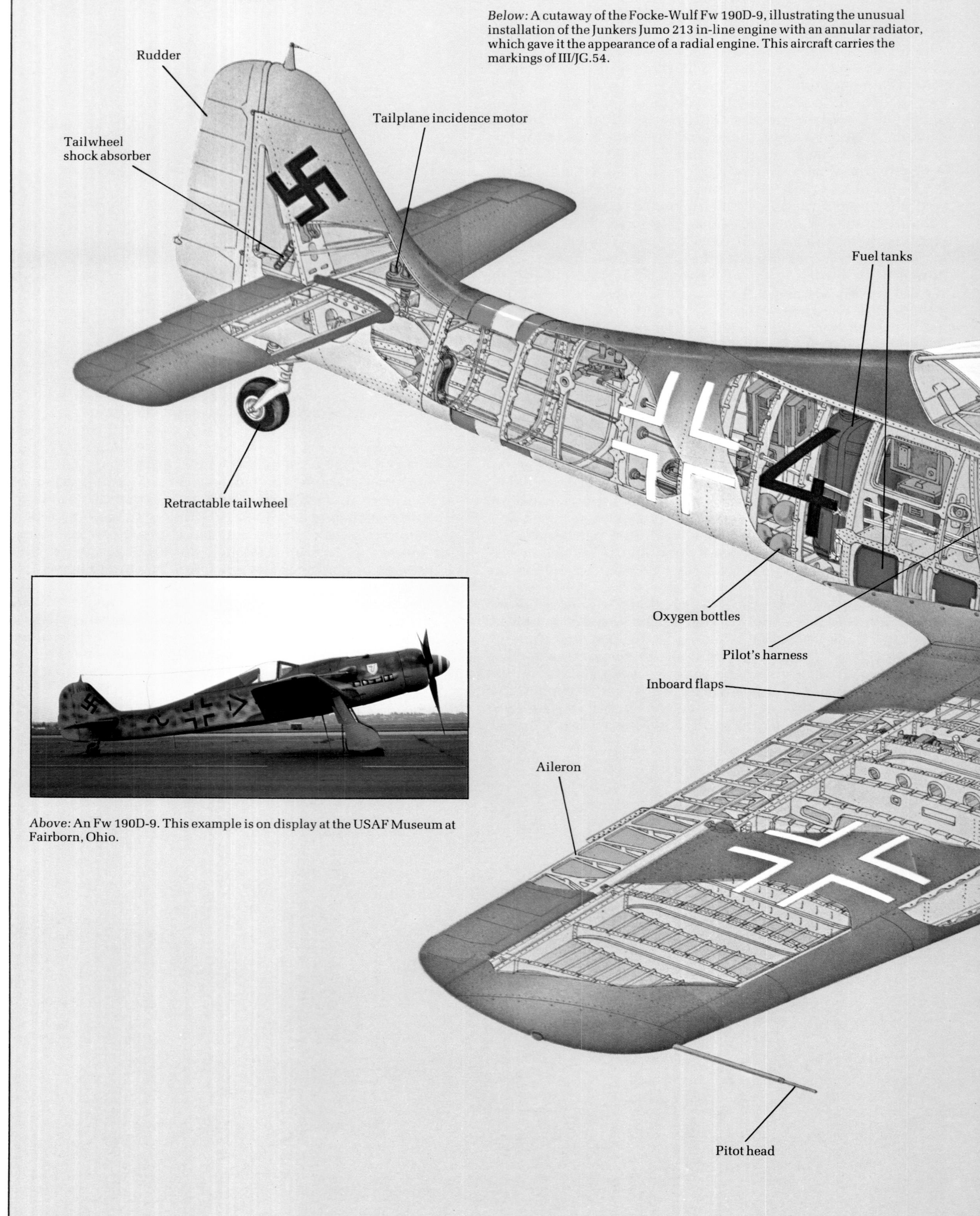

Above: An Fw 190D-9. This example is on display at the USAF Museum at Fairborn, Ohio.

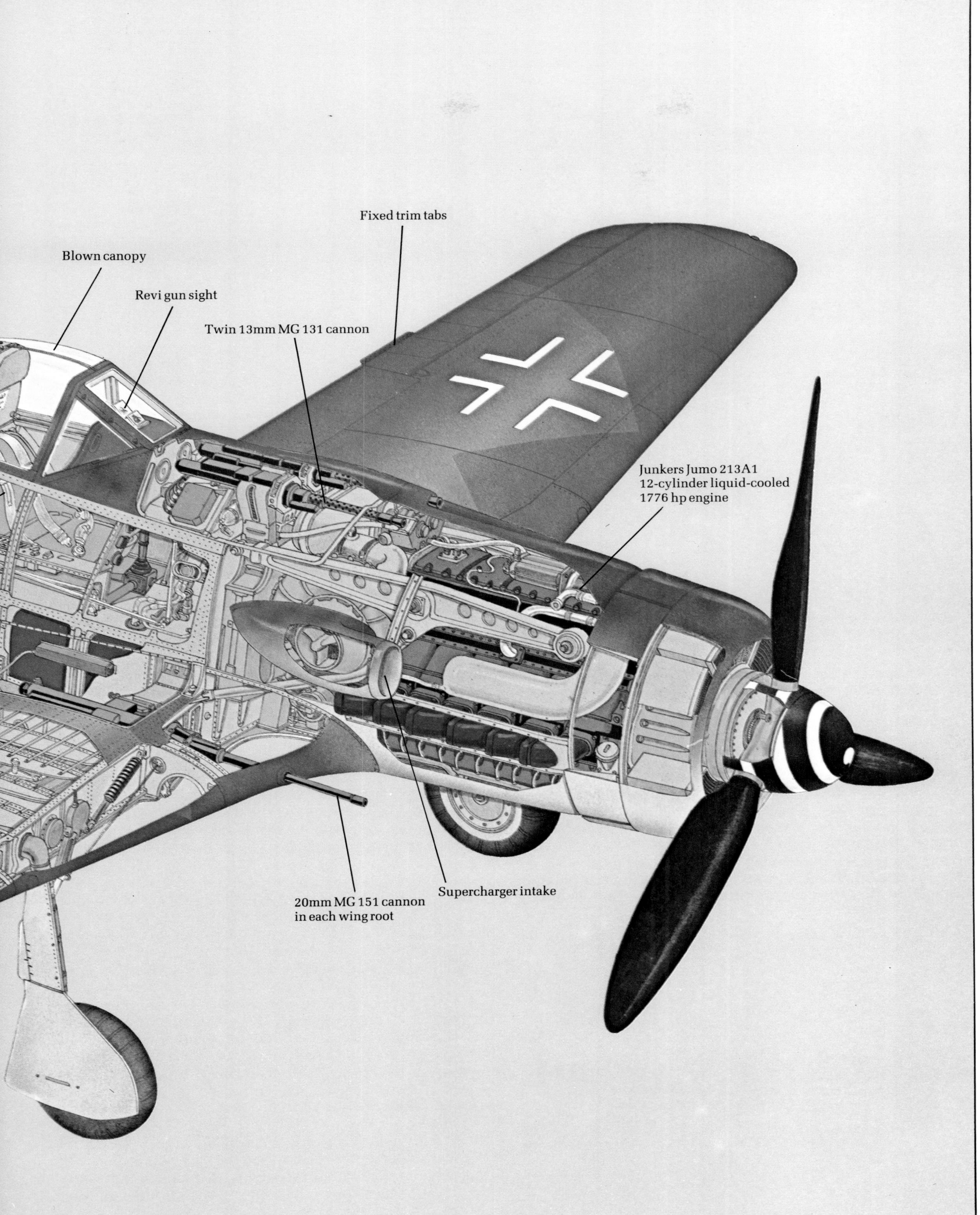
Fixed trim tabs
Blown canopy
Revi gun sight
Twin 13mm MG 131 cannon
Junkers Jumo 213A1
12-cylinder liquid-cooled
1776 hp engine
Supercharger intake
20mm MG 151 cannon
in each wing root

Above: Searchlights formed an important part of the German night defense screen against Allied air attack.

On 6 September 1942 Fw 190s of II/JG.26, led by Hauptmann Egon Meyer, shot down the first B-17 to fall to a Fw 190. By November the American bombers were penetrating further and had embarked on their daylight strategic campaign, but by then Meyer and his pilots had evolved the frontal attack which avoided the massed rearward defensive armament of the bomber formations. By sweeping ahead of the box formations and then climbing above to turn and dive head on, the German fighters faced less concentrated fire from the B-17s and B-24s, but at the same time with closing speeds rising toward 500mph they had less time to select their target and fire. But the heavy caliber weapons of the Fw 190 proved adequate for even the briefest of encounters and American losses mounted. The advent of the American long-range escort fighter presented problems but until they were fitted with additional long-range tanks enabling them to go all the way to the target and back with the bombers, the defending fighters played a waiting game. Defense of the Reich by day was strengthened by the recall of units from other fronts as well as the use of the night fighter force, the first eight BF 110s of II/NJG.1 going into action on 4 February 1943.

Below: The unusual twin engined Do 335A-1 was to be developed as a day and night fighter. It had not reached production status when the war ended.

Although losses were high the Americans persisted but concern was mounting. This peaked in October 1943 when 60 B-17s failed to return from Schweinfurt and well over 100 were severely damaged; the Fw 190s, Bf 109s, Ju 88s and Bf 110s and the recently introduced Me 410, had a field day especially after the escorting P-47s had turned back when reaching the extremity of their duration. By a quirk of fate it was the beginning of the end for the German defending fighters, for although it was a victory in one battle, the signs of defeat were growing. Hitler continued to interfere and Goering was virtually a spent force, drugs having reduced his ability to comprehend even the simplest strategy or accept facts presented to him. When Galland reported to him after the Schweinfurt raid that P-47s had escorted the bombers as far as Aachen and proof existed in the form of a shot down fighter, he refused to believe it and stated that the pilot must have glided to Aachen after his aircraft had been damaged.

The introduction of long-range tanks, and the debut of the P-51 in the long-range escort role in December 1943, saw the scales tip back toward the raiders. Throughout 1944 daylight raids continued but although German fighter production reached a peak of 2995 machines per month by September 1944, lack of trained pilots, a shortage of fuel and disruption in lines of communication, outweighed any advantage this normally might have given. New weapons in the form of air-to-air missiles fired into the massed bomber formations, the introduction of the Me 163 rocket fighter and Me 262 jet fighter, all brought new hope to the Luftwaffe, but surviving veterans knew in their hearts there was little hope, and the courage shown by young pilots with only a few hours in their log-books was no insurance against the highly trained and well equipped Allied air forces.

The Me 262 could have made a much greater impact, but again it was dogged early on by engine problems plus interference from Hitler, and when it did reach operational units, pilots with the right kind of experience to exploit its performance were very few. But credit must be given to the German air force for not only introducing the first operational jet fighter, but also for the formation of a jet bomber equipped squadron which operated against England as well as Allied airfields in Belgium.

As the day fighter Gruppen fought a withdrawing action across the Continent, the night fighters were faced with similar moments of glory and frustration. Since the early days of 1941 the techniques of night interception had improved beyond all recognition. Airborne radar installed initially in Do 217s, Ju 88s and Bf 110s had been improved and perfected and although this met opposition due to the sacrifice of some performance, it was soon realized that the aircraft and their fire power were still more than a match for the RAF's main force of Wellingtons, Lancasters and Halifaxes, whose rifle caliber machine guns were really of very little use unless the unwary allowed themselves to get too close. Those who had at first eyed the night fighter force with some suspicion, among them being Helmut Lent who was to become one of the first night fighter aces, were converted.

Night fighters took a steady toll of RAF bombers and by mid 1943 over 95 percent of the force operating was equipped with airborne radar. During the onslaught by Bomber Command in 1943 scientific measures and counter measures tilted the scales one way and then the other. On occasions when the Allies had the upper hand in jamming radar, a new tactic was tried by the

Above: A Ju 88G-1 night-fighter version of the famous bomber.
Right: The Ju 88 was also used in shipping strikes; the aerial arrays on this A-6/U are for FuG Hohentwiel equipment.

Luftwaffe whereby free-ranging day fighters operated in what were known as *Wilde Sau* roles. Most of these were Bf 109s or Fw 190s which patrolled in the area of the bomber stream and relied on the pilots' eyesight aided by flares and searchlights to locate the bombers.

Crews however preferred *Zahme Sau* operations in which twin engined long-duration fighters would roam free from ground control, outside their delegated boxes and use their on-board equipment to locate stragglers from the main stream. Sometimes they would use ground stations to place them in a favorable position in relation to the incoming bomber force, then the radar operator would take over. Interceptions might start well out over the North Sea, during the approach to the target, or even when the bomber turned for home, for although by then the bomb load would be gone, the crew might be relaxing their vigilance and in any case a destroyed bomber and its crew could not operate on another day. The night fighters'

Below: If the He 219 had been available in greater numbers it would have had a tremendous impact in the night fighting. This is an He 219A with SN 2 radar.

war developed into one where radar and radio aids played a major role, and from 1944 until the end of hostilities such devices were developed to a very high degree by both sides thus laying the foundations for today's modern electronic warfare.

The fighters' heavy firepower was further augmented in 1943 by the introduction of vertically firing 30mm cannon known as *Schräge Musik*. This weapon was lethal to the bomber. The technique was to locate the target by radar, creep up in the blind spot beneath the tail, sit under the bomb bay, and then fire. There was very little defense apart from vigilance and downward firing .303 machine guns proved totally inadequate. The major danger to the night fighter was getting too close before opening fire, and a good vertical separation was essential.

Despite losses inflicted by the night fighters and ground defenses, there were only rare occasions when they were above an acceptable rate to the RAF. One of these was on the night of 30 March 1944 when 94 bombers from a force of 795 attacking Nuremberg were shot down. At this time it is interesting to reflect that the Nachtjagdgeschwadern had only 376 available crews for 361 serviceable fighters, and by the end of the year although 913 night fighters were available only 599 could be crewed, such was the poor state that the German administrators had allowed themselves to be put in.

In a desparate attempt to stem the flow many odd designs were to be seen coming from the drawing boards of the German aircraft industry. The Bachem Ba 349 Natter was one, in which a nose battery of 24 missiles was mounted in what was virtually a missile launched from an 80 foot ramp and powered to a height of over 38,000 feet by a Walter bi-fuel rocket. Only 36 had been completed by the time the first launching area was overrun, but initial test flights had indicated that the rocket fighter might well have been a success. A utility fighter powered by a single jet engine mounted on its back and designed to be flown by those with limited experience of powered flight or even just of gliders, was ordered to be put into production. This resulted in the Heinkel He 162, but although JG.1 was formed by April 1945 it saw no action, which was perhaps just as well for its inexperienced pilots.

In March 1945 Hitler at last gave absolute priority to Me 262 production with SS General Hans Kammler in charge of all jet-propelled aircraft production. In the first four months of 1945 865 Me 262s were produced making a grand total of 1433 of which less than 100 saw operations. Galland formed a new fighter unit Jagdverbande 44 equipped with the Me 262 early in 1945, and chose the cream of the fighter aces to fly the aircraft. The closing weeks saw some considerable successes being achieved although at any one time there were only fifteen aircraft ready for action. Some ten of the jets were fitted out with radar and used to defend Berlin against night bombers, but by this time it was all too little and far too late.

The assault by the USAAF and RAF on oil refineries, lines of communication, rail systems, airfields, factories and utility plants, brought increasing pressures which the Luftwaffe just could not resist. Eventually a serious shortage of fuel, lack of pilots and the Allied advance which overran radar stations negated the night and day fighter forces, although some units continued to put up spirited opposition until the very end.

Left: Planned to succeed the Bf 110 the Me 410 was not the success hoped for and saw relatively little use.
Below left: The so called 'Peoples Fighter,' the He 162A-2.
Below: The only rocket-powered aircraft ever to see service, the Me 163 Komet.

The Dornier Do 26 was originally built for Lufthansa as a mail plane. Only five were constructed and they were impressed for use by 1/KüFlGr.506, and mostly operated in Norwegian waters.

NAVAL AVIATION

The German desire for a strong navy stemmed from Kaiser Wilhelm II's envy of the British Fleet which dominated the seas during his early life. Although lacking experience in the design and building of large warships, the Germans quickly learned, and by the outbreak of World War I had the makings of a fleet that was to challenge the might of the Royal Navy. By the time of World War II, the fleet had learned a lot and had grown in stature to a point where it was a force that had to be quickly countered or contained. Unlike most major navies the Germans had not chosen to build a force of aircraft carriers and, although a carrier was being built at the start of the conflict, they never had such a vessel in service.

However, in 1939 a small maritime air force existed under the control of the Kriegsmarine. Its main task was that of reconnaissance and it was known as the Seeluftstreitkräfte which literally translated means Fleet Air Arm. The majority of the aircraft were seaplanes equipped only for reconnaissance and very lightly armed for their own defense, their task being the monitoring of sea lanes feeding German ports, which was not considered to be part of the Luftwaffe's duties. Little thought had been given to any naval role the Luftwaffe might be called upon to perform for as previously stated the air force was considered primarily to be a tactical force supporting the army.

Most of the aircraft under the control of the Führer der Seeluftstreitkräfte were based in the Baltic and on the North Sea coast and comprised mainly obsolescent types which had first flown in the mid 1930s. These included the He 59B, He 115 and Dornier Do 18, all of which were to perform adequately and proved their worth as did many similar vintage machines that it would have been easy to condemn on paper.

One task which fell to the He 59 was the air sea rescue role with the Seenotdienstaffel where in some cases they were painted overall white and carried civil registration as well as the red cross. It was such an aircraft that caused controversy on 9 July 1940 when it was found to be monitoring shipping and radioing reports to Luftwaffe strike aircraft. The RAF immediately stated that in future such pseudo-civil aircraft would be considered legitimate military targets and shot down if they appeared near convoys.

Like many German aircraft the He 59 had served in Spain where it was used as a night bomber and a potential torpedo strike aircraft although by the time World War II started considerable rethinking was needed when it came to dropping torpedoes from slow flying biplanes. The He 59 was however a workhorse and used in training roles as well as clandestine operations including the dropping of agents, mine laying in the Thames Estuary and other coastal areas, and in tactical support. One of the most notable examples of this last role was on 10 May 1940 when 12 He 59s carrying a force of 120 troops took off from Lake Zwischenahn near Oldenburg and landed either side of the Willems Bridge near to the center of Rotterdam. This bridge, together with those over the Maas at Leeuwen and Jan Kuiten were secured for the loss of only four Heinkels; a small price to pay for the advantage secured for the advancing German army.

Another seaplane success in 1940 was the capture on 5 May of the British submarine HMS *Seal* by Leutnant Günther Mehrens flying an Arado 196A-3. The submarine under the command of Lieutenant-Commander R Lonsdale, had been damaged by mines and was unable to dive. Mehrens attacked with such ferocity that the submarine commander surrendered, whereupon the Arado landed alongside, picked up the unfortunate skipper and flew him to interrogation and captivity. The *Seal* was taken in tow to Friedrichshafen by a Kriegsmarine ship summoned to the scene by the jubilant seaplane crew.

The Arado Ar 196 was the type issued to most major German

Right: Heinkel He 114C-1 of Rumanian Escadrilla 102.
Below: A Heinkel He 177A-5 of II/KG.40 about to set off on a shipping strike from Bordeaux-Mérignac, in 1944.

warships including the *Gneisenau*, *Lützow*, *Scharnhorst*, *Prince Eugen*, *Tirpitz* and *Bismarck*. The *Bismarck*'s aircraft were used during the action in the Atlantic, when they shadowed the RAF flying boats sent to monitor the battleship's moves.

Bordfliegerstaffeln 1/196 and 5/196 were the first land-based units to receive the Arado and used them in the Bay of Biscay under the control of Fliegerführer Atlantik where they supported U-Boats to and from their bases to the convoy routes. In this capacity they caused RAF Coastal Command, then using Whitley aircraft, serious problems and the threat to the patrolling bombers was not finally removed until the long-range Beaufighter came on the scene and proved more than a match for the small seaplane.

Norway and the Aegean were also happy hunting grounds for the seaplanes which in addition to reconnaissance duties could also harry shipping and troops with their small bomb loads. Operating as part of Luftflotte 1, Fliegerführer Ostsee had 2/SAGr 125 equipped with the Ar 196 and these were used against Russian targets as well as convoys sailing in Northern waters. Despite its frail looks the Arado was a sturdy, reliable aircraft and was maneuverable enough to surprise many fighter pilots. It remained in service throughout the war and was still front line equipment for one unit in 1945.

Right: Werner Baumbach one of the Luftwaffe's most successful maritime strike pilots.
Below: A KG.100 He 177A-3/R2 with two-tone gray upper surfaces and all-black under surface.

The Seeluftstreitkräfte gradually encountered increasing opposition to its activities and despite the enthusiasm of its officers and men, there was a constant fear that either the Kriegsmarine or Luftwaffe would absorb or take over its tasks. These fears materialized in July 1942 when it was dissolved. But by this time it had made a significant contribution in the mining of coastal waters and this was duly acknowledged by Goering.

The man behind this campaign had been General Joachim Coeler who first devised the idea in 1939 and then fought an uphill battle against the Kriegsmarine until the operation was

Below: The popular twin float He 115B-1 was used extensively by coastal patrol units. This one is from KüFlGr.106.

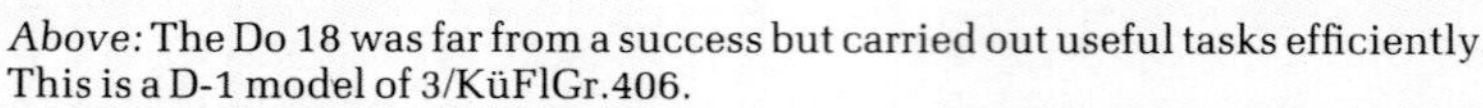

Above: The Do 18 was far from a success but carried out useful tasks efficiently. This is a D-1 model of 3/KüFlGr.406.

Above right: This giant six-engined Bv 238V1 was destroyed on Lake Schaal by P-51s in April 1944.

finally given the unconditional go-ahead by Oberkommando der Kriegsmarine whereas prior to this individual area commanders had had to approve Coeler's operations. Although he operated under some restrictive limitations Coeler was able to prove that sea mining was very effective with losses to aircraft being minimal. Such was the strength of his argument that Goering eventually created a Luftwaffe unit with the specific task of mining. This was Fliegerdivision 9 and came into being in February 1940. Total responsibility for the task was immediately the major function of the new unit and it was thus instrumental in sealing the fate of the Seeluftstreitkräfte. The disintegration of the service and its ultimate demise can thus be traced directly to one of its keenest supporters and most able officers. Aircraft operated were taken over by the Luftwaffe and many of the original naval airmen also transferred their allegiance, although throughout the war it was not unusual to have a mixed naval and Luftwaffe crew operating together.

In the spring of 1939 General Hans Geisler became responsible for the formation of an anti-shipping strike force which was also to be capable of attacking naval objectives. It was felt that neither the Kriegsmarine nor Seeluftstreitkräfte had the experience to adopt this role so it became part of Luftflotte 2 with a former naval officer, Major Martin Harlinghausen, as its operations officer. He was another officer with experience from the Spanish Civil War and this was reflected in all future Luftwaffe anti-shipping operations. One of the earliest techniques introduced by Harlinghausen was based on the old naval principle that ships presented the best targets when approached directly from abeam; and with his pilot Hauptmann Robert Kowalewski he was very soon leading by example with the Staff Flight in shipping strikes. Approaching at low level the aircraft presented very difficult targets for ships' gunners, but at the same time the ships with their massive superstructures were silhouetted against the horizon and gave bomb aimers a considerable margin for error. The success of these operations, which were initially carried out by He 111 and Ju 88 aircraft operated by two Gruppen of KG.26 and one of KG.30, can be judged from their claims of over 1,300,000 tons of Allied shipping sunk during the first year of the war. Postwar records indicate that this was more than three times the amount lost to air attack, nonetheless it still represents a considerable figure for such a force.

Above: A Heinkel He 60 floatplane which saw service in 1935 and the Spanish Civil War.

Above left: The Fw 200 Kondor became the scourge of the Atlantic convoys until escort carriers came into service with the Allied navies.

Range was of course a problem for the He 111s and Ju 88s but this was resolved by the introduction of the Fw 200 Kondor which immediately extended operations from 600 miles to over 1000 thus bringing a new threat to convoys operating in the Atlantic. The man tasked with bringing this former civil airliner into the Luftwaffe was Oberstleutnant Edgar Petersen who was ordered by General Hans Jeschonnek to establish a long-range anti-shipping squadron using ten modified Fw 200s. The first patrol was in April 1940 when the Fw 200s accompanied He 115 flying boats of Küstenflieger Gruppe 506 on reconnaissance over the North Sea. Petersen's aircraft operated as a self-contained Staffel until the end of April 1940 when they formed into 1/KG.40. Two months later I Staffel was redesignated I Gruppe and re-equipped with the Fw 200C-1 before moving to Bordeaux-Mérignac from where it saw action during the Battle of Britain.

The Kondor was the only long range maritime aircraft used by the Luftwaffe and operated in Iceland, Norway, Russia and the Atlantic where it earned a deadly reputation. As the war progressed and merchantmen were protected first by fighters launched by catapult from their decks, then by small escort carriers, losses mounted but they never reached sufficiently serious proportions to cause the Fw 200 to be withdrawn or curtail its operations. As convoy defense increased the Kondors had to revise their tactics, which changed from singleton aircraft to formations of up to six led by a reconnaissance shadow aircraft which stayed outside the range of aircraft defense. Such changes also serve to underline the Allied countermeasures, for by mid 1943 attacks were having to be made from 9000 to 10,000 feet, a far cry from Harlinghausen's low-level attacks. The growing anti-shipping force which by now comprised three Gruppen was used in an attempt to blockade Britain, and in this role it worked very closely with Dönitz's U-Boats. The loiter time of the Fw 200 enabled it to shadow convoys and report their movements to U-boat captains who could then work out the most profitable interception course. Sometimes the roles were reversed and the U-Boats called upon the Luftwaffe to mount strikes against convoys. These actions caused many losses to the British until

Below: The Hispano-Suiza 404 cannon in the dorsal turret gave this Do 24T-1 a certain amount of protection, although overall it was very vulnerable to fighter attack.

Above: An He 115B-1 of KüFlGr.406 in flight over Norway.
Above left: The ubiquitous Ju 52, this time on floats, was to the Luftwaffe what the C-47 was to the Allies.

the so-called 'Black Gap', where U-Boats could operate freely, was closed by long range patrol aircraft.

During 1941 a complete re-organization of Luftwaffe commands was carried out, one aim being to increase the concentration of anti-shipping units along the European coast. When this objective failed to reach the aims hoped for many of the units were dispersed to the Mediterranean, Norway and inevitably the Russian front where they were used in conventional bombing raids against coastal shipping and harbor installations. In the background there was a simmering political argument as to who should control the anti-shipping units. Hitler intervened in January 1941 to give Admiral Dönitz control over I/KG.40 but this was reversed in March, although in reality it was not a true reversal since Harlinghausen who now took over the reins was a former navy man and in his capacity of Fliegerführer Atlantik was primarily responsible to Dönitz for supporting the U-Boat campaign. When Harlinghausen was wounded in October 1941 his command passed to a minor deputy which indicates that the future of anti-shipping in the eyes of the Luftwaffe was already beginning to deteriorate. But on his return to duty he became head of a department looking into the use of aerial torpedoes and by January 1942 he was in command of I/KG.26 (equipped with He 111-6s) which operated against shipping with this weapon. This proved to be an effective move and when the aircraft moved against the convoys operating on the Arctic route, the He 111s took a very heavy toll. Operations in this theater mirrored those in the Atlantic and considerable efforts were made to stem the flow of supplies to Russia. But limitations with the Heinkel were soon evident as the pendulum swung against the Luftwaffe, and improved defenses coupled with tactical limitations saw the gradual decline in the use of the aerial torpedo.

One new aircraft which, after a disappointing start caused mainly by structural problems, proved to be successful and popular with crews was the Blohm and Voss 138. With a crew of six and an 18 hour endurance this was the closest the Luftwaffe came to matching the British Short Sunderland. Like the Sunderland the Bv 138 flying boat could also give a good account of itself as was shown when one aircraft fought a 90 minute battle with Sea Hurricanes when it was shadowing a PQ convoy in the Arctic. Bv 138s ranged far and wide and it was not unknown for them to be refueled by U-Boats at sea, thus increasing their patrol times. One notable operation occurred in 1943 when a pair of the cumbersome flying boats operated from the Soviet island of Novaya Zemlya on which U-Boats had set up a forward base. The aircraft was able to monitor movements in the Kara Sea for a three week period before moving to a more secure base. Following the Bv 138 into service was the Bv 222 which was the largest flying boat to serve in World War II. Although never available in great numbers its main task was trooping and, in the later days of the conflict, reconnaissance.

There were of course many other 'boats worthy of mention, among them being the Dornier 18 and 24, the former featuring in an early action when an aircraft from 2/KüFlGr.106 spotted a British force including the *Ark Royal*, *Hood*, *Rodney*, *Nelson* and *Renown*, and was able to send a position report before falling victim to a Skua aircraft from the *Ark Royal*, thus becoming the first Luftwaffe aircraft to be destroyed by British aircraft in World War II. The Do 18 also saw service in the Battle of Britain and although gradually phased out during 1941-42, it did useful work in the air sea rescue role. Its larger three engined brother, the Do 24, had a chequered career and was used by the Dutch against the Japanese as well as in Luftwaffe service. Its main task was reconnaissance and rescue and it had a fairly uneventful war.

Like most other fields of operations the maritime strike force produced its personalities one of whom was undoubtedly Oberst Harlinghausen, but perhaps the best known is Werner Baumbach who became General of Bombers by the end of the war. He served with I/KG.30 from the very outset of the campaign in 1939 and moved with that unit from the North Atlantic to the Mediterranean during which time he devised improved tactics and carried them out to such effect that he was decorated with the Knight's Cross with Swords. By mid 1943, however, Baumbach's and Harlinghausen's methods, although still sound in theory, were proving harder to carry out and a new anti-shipping weapon was desperately needed. This came in the form of a pair of air-launched guided weapons; the Fritz-X stand-off bomb and the Henschel 293 glider bomb.

The glider bomb, which had a 500kg warhead, was released by the carrier aircraft at a height of 5000 feet and using its own liquid fuel rocket, accelerated to 370mph in a 12 second engine

Above right: The single-engined Junkers W 34 could also be fitted with wheels.
Below: A Bv 138B-1 on the step; the Bv 138 was the Luftwaffe's equivalent of the Sunderland.
Right: The Arado 196A-3 was a popular, versatile and very maneuverable floatplane which was used throughout the war.

burn, after which it descended in an accelerating dive to its target. Controlled by a small joy-stick on board the parent aircraft it had an effective range of about five miles and a flare attached to its tail gave visual indication of its position. Low impact speed made penetration of armor difficult so its main use was against merchantmen. Its first operational use was in the autumn of 1943 when Do 217E-5 aircraft of II/KG.100 operated in the Mediterranean with little success. By November the Do 217s had been replaced by the He 177A-5 and against convoy SL139/MKS30 they sank one ship but lost three aircraft. Five days later the result was even less favorable when four out of eight He 177s including the Gruppenkommandeur's aircraft failed to return from a shipping strike off Bougie. These losses saw a switch to night operations when a pair of aircraft would illuminate the target with flares and another pair would attempt to guide the glider bombs to it. This reduced losses but also had the same effect on the strike rate, thus reducing the whole operation to the level of a nuisance raid.

The Fritz-X was an entirely different concept being a free-falling bomb with small wings halfway along its length and a total weight of about 1500kg. It was usually released at a height of 16,000 feet and aimed by the bomb aimer guiding it to the target using his bomb sight and making adjustments by radio-controlled stabilizers during its final trajectory. Once again visual acquisition was by a tail flare.

Both these weapons had limited success though their carriers were not so vulnerable as they were for example in a low-level torpedo attack. Once again, however, it was the story of an advanced concept weapon suffering because of bad forward planning which failed to provide a suitable carrier

Above: Known as the 'Flying Clog' the Bv 138 was used in most theaters with considerable success. This is a C-1 of SAGr.125.
Above right: Third prototype of the He 60C during early trials.
Right: The lumbering He 59 was outdated by the start of the war, but proved to be successful in the roles chosen for it. This is a B-2 in the Middle East.

aircraft. However, credit must be given to the Germans for introducing such advanced (for the time) weapons and tactics which only failed because they were too late.

The effect the Luftwaffe maritime units had on the last two years of the war is negligible when taken in its widest context. After the European invasion units were used against land targets and in mining operations, but although some ships were sunk and problems caused to military movements, the force was fairly ineffective. The last few months brought the maritime units the same problems as those facing the rest of the Luftwaffe, plenty of aircraft, inexperienced crews, and little fuel, the familiar trio which in no way could be combined to produce viable results.

As far as maritime units are concerned, it is sufficient to record that lack of foresight in planning maritime operations, inter-service rivalry, the shortage of modern seaplanes and flying boats, the continual use of aircraft against land targets by crews trained in maritime operations, the late introduction of a suitable aerial torpedo, and the totally misguided belief that the few units involved could put the British navy out of action, all played significant parts. However, like their counterparts in other units and theaters, the crews gave their best when in their hearts many must seriously have doubted the wisdom of their leaders.

Tornadoes of the Luftwaffe at the Tri-National Tornado Training Establishment RAF Cottesmore.

A COUNTRY DIVIDED

When the war ended in 1945 German aircraft designers had some revolutionary ideas on their drawing boards, and in some cases in prototype or engineering mock-up form. They were quickly shared out among the victors, analyzed and discussed with German engineers and scientists before being incorporated into postwar Soviet, British and American military aircraft, where the potential or idea originated by the German concerned, was thought to be more advanced than the line being pursued by his Allied contemporary. One particularly significant aspect of this is in the space race, and there would be few who would argue that work carried out by Germans has not laid the foundations for Soviet and US scientists to quicken the pace of their own programs to investigate space for both peaceful and warlike means. However, with victory came unrest and the sadness of seeing a country divided among the victors.

The military situation prevailing in Germany after 1945 was similar to that in the period after the 1918 war, with construction of powered aircraft and the formation of an independent air force being banned. In the years immediately following World War II the whole of Germany was controlled by the four power agreement between the United States, Great Britain, France and the USSR, each of the powers operating its own armed forces within its own sectors. Any military forces or work associated with military hardware was banned. Indeed the design and construction of light civil aircraft and the operation of any German airline was also prohibited. German nationals wishing to follow a career in these fields were forced to do so abroad.

On 23 May 1949 the three western sectors were integrated to form the Federal Republic of Germany, with a new capital in Bonn; Berlin the traditional capital was geographically isolated inside the Soviet sector, and split into four sectors under the controlling powers. The Soviet-occupied sector of Germany became the German Democratic Republic (DDR), but it did not receive diplomatic recognition from the West. With West Germany's long-term economic and political stability assured, the Western powers relaxed some of the controls over military activities, and set about the task of clearing the way to West Germany's rearmament as a partner within the proposed European Defense Community. In the event the EDC failed to materialize, and it was not until ratification of the Treaty of Paris in October 1954 that the first steps were taken toward the reforming of the Luftwaffe and West Germany's formal joining of the North Atlantic Alliance (NATO).

Ambitious plans had been made for Germany's proposed armed forces, but these proved to be not entirely realistic when the time came to implement them and considerable revision was needed. The two essentials were to find suitable hardware and the personnel to operate it. Finding the former was the lesser problem, since there was a host of countries willing to sell armaments to Germany. In any case West Germany had, with massive aid, already re-established itself as a major financial and industrial base, and self-interest dictated that much of the vast quantity of hardware needed should be produced by German industry even if it was not of indigenous design. Apart from the immediate financial and employment gains, the long-term benefits enabling German industry to regain its traditional role as leader in the field of advanced technology were not only attractive but necessary.

In respect to aviation, however, many of the aircraft needed at first were purchased from abroad, especially older combat types approaching obsolescence in the massive arsenal of the USA. Such equipment would fill the gap in the formative years, but for the future large numbers of newer types would have to be obtained. In addition to the USA, Britain also supplied a number of new aircraft from its then bouyant industry, the majority of these going to the Navy's air arm, the Marineflieger.

Meanwhile, most of the famous German aviation companies whose names had been household words up to 1945 still existed; Messerschmitt, Focke-Wulf, Henschel, Heinkel, and Daimler-Benz to name just a few, were engaged mainly in the production of light motor vehicles, but very eager to return to aviation fields. Logically the solution was to make direct purchases in small quantities from overseas sources of the aircraft needed for the short-term operational requirements, while reorganizing German industries into suitable groupings both internally and with partners abroad so that major programs could be undertaken in Germany. Two subsequent outstanding examples of this practice have been the NATO F-104 Starfighter and trinational Tornado programs.

Manpower was to prove a more intractable problem, since having large amounts of hardware without trained personnel to operate it does not deter aggressors or win wars. Although the Bundeswehr's assessment of equipment levels was realistic

Below right: The first Fouga CM170R Magister delivered to FFS-A at Landsberg in 1957.
Below: Postwar Luftwaffe pilots were trained in America and Germany on Harvard aircraft.

enough, its hopes that large numbers of ex-servicemen would respond to the invitation to resume their military careers and so form a nucleus of semi-trained personnel, were sadly over-optimistic. After some ten years out of the armed forces fewer men than hoped for were willing to chance sacrificing new found prospects and prosperity for a late and uncertain start in another job. Also, in the intervening years the rate of technological progress had considerably outdated much of the experience such recruits could offer. In particular, many experienced pilots or other aircrew from the war years were too old or unfit to start flying again in significantly more advanced aircraft than those they had last encountered.

For obvious reasons, the German public at large was apathetic toward anything military, added to which there was a significantly vocal section of the population totally opposed to any form of rearmament. The Luftwaffe's plans to have 1326 aircraft, and 80,000 personnel and possibly about 1300 former pilots to form the backbone of the force, by 1960, had to be carefully looked at and revised. (In fact by 1960 the new Luftwaffe had 800 operational aircraft and some 62,000 personnel, which by any standard is good growth from scratch in a five year period.) The revised plans called for the cutting back of aircraft numbers and extending the period of build-up to allow sufficient time to train a correspondingly larger number of new, but in the main younger, recruits. Similar revision of plans also affected the army and navy.

Above: Former West German Chancellor Willi Brandt and General Johannes Steinhoff, Commander of the Luftwaffe in the late 1960s and early 1970s.
Below: A line-up of Piaggio P.149D trainers built under license by Focke-Wulf, and used for flying training.

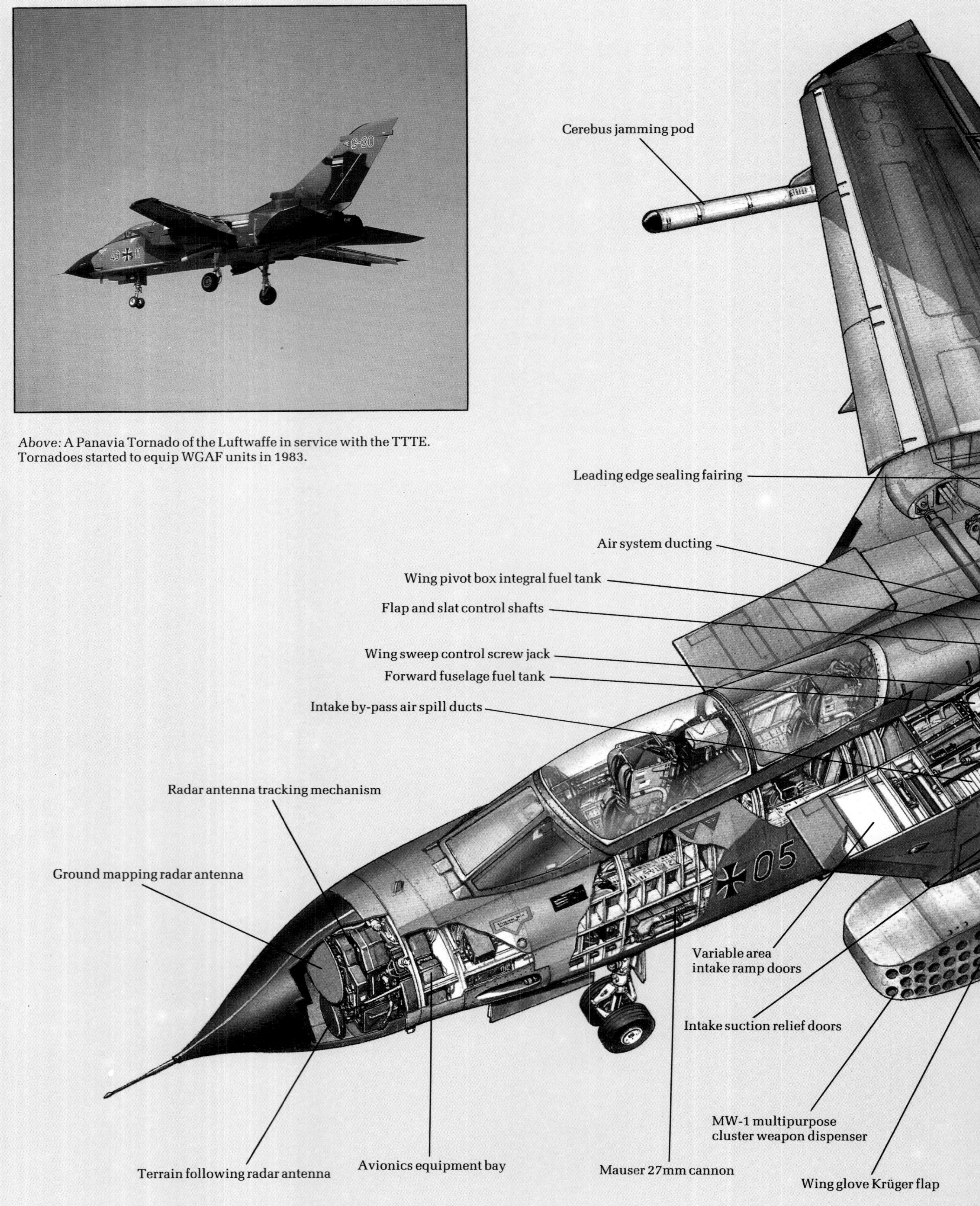

Above: A Panavia Tornado of the Luftwaffe in service with the TTTE. Tornadoes started to equip WGAF units in 1983.

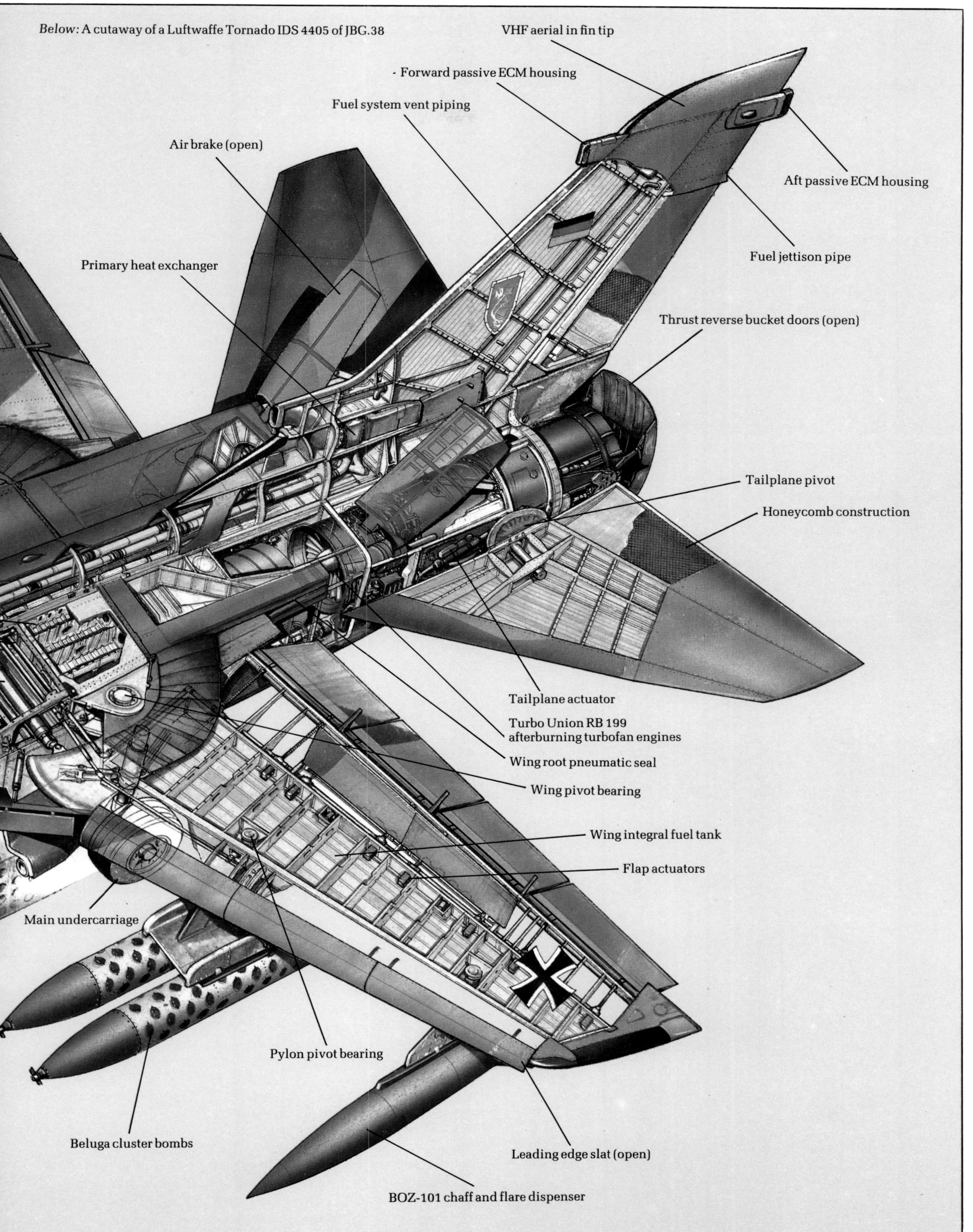

Below: A cutaway of a Luftwaffe Tornado IDS 4405 of JBG.38

24 September 1956 was chosen as the official birthday for the new air force, and it was hoped to commence training during 1954 at Luftwaffe aircrew training schools set up in Europe by the USAF at Landsberg and Fürstenfeldbruck. There was however a political set-back which caused delays until the ratification of the 24 October 1954 Treaty of Paris by the Bundestag. As soon as this was done the first pilots reported to Landsberg where they were checked out on Piper L-18Cs, before progressing to the Harvard (Texan T-6G), and later the Lockheed T-33A which were based at Fürstenfeldbruck.

The lessons learned in World War II that the Luftwaffe was not able to fulfil the requirements of the Navy, had been digested by the German Ministry of Defense who insisted that if Germany was to be an important partner in NATO its navy must also have its own air arm. The first batch of pilots went to Pensacola, Florida, in 1956 for training while observers went to England to train with the Royal Navy's Fleet Air Arm.

The new Luftwaffe did have a nucleus of experienced leaders and former Luftwaffe officers, led by Generalleutnant Josef Kammhuber as Inspekteur der Luftwaffe, and supported by such well known pilots as Adolf Galland, Johannes Steinhoff – who at the age of 32 in April 1945 had been pulled severely injured from the burning wreck of a Me 262 and must have thought his flying career was over – Dieter Hrabak, Werner Panitzki, Gerhard Barkhorn, Walter Krupinsky and Herbert Wehnelt. These men had already undertaken refresher training in the USA and Britain and received their wings. During their training time they had had the chance to evaluate several aircraft of interest to the Luftwaffe and their experience enabled them to become very influential advisers on the aircraft procurement program.

Ten former World War II Luftwaffe pilots started their training at Landsberg in January 1956, among them being Oberleutnant Werner Forster who had originally enlisted at 16, flown Bf 109s, Fw 190s and the He 162, and now at 29 was the youngest of the old brigade recruited as pilots by the Luftwaffe. The two oldest were both 40-year-old veterans, Major Fritz Schröter who had enlisted in 1936, and Hauptmann Heinz Dudeck. The others were, Werner Siebert (36), Gerhard Limberg (36), Günter Ludigkeit (37), Axel Stuth (34), Hans Klaffenbach (32), Horst Bauer (31) and Klaus Neumann (33). All ten were presented with their wings at the official birthday parade on 24 September 1956 on which occasion there was a symbolic hand-over of one of each of the three training aircraft. These had officially been taken on charge in June and July but the event at Fürstenfeldbruck was the first time they appeared resplendent in the readopted World War I style crosses.

Below: Brigadier General Barkhorn commanded JG.52 in World War II and scored 301 victories on the Eastern Front. He rejoined the Luftwaffe from its re-formation in 1956.

The recruitment of suitable young men for aircrew training was to remain a problem for the next ten years, but this was not the case with aircraft, since the Western powers had a veritable arsenal of modern types on offer, and the USA stepped in to provide a large batch of proven machines until German industry had gathered enough momentum to start building its own designs and others under license. The inventory did in fact become something of an embarrassment, with many new aircraft being placed in store until the units they were intended for were formed. This process was slower than had been envisioned and some of the aircraft were sadly destined never to leave their storage areas until they were disposed of in favor of more advanced designs.

Army and naval aviation developed at a slightly slower pace than did the Luftwaffe, with the air arms of these two services respectively reaching operational status in 1957 and 1958. Aircrew for the army services were trained in Germany and the USA, but most of the Marineflieger crews did their training in Britain. By 1959 all three services, although not by any means at full-strength, were ready to take their place alongside their NATO allies. Equipping from scratch can be a problem, with political and economic factors playing vital roles in the final choice of hardware, and such was the case with the German air services.

Under the Mutual Defense Aid Program (MDAP) the Americans supplied 450 F-84F Thunderstreaks, 108 RF-84F Thunderflashes, 88 Texan T-6Gs and 192 T-33s. The British, French and Italian aircraft industries also profited although most of the types concerned were scheduled to be license built. Most of the British aircraft were Armstrong-Whitworth Sea Hawks type 100/101 of which 68 were ordered for the Bundesmarine squadrons, and the Fairey Gannet AEW for which there was a requirement for 15 aircraft plus one dual controlled trainer. Of the 33 Pembrokes and fifty Sycamore helicopters the majority served with the Luftwaffe alongside two DH Heron VIP transport aircraft. Canada supplied 75 Canadair Sabre Mk Vs free of charge, and this aircraft proved so successful for the Germans that later on they placed an order for 150 of the later Mk VI, which equipped the day fighter squadrons enabling the earlier Mk Vs to be released to the operational training units.

In addition to the flying units a material and procurement command was set up with headquarters at Münster and Karlsruhe, with a brief to supervise radar, radio and other installations as well as airfields. The Air Force General Office was also established with a responsibilty for routine administration. Even when the first formative steps were being taken the future was very much in the minds of the planners. The *ab initio* trainer to replace the Piper L-18C was to be the Italian Piaggio P149D, and the French CM 170-1 Magister was the choice to replace the Texan/Harvard. The first of 76 of the Italian aircraft was delivered in May 1957 and a further 190 were subsequently built under license. By this time some Luftwaffe pilots had been receiving instruction and conversion to the Magister with the Armée de l'Air at Salon-de-Provence.

By the end of 1960 the Luftwaffe had five fighter-bomber, three fighter and two reconnaissance Geschwadern operational within NATO, with logistic and transport support coming from Noratlas and C-47 transport aircraft which equipped Luft Transportgeschwadern (LTG) 61 and 62 based at Neubiberg and Wahn. LTG.62 later moved to Celle and a new unit LTG.63 brought their Noratlas to Ahlorn, which incidentally had also been the home base for the first fighter wing JG.71 flying Mk VI Sabres.

Tradition is an important part of any fighting service and this was not overlooked in the formation of the Luftwaffe. Kammhuber sought permission to use the names of three of Germany's leading World War I aces on three flying units. This was readily given by the President of the Republic and at a ceremony at Ahlorn on 21 April 1961, the names Richthofen, Boelcke and Immelmann were given to JG.71, JaboG.31 and AufklG.51. Sleeve badges (Ärmelstreifen) were received for the respective units by Oberstleutnant Hartmann (the highest scoring German ace of World War II), Oberst Barkhorn, and Oberstleutnant Graseman. By this time, however, the aircraft equipping front line units were obsolete when compared with the majority of the NATO air forces' inventories, so thoughts had to be turned to a replacement to carry the Luftwaffe through the 60s and into the next decade.

The Mach 2 English Electric (as it was then) Lightning was on the verge of entering service with the Royal Air Force, and appeared to have a very good potential within the European air forces. The manufacturers had high hopes that with support from the British Government they could make serious inroads into what was a lucrative market. But the problem at that time was the short range of the Lightning and the British government's reluctance to spend on its development, since they saw it as only a stop-gap airframe with a maximum of ten years RAF service. They were also anxious to push the Saunders-Roe SR53 which the RAF had indicated they did not want but looked to be arousing some interest in West Germany.

In America Lockheed had already made plans to produce the F-104 in quantity when the USAF dramatically cut its requirements as the aircraft did not fulfil the operational parameters they had specified. The F-104 had the ability to get to Mach 2 very quickly, but had severe limitations in many other directions, furthermore many NATO air force pilots who had flown both it and the Lightning were very much in favor of the British machine. But the Americans realized that if West Germany selected the Lockheed fighter, there was a very good chance that, in the interests of standardization, most NATO countries would follow their lead. An aggressive but polished American sales campaign, which offered the opportunity for licensed production in Germany and Holland, as well as training in the USA, quickly established a foothold that it was impossible for the British company to match without the help of government support.

Despite reports from test pilots that the Lightning was a far better aircraft, the government still refused to help and in fact made it patently obvious in Bonn that in their view the Lightning was not a suitable aircraft for West Germany's needs. So in 1958 the decision was taken to accept the American fighter which was to become the backbone of Europe's NATO air forces. It is very likely that despite the numbers sold the cost per aircraft to the Americans was higher than the Germans paid, but this was offset by keeping plants in America in production and providing a good return as far as spares and back-up support was concerned. The first of 30 two-seat F-104Fs reached Fürstenfeldbruck in the late spring of 1960 and were followed by 60 of the planned 600 F-104G models. The first unit to re-equip was JaboG.31 *Boelcke* which became operational with the F-104 on 20 February 1962. At the same time as the purchase of the F-104s was made the West Germans also decided that they would use the Fiat G 91 as a close-support aircraft.

The first batch of two-seat and single seat F-104s was supplied direct from America, but the majority of the remaining 599 were to be license built, the first German constructed aircraft making its maiden flight on 5 October 1960 by which time aircraft from Waffenschule 10 had been displaying the Luftwaffe markings on the new shape in German skies since 1959. Problems with the aircraft started to be encountered in 1962 and gradually increased as more units converted from the F-84F and RF-84, this change being quite a leap for pilots and one that certainly contributed to the reputation that the Luftwaffe's F-104s started to earn.

By 1965 the loss of every Starfighter was an increasingly acute embarrassment. By the end of the year 30 had crashed during the twelve months bringing the total to 50 since its introduction into service. But the situation must be taken in its true perspective. A program as large as the F-104 for Europe was bound to suffer political repercussions, especially in Germany which was operating the largest number of aircraft. It was good material for those who were against re-arming, opposed to America for one reason or another, or had not seen the F-104 as a suitable aircraft in the first place. The truth is that even a modest percentage loss rate for a type of which many hundreds are in service naturally amounts to a noticeable number, whereas a much higher percentage loss rate for another combat aircraft operated in lower numbers barely makes the news. In fact other NATO countries which operated exactly the same model F-104 as the Germans, did suffer higher percentage losses than were experienced by the Luftwaffe or Marineflieger.

Nevertheless, German losses did to some extent result from the continued shortage of experienced pilots and maintenance personnel, as well as contributory factors such as crowded airspace over central Europe, difficult terrain and bad weather conditions especially in southern Germany. Certain modifications were carried out to the aircraft's mechanical and avionic systems, and during 1967 the retrofitting of Martin Baker zero-zero ejection seats was started. Steps were also introduced to improve the flying training methods, and from the mid 1960s the loss rate of the F-104 began to fall, and by the time the aircraft was phased out of service in 1985, its record was no worse than any other type.

In 1962 Kammhuber retired from the post of Inspekteur der Luftwaffe following a distinguished career in the service of his country. His place was taken in October by Generalleutnant Werner Panitzki who had also served as a pilot in World War II flying bombers in the French, Norwegian and English theaters and ending as a staff officer with Luftflotte 3. Unfortunately he took up his post at a time when there was much political controversy and this led to his own retirement after only four years in the top seat. Many of the problems centered around the provision of aircraft and personnel, for although a year after his appointment manpower had reached 92,000 and a decision

Below: The F-104G earned a somewhat sinister reputation for accidents in Luftwaffe service. This one is a JBG.31 aircraft.

Above: A Westland Sea King Mk 41 of MFG.5.
Above left: A German Army MBB Bö 105P helicopter.
Left: The F-86 was popular with Luftwaffe pilots, this is an F version.
Below: A pair of Bundesmarine F-104Gs of MFG.2.

had been taken to undertake most of the Luftwaffe's flying training in the USA where weather conditions were very much better, the Starfighter problem was beginning to manifest itself and it was difficult to attract skilled personnel. In 1964 the decision to buy Transall C-160 transport aircraft instead of the American C-130 Hercules brought further political pressures which only added fire to those surrounding the F-104 deal and the acquisition of the Fiat G 91R which it was widely known was not favored by the Luftwaffe. Real or contrived shortcomings as far as aircraft were concerned, had to be lived with and overcome and when Panitzki went, the task fell on the shoulders of Generalleutnant Johannes Steinhoff.

Under his guidance the late sixties and early seventies proved a decisive period with much being achieved in the procurement of men and machines as well as the reorganization of commands to meet the continuing changing NATO requirement for an air force that was right in the front line of any conventional attack from the Eastern Bloc with designs on taking control of Europe.

Also contributing to this NATO commitment is the Marineflieger whose main task in conjunction with other maritime forces, is to defend the Baltic approaches. The special requirements of naval aviation are well catered for by having a separate organization with tactical control in the hands of the Bundesmarine, but logistic support still comes from the Luftwaffe. The original British built Sea Hawks and Gannets started to be replaced in 1965 by the F-104 and Breguet Atlantique, as well as an expansion – following the trend of most navies – into the field of helicopters. The Bundesmarine is the smallest of the three German forces, with some 200 aircraft and 35,000 personnel, and at its peak the Marineflieger operated approximately 100 F-104Gs and TF-104Gs, but like the Luftwaffe opted to replace these with the Tornado which at the time of writing is just becoming fully operational.

In terms of manpower, the army is the largest of the three forces and is organized into three Korps each with its own aviation command. The Heeresflieger (the army air service) is equipped with about 550 helicopters which are used for transport, battlefield observation, ground attack, casualty evacuation (casevac), liaison and other communication duties, in other words very much in line with army operations of all the NATO member countries. The Korps headquarters are at Münster, Koblenz and Ulm, and cover six regions (Wehrbereich 1-6). Apart from the various aviation regiments directly attached to each Korps, various squadrons are attached at divisional levels (Heeresfliegerstaffeln 1-12). Training is carried out at the helicopter training center (HFS(L)) and there is a weapons school (HFWS) at Buckeburg.

In 1967 Steinhoff instituted a reorganization program for the Luftwaffe in which units were regrouped in accordance with their tactical mission. (At this time the strength of the Luftwaffe had reached 96,000 men and 13 combat wings.) The two main commands, Luftwaffengruppe Nord and Luftwaffengruppe Süd, were retained but each of them was structured to comprise one Attack, one Defense and one Support Division; a separate transport unit under the control of the Defense Ministry existed to look after all aspects of transport support. Thoughts also had to be given to future equipment to keep the Luftwaffe on par with other air forces. While this was being assessed from what was on offer in the international marketplace, it was decided to extend the F-104s' service life well into the seventies. In the event it was to be the early eighties before this aircraft was phased out of front-line service. To offset the high attrition rate suffered by the F-104 (over 200 were lost during service), it was necessary to reopen the production line and a further 50 aircraft were produced.

In 1968 it was decided to purchase 88 McDonnell Douglas RF-4Es to re-equip two reconnaissance wings (AufklG.51 and 52) thereby releasing their RF-104Gs for conversion to standard G models and subsequent re-issue to fighter and fighter-bomber units. The initial batch of Phantoms was delivered in 1971 and equipped four 15-aircraft squadrons, with four machines being retained for training and trials purposes and the balance held in reserve. As it had done with many other air forces the Phantom proved popular with the Luftwaffe, so in 1971 a further 175 aircraft were ordered. These were F-4F and modified F-4E models to be used in defense and ground attack roles with JG.71, JG.74, JBG.35 and JBG.36, the equipping of the four wings being completed by 1976.

Below: The mainstay of the tactical transport force is the C-160 Transall, this example was photographed in 1985.

At the same time a replacement had to be found for the Fiat G-91 and a decision was taken to opt for the Dassault-Breguet/Dornier Alpha Jet. The unpopular Fiat of which the Luftwaffe eventually purchased 345, started to be phased out in 1980 as the first of 200 Alpha jets came on to the inventory. In addition to operational training for future Tornado navigators, the aircraft was also destined for the strike role in which configuration it operates as a single-seater, the rear cockpit being equipped with electronics.

The seventies was a busy time for the German air forces. New aircraft, revised training and new equipment in the form of ground launched missiles were introduced and another reorganization took place. The Marineflieger took delivery of 22 Sea King Mk 41 helicopters as well as being involved in more-or-less constantly updating their 20 Breguet Atlantiques. With changing NATO strategy which turned from a full-scale nuclear retaliation possibility to a flexible response situation, the Luftwaffe was regrouped in late 1970 by functional commands rather than geographical location. Although by the very nature of the fact that most of its bases were either in the north or the south, with the USA and Britain as well as detachments from other air forces looking after the center, the new commands were still to a certain degree located within previously defined areas.

Overall control is exercised by the Führungsstab der Luftwaffe which is subordinate to the Federal Defense Ministry in Bonn, and is supported by management and security groups. The three functional commands control all other operations, with operational flying coming under Luftflottenkommando which includes tactical and air defense divisions. Transport, ground training, flight safety, electronics, cartography and records are grouped within the Luftwaffenamt and finally control of logistics for both the Northern and Southern support groups, as well as radar regiments, supply bases and miscellaneous support formations, are under the auspices of Luftwaffe Unterstutzungskommando.

The Luftwaffe reached its peak strength in the sixties but as aircraft and systems became more cost-effective this gradually reduced. By 1975 it had fallen from around 110,000 personnel to about 106,000 with 1100 strike and fighter aircraft plus 150 helicopters, and 450 assorted other types, some of which were permanently based in America where flying training up to operational standards is carried out. Among the aircraft used in this role were 44 Cessna T-37Bs, 45 T-38A Talons, and 110 TF-104G Starfighters. Conscription does of course affect the numbers over a given period and in the years since 1975 the overall strength in personnel has very much reflected this. But the fall off in aircraft quantities is indicative of the growing effectiveness of the modern combat machine, and changes in global strategy.

Among the changes was the original 1978 plan to provide a European airborne early warning program in which Germany made a major (28 percent) contribution. This development was introduced during the 1983-86 period when 11 NATO nations subscribed to the provision and operation of 18 Boeing E-3A aircraft and their associated ground control and command centers to provide early warning of low-level strikes being mounted from behind the Iron Curtain.

Tactical elements of the Luftwaffe also have two wings of Pershing 1A surface-to-surface missiles (SSMs) each with four squadrons and associated launching ramps, while fighter bombers have the ability to deliver tactical nuclear weapons. It

Above: A colorful RF-4E Phantom of AufklG.51 'Immelmann.' Note the camera mounted in the nose of this reconnaissance Phantom.

is also very likely that following the agreement of Britain to allow Ground Launched Cruise Missiles to be deployed in that country from 1983, Germany will follow suit, although as in Britain there has been political pressure to review the original 1979 tentative arrangement.

The first of 100 Tornadoes for the Marineflieger were delivered in July 1982 to MFG.1 at Schleswig-Jagel in Northern Germany and these will be followed by MFG.2 replacing their Starfighters with the Tornado in early 1986. The navy thus just beat the Luftwaffe into introducing this swing-wing multi-role aircraft into service. The first Luftwaffe unit to take the aircraft was JBG.31 at Nörvenich on 1 August 1983.

One year later JBG.32 also received the Tornado at Lechfeld in southern Germany. The former group operates in conjunction with RAF Tornadoes within the 2nd Allied Tactical Air Force, and the latter forms part of the 4th Allied Tactical Air Force, partnered by JBG.33 at Büchel. JBG.34 has yet to receive its aircraft but supply is imminent at the time of writing in early 1986. All four Gruppen which formerly operated F-104s would fly a variety of strike missions including counter-air and anti-armor operations. Their aircraft are usually equipped with a different ECM and weapons fit than Tornadoes in British service. The main task in the event of war that would fall to the Marineflieger's Tornadoes would be anti-shipping strikes in the Baltic for which they would use the MBB Kormoran anti-ship missile.

By the time delivery of the 100 aircraft for the navy and 200 for the Luftwaffe is complete, thoughts will no doubt have been once again turned to their replacements. There can be little doubt that this will be a product of the combined European aircraft industry, together with American support aircraft. Foremost in the protection of the democracy and peace that has been preserved through NATO and its member nations' contributions since 1948, will be the German air forces, which once again have risen Phoenix-like from the flames of defeat to a position of strength and respect in the free world.

Below: Long-range maritime work falls to the Breguet 1150 Atlantique. Note the magnetic anomaly detection equipment in the tail boom.

East Germany

Although having its own identity and national markings, the East German Air Force like those of Poland, Bulgaria, Hungary, Rumania and Czechoslovakia operates as part of the Warsaw Pact organization and operates very much under the control of the Russians. Equipped almost entirely with Russian-built aircraft, using Russian as a common military language, and conforming to Russian training and operational procedures, it is controlled entirely by the Soviet Union from Moscow. There are national commanders at various levels but they are under the overall command of a Russian, and despite cosmetic changes made during the last decade to give emphasis to 'local' control, this is not so in practice. The operations and equipment of all air forces within the Warsaw Pact remain primarily an aspect of Soviet air power and do not have the degree of flexibility and independence that the West German air force is able to exercise within the NATO organization.

The German Democratic Republic (DDR) comprises the area of East Germany occupied by Russian forces in 1945, and can trace the origins of its air force to the formation in 1950 of a small air arm established as part of the People's Police (Volkspolizei). The Volkspolizei-Luft, or VP-L as it is abbreviated, operated Russian light aircraft such as the Yak-18 and Po-2 as well as a few ex wartime Fieseler Storch Fi 156C monoplanes, which must have brought memories to the original pilots who were all former Luftwaffe pilots from World War II repatriated from Russia after a suitable period of political indoctrination.

The first Commander-in-Chief was Major General Heinz Kessler who had joined the Free Germany Committee in Moscow after the Battle of Stalingrad during which he had seen action as a member of the Wehrmacht. His Chief of Staff was Major General Heinz Zorn, also a former Luftwaffe officer and their first headquarters was established at the historic seat of German aviation, Johannisthal. Five regional commands were established and using the nomenclature VP-L Inspektionen, embraced the whole of the DDR linking with similar control areas in the bordering countries of Czechoslovakia and Poland. It is interesting to reflect that virtually all flying was confined to the eastern areas of Germany which perhaps reflected lingering doubts by the Soviets as to the exact loyalty of some of the pilots of the VP-L, most of whom received their training in the Soviet Union, under a program established in 1952 which saw some 250 new pilots added to the original Luftwaffe veterans. The Russians' hesitancy was perhaps justified in their eyes when in 1953 dissatisfaction with the Communist régime and

Right: The MiG 21U is a trainer version of this obsolescent Russian design. About 100 of various types remain in use.
Far right: MiG 21PFs of an East German Jagdfliegergeschwader form an impressive line-up.
Below: There are about 225 MiG 23s of the S and MF series currently in service with the DDR air force.

225

823
942

681

Above: The MiG 21 single-seater is gradually being phased out but about 100 still remain in front-line service.
Above right: An An 24 of a transport unit carries out a practice low-level drop.
Below: Three attack squadrons are equipped with Mi 24 gunship helicopters, 30 of which had been delivered by April 1986.

Above: Two-seat MiG 21Us and single-seat PF versions at a DDR training school.

the continuing presence of Soviet occupation forces, led to a revolt by East German industrial workers resulting, among other things, in the immediate withdrawal of the small number of MiG 15 fighters that had been used to form the nucleus of a VP-L combat unit, and a shelving of plans to carry out an expansion program.

Following the quelling of the uprising, the military aspect of the VP-L was lowered in tone, and a new aviation organization known as the Verwaltung der Aero Klubs (VdA) was formed and received widespread publicity. The 'Clubs' were set up at Cottbus, Bautzen and Drewitz, and were organized on military lines, each having its own supply, motor transport and maintenance units. Every 'Club' had ninety aircraft formed into three Geschwadern each of three Staffeln. The aircraft were mainly Yak 11 and Yak 18 trainers supported by An 2 transports although the Yaks were gradually replaced by Zlin 26 trainers and Mraz M.1C Sokol communications aircraft supplemented the An 2s.

Toward the end of 1956 with political harmony seemingly re-established, the VP-L and VdA were amalgamated to form the Luftstreitkräfte, and in January 1957 the MiG 15 UTI two seat trainer and its single seat fighter cousin the ubiquitous MiG 15 were returned to the fledgling combat units which by this time had a strength of 10,000 personnel.

In the formative days of the new East German Luftwaffe, all personnel were selected from the Federation of East German Youth and the Popular Sport Federation. Pilot training was initially undertaken at Kamenz and Cottbus with jet conversion being carried out in the Soviet Union. But this scheme was gradually relaxed and by the early 60s most of the flying training was being carried out from East German training schools, some of which were refurbished World War II Luftwaffe bases, and others being part of the Soviet expansion program which provided new airfields, the prime use of which was by Soviet forces but sometimes on a shared basis with the Luftstreitkräfte.

By the end of 1958 the East German air force was operating

Above: Generaloberst Heinz Kessler, the first Commander in Chief of the DDR air force.
Below: The Aero L-39 Albatross is the current jet conversion trainer.

approximately 200 MiG 15 and MiG 17 fighters, and although predictions were that within two years its aircraft strength would reach some 1200 machines, reality was a little different as problems in recruiting and the country's poor economic recovery began to take effect. The problems were eased by massive injections of Soviet aid to industry and the introduction of conscription in 1962. The Soviet aid helped establish new State Factories in the Dresden area where Russian aircraft are built under licence, and an aircraft development center at Pirna-Sonnestein.

For the first few years of its existence there can be little doubt that the Luftstreitkräfte was nothing more than a training organization closely under the control of the Soviets but by the early 1970s it had started to be re-equipped with more modern front-line equipment, although this was confined to fighter and ground attack aircraft supported by helicopters, the latter being operated in small numbers by the air force and exclusively by army support and navy units.

In the mid 1970s, personnel stood at 30,000 and operational aircraft strength was 480 fighters and fighter bombers, the biggest quantity being 300 MiG 21s, the balance made up of the MiG 17, 19, 23 and a few Su-7s. Helicopters were mainly Mi 1, Mi 2, Mi 4 and Mi 8, with An 2, An 14 and Il 14 making up the supporting transport elements. Trainers comprised the L 29 Delphin, Zlin Z 226, Yak 11 and 18 with a few MiG 15 UTI lingering on. The army uses the Mi 24 helicopter gunship exclusively as well as manning two battalions of SA 2 Guideline SAM launchers and anti-aircraft artillery. The navy's fleet is a total helicopter one comprising the proven Mi 1, Mi 4 and Mi 8, whose prime task is coastal anti-submarine work and communications.

The air force is organized into two air defense divisions, a flying training division and two transport and communication units. The 20 or so fighter and fighter/bomber squadrons appear to be soldiering on with aircraft that by Western standards are obsolete. It is not easy to obtain accurate information about the East German air force, but it does look as though that in 1986 the backbone of the fighter force was some 200 MiG 23s and 120 MiG 21s of various versions, as well as some three dozen MiG 17s which are probably retained for operational work but also providing a shadow squadron support role. The MiG 23 and 27 will no doubt gradually replace the other ageing fighters, but there is evidence to suggest that as part of an overall Soviet strategy, the role of the East German air forces is still very much seen as a training one, albeit with a defense and strike capability which must be considered – in view of its present equipment – as very limited. But on the other hand, the wrong impression can be gained by attempting to isolate what is essentially only a small element of a major air force. The East German air forces are an integral part of Soviet air power. They operate as a Warsaw Pact air force, and are therefore impossible to assess as an independent air force, which quite clearly they are not.

Right: An Mi 24 firing an antitank missile, has a formidable fire power and is armed with rockets, cannons and guided missiles.
Below right: A trio of Mi 24s, bomb and missile armament under the stub wings.
Below: A MiG 21 being refueled in typical operational conditions.

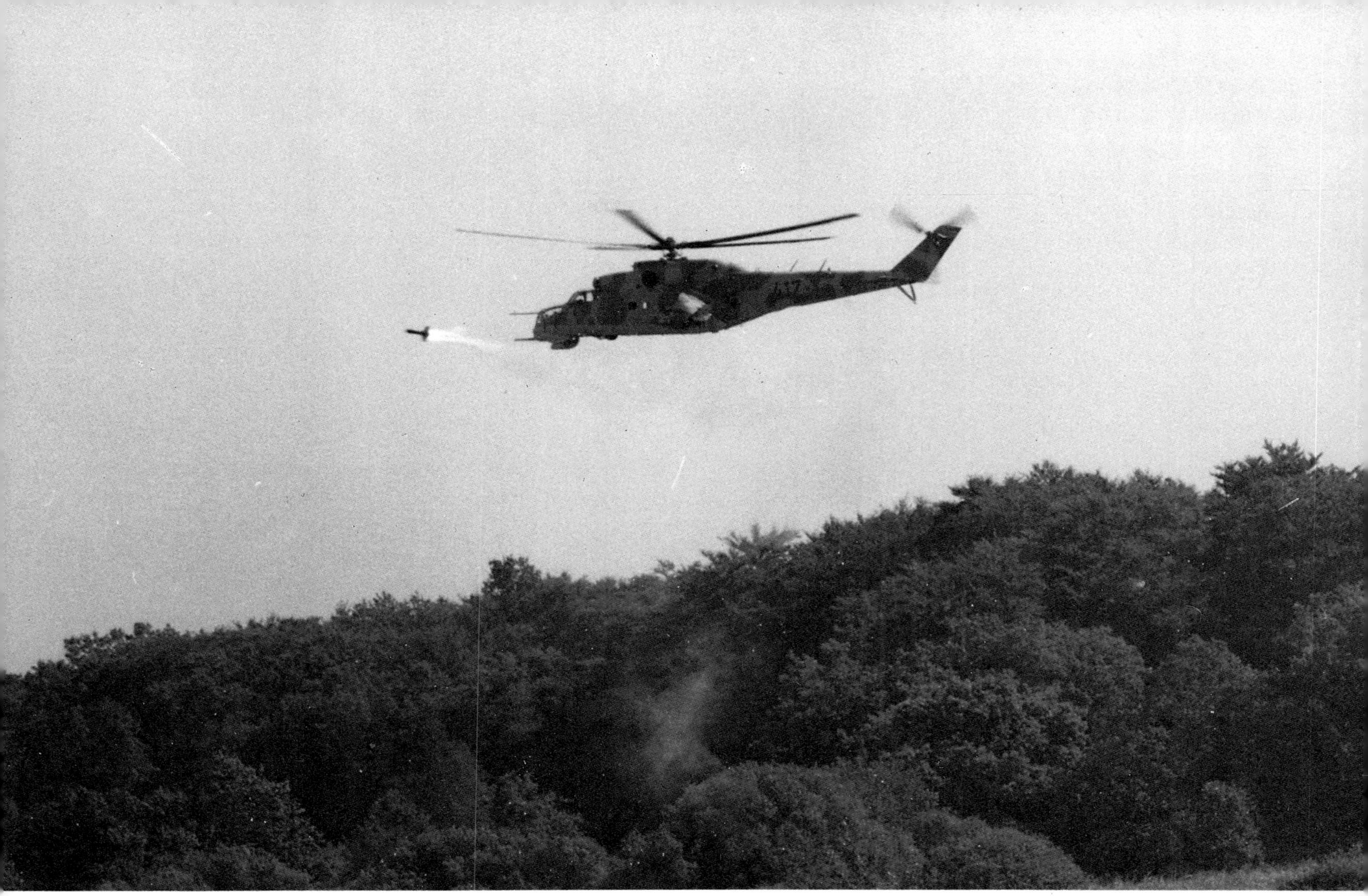

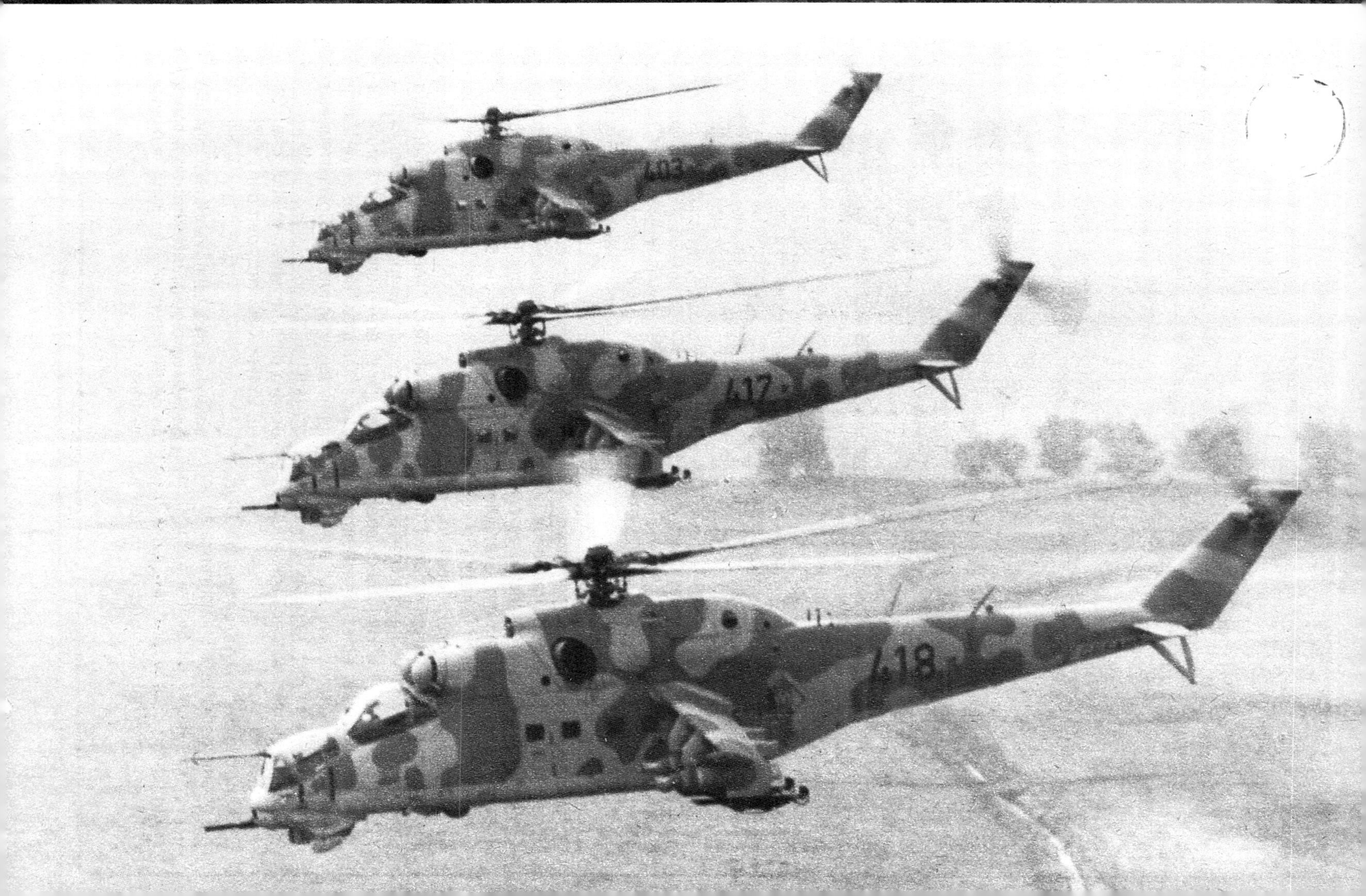
403
417
418

GLOSSARY

German Air Force Organisation

The basic flying unit was and is the Staffel or squadron. During World War II a Staffel would have a nominal strength of 9 aircraft. There would be 3 Staffeln and a headquarters flight in a Gruppe or wing (total 30 aircraft, usual abbreviation Gr.) and normally 3 Gruppen, but on occasion more, in a Geschwader (somewhat confusingly usually translated as group, usual abbreviation G.) Each Staffel would be led by a Staffelkapitan and each Gruppe by a Kommandeur. Larger formations incorporating units of all types were Fliegerkorps and Luftflotten (air fleets).

German Air Force Ranks

Oberfähnrich: Ensign
Leutnant: Lieutenant j.g. or 2nd Lieutenant
Oberleutnant: Lieutenant
Hauptmann: Captain (Army)
Oberstleutnant: Lieutenant Colonel
Oberst: Colonel

Navy Ranks

Korvettenkäpitan: Commander
Käpitan-zur-See: Captain (Navy)

Technical Terms

Aufklarung: reconnaissance
Bordflieger: coastal air force unit
Eindecker: monoplane
Etappen Flugzeugparke: zone base
Experte: ace pilot
Fliegerführer: air force officer commanding an area
Heeresflieger: Army Air Corps (West Germany)
Jagdstaffel -gruppe etc: fighter squadron, wing etc (usual abbreviation J.)
Jagdbomber: fighter bomber (Jabo)
Kagohl: Kampfgeschwader der Obersten Heeresleitung – Army High Command Battle Group
Kampfgeschwader -gruppe etc: bomber group wing
Luftflotte: air fleet
Luftschiffe: airship
Luftstreitkräfte: air force or air service
Marineflieger: naval air service
Nachtjagdgeschwader: night fighter group (NJG.)
Regia Aeronautica: Italian Air Force (WW2)
Reichsluftfahrtminesterium: Air Ministry (during the Nazi era)
Reichsverkehrministerium: Transport Ministry (Nazi era)
Stab: staff or headquarters unit
Stuka: In full Sturzkampfflugzeug or dive bomber aircraft (usual abbreviation St.)
Zerstörer: Literally destroyer, the designation given to heavy fighter units, often Bf 110 units, during WW2 (usual abbreviation Z.)

In unit designations Arabic numerals are conventionally used to designate Staffeln and Roman numerals show Gruppen. Thus 4/JG.46 is the fourth Staffel of fighter Geschwader 46. The 4th Staffel would be the 1st Staffel of the second Gruppe of the Geschwader. If the second Gruppe as a whole was meant the designation would be II/JG.46.

BIBLIOGRAPHY

It is of course not possible in a book of this size to cover in great depth every facet of the history of the German air forces; indeed any book attempting this within one volume would be an enormous tome and commercially unviable.

There have been, and no doubt in the future will continue to be, deep and purposeful studies of various aspects of German aviation, as well as books covering certain campaigns, actions and individual achievements. The reader who wishes to specialise in one particular aspect will know the path to follow; the following publications will enable those who seek deeper information or wish to follow up an aspect of interest that this book has aroused, to do so.

The German Air Weapon 1870-1914 Vol I John Cuneo
1914-1916 Vol II John Cuneo
Pictorial History of the German Army Air Service Alex Imrie
Zeppelin Raymond Laurence Rimmel
Air Forces of World War I and World War II Christopher Chant
Der Deutsche Luftwaffe 1914-1941 Dr Christian Zenter (ed.)
Aces High Alan Clark
Air Aces Christopher Shores
The Great War at Sea 1914-18 Richard Hough
Early Aviation Sir Robert Saundby
Luftwaffe War Diaries Cajus Bekker
Pictorial History of the Luftwaffe Alfred Price
The Luftwaffe at War A. Galand, K. Reis, R. Ahnert.
The Luftwaffe (part of Ballentine's **History of World War II**) Alfred Price
Hitler's Luftwaffe Tony Wood, Bill Gunston
Blitz over Britain Alfred Price
Battle over Britain Francis Mason
The Luftwaffe Handbook Alfred Price
First of the Few Dennis Winter
Encyclopedia of German Military Aircraft Bryan Philpott
Luftwaffe Photo-Albums Bryan Philpott
Luftwaffe Camouflage of World War II Bryan Philpott
History of the RAF Chaz Bowyer
In Enemy Hands Bryan Philpott
German Fighters of World War II Bryan Philpott
Osprey AirWar series Various authors
Air Power Anthony Robinson (ed.)
Dora Kurfürst und Rote 13 Karl Reis Jr
World Combat Aircraft Directory Norman Polmar
Kampfgeschwader 'Edelweiss' Wolfgang Dierich
Geschwader 27 Hans Ring
Fighter! Werner Held
The Defense of the Reich Werner Held & Holger Nauroth
Goering – Air Leader Asher Lee
Warplanes of the Third Reich William Green

The following aviation magazines also contain useful articles about the German air force, its aircraft and personnel: *Air International, Aircraft Illustrated, Aeroplane Monthly, Aviation News, Cross & Cockade, Warbirds International, Jagerblatt* (Magazine of the German fighter pilots association), *Air Pictorial, Air Extra, FlyPast.*

Right: A Ju 87G-1 fitted with two 37mm *Flak* 18 cannons.

INDEX

Page numbers in *italics* refer to illustrations.

Acknowledgments

The author would like to acknowledge the help given in the preparation of this book by the Embassies of the FDR and DDR, the Bundesarchiv at Koblenz, the staff of the Air Historical Branch R.A.F., the Public Records Office, the Imperial War Museum, the R.A.F. Museum and Mrs Heather Cook for help in translating.

The author and publisher would like to thank David Eldred who designed the book, Jean Martin who did the picture research and Ron Watson who compiled the index, as well as the following agencies and individuals who supplied illustrations:
Mike Badrocke (artwork): pages 30-1, 38-9, 50-1, 78-9, 134-5, 152-3
Gordon G Bartley: page 149 (top)
Bison Picture Library: pages 7 (top two), 58 (top), 74 (both), 76 (bottom), 81 (top left), 82 (bottom), 83 (bottom), 86, 87 (bottom two), 89, 90 (top left), 91 (top), 94, 102 (top), 118 (bottom), 119 (bottom), 123 (both), 130 (top left), 150 (top)
Austin J Brown/Aviation Picture Library: pages 70-1, 82 (top), 156 (bottom), 157, 172, 175, 176 (top), 177 (bottom), 178, 179 (bottom)
Tony Bryan/Peter Sarson (artwork): pages 172-3
Bundesarchiv: pages 2-3, 84, 84-5, 106, 106-7, 108, 108-9, 109 (top), 111 (top), 112 (top), 116 (top), 117 (both), 120, 121 (center), 122 (bottom), 128, 135, 162-3, 164 (top right)
CB Collection: pages 32 (top), 43 (top)
P Chinnery Collection: pages 176 (bottom), 179 (top)
Archiv Gerstenberg: pages 15, 17 (top), 19, 20, 22, 47 (bottom), 59 (top), 73 (bottom), 88 (bottom), 98, 141, 147 (top), 161 (center)
Stuart Howe: pages 26 (bottom), 27 (top), 31 (top), 118 (top), 130 (bottom), 149 (bottom)
Imrie Aeronautical Collection: pages 8-9, 14, 16-17, 18, 18-19, 28 (top), 29 (bottom right), 32 (bottom), 33 (top), 36 (top), 40 (top), 41 (top left), 44-5, 47 (top), 48 (both), 50, 56-7, 59 (bottom), 60 (top), 61 (both), 62 (top right), 63 (top right), 64 (top left), 66 (top right), 67 (both), 69 (top), 90 (top right), 92, 95 (both), 97 (bottom), 99 (bottom), 101 (bottom), 103, 154 (top), 155 (bottom), 163 (top left), 167 (top)
Bildarchiv Juergens: pages 180-1, 181 (both), 182, 182-3, 183, 184, 184-5, 185, 186, 187 (both)
MAP: pages 26 (top), 29 (top), 33 (bottom), 41 (top right), 58 (bottom), 60 (bottom), 63 (bottom), 65, 66 (top left and bottom), 68 (both), 80, 81 (bottom), 99 (top), 150 (bottom), 152, 154 (bottom), 155 (top), 158-9, 163 (top right)
Peter March: pages 4-5, 7 (bottom), 27 (bottom), 30 (top), 35 (both), 38 (both), 91 (bottom), 114 (bottom), 130 (top right), 156 (top)
MARS, Lincs: pages 11 (bottom), 21, 55, 69 (bottom), 75 (top and bottom), 83 (top), 87 (top), 114 (top), 115 (both), 131, 138-9, 139 (top and bottom), 148 (top)
Frank Marshall: pages 127 (top), 148 (bottom)
Peter Newark's Historical Pictures: page 53
Bryan Philpott: pages 29 (bottom left), 41 (bottom), 43 (bottom), 46 (top), 54, 64 (bottom), 73 (top and center), 76 (top), 77 (both), 81 (top right), 85, 88 (top), 93, 97 (top), 100, 101 (top), 104-5, 107, 109 (bottom), 110 (both), 112 (bottom), 113 (both), 116 (bottom), 119 (top), 121 (top), 122 (top), 124-5, 128-9, 129, 132, 132-3, 133, 134, 136, 137 (top), 140, 140-1, 142 (top), 144-5, 146 (both), 147 (bottom), 151 (both), 155 (center), 160 (both), 161 (center and bottom), 162 (top two), 164 (top left and bottom), 165 (both), 166, 167 (bottom)
Rolls Royce Ltd: pages 168-9
Royal Aeronautical Society, London: pages 6, 11 (top), 12, 12-13, 23, 24-5, 28 (bottom), 36 (center), 36-7, 37, 40 (bottom), 42 (bottom), 51, 52-3
Rolf Steinberg: pages 34 (all three), 46 (bottom)
VFW-Fokker GmbH, Bremen/MARS Lincs: pages 142 (bottom), 143
RL Ward Collection: pages 62 (top left), 64 (top right), 79, 96-7, 102 (bottom), 111 (center), 121 (bottom), 126, 127 (both), 137 (bottom), 177 (top)
German MOD: pages 170 (both), 171 (both), 174
WZ Bilddienst: pages 1, 48-9 (top)

Front jacket:
Top left: Peter March
Top right: Bildarchiv Juergens
Inset, right: artwork by Mike Bailey
Bottom right: Bison Picture Library
Bottom left: Austin J Brown/Aviation Picture Library
Inset, left: artwork by Mike Bailey
Center left: MARS, Lincs
Center: Archiv Gerstenberg

Back jacket: Bison Picture Library